Psychotherapy for Neuropsychological Challenges

Psychotherapy for Neuropsychological Challenges

Albert S. Aniskiewicz

JASON ARONSON
Lanham • Boulder • New York • Toronto • Plymouth, UK

Published in the United States of America
by Jason Aronson
An imprint of Rowman & Littlefield Publishers, Inc.

A wholly owned subsidiary of
The Rowman & Littlefield Publishing Group, Inc.
4501 Forbes Boulevard, Suite 200, Lanham, Maryland 20706
www.rowmanlittlefield.com

Estover Road
Plymouth PL6 7PY
United Kingdom

British Library Cataloguing in Publication Information Available

Library of Congress Cataloging-in-Publication Data

Aniskiewicz, Albert S.
  Psychotherapy for neuropsychological challenges / Albert S. Aniskiewicz.
    p. ; cm.
  Includes bibliographical references.
    ISBN-13: 978-0-7657-0389-7 (cloth : alk. paper)
    ISBN-10: 0-7657-0389-0 (cloth : alk. paper)
  1. Psychotherapy. 2. Brain—Diseases—Psychological aspects. 3.
Neuropsychiatry. I. Title.
  [DNLM: 1. Nervous System Diseases—psychology. 2. Psychotherapy—
methods. WL 140 A599p 2007]

  RC480.5.A633 2007
  616.89'14—dc22   2007001109

Printed in the United States of America

♾™ The paper used in this publication meets the minimum requirements of
American National Standard for Information Sciences—Permanence of Paper
for Printed Library Materials, ANSI/NISO Z39.48-1992.

For Linn

Contents

Acknowledgments

With grateful appreciation...

To my patients who have invited me into the moments of their lives—their joys and sorrows, their fears and hopes. You have been among my best teachers.

To Dr. Christopher Colenda, Dr. David Kaufman, and Dr. Jed Magen who know that leadership in academic medicine is providing opportunity and then support for others to succeed.

To Dr. William J. Mueller, my colleague, mentor, and friend—you set the standard for what it means to be a psychotherapist.

To my family. Without your love and support there would have been no professor, there would have been no book. For Stanley and Stella Aniskiewicz, and Mary A. Jackiewicz—how I wish you were here to see how it is all turning out.

To my daughter Alena. You have been, you are, and you forever will be the joy of my life.

To my wife Linn. Your life is a lesson in grace under pressure. You taught me how to find joy, happiness, and our dreams in the difficult. You are an inspiration for hope, and I hope this book has been faithful to your teachings.

Permissions to Reprint

Part I

AN ATTITUDE OF MIND

Introduction

In the middle of the journey of our life
I found myself astray in a dark wood
Where the straight road had been lost sight of.

—Dante

Dante's poetry provides a timeless metaphor for the darker side of human experience ultimately shared by all at some time in our journey. Perhaps unexpectedly thrown off course having been stricken by illness or touched by other personal tragedy, feeling alone, lost, facing inexorable struggle; indeed the time does come when what had been someone else's crash with fate becomes our reality. In a beautifully written yet compellingly accurate description of his own struggles with depression, *Darkness Visible*, the novelist William Styron (1990) calls upon Dante's "vast metaphor" to represent the "fathomless ordeal" and "black struggle" known by those who have suffered the descent into depression's dark wood. The metaphor is equally applicable to the neuropsychological challenges that are faced by people who have been stricken with conditions or traumas that affect the brain and central nervous system.

Consider the experience of a young father diagnosed with multiple sclerosis whose struggles to maintain his job with a construction firm depleted his reserves, leaving little of him available for his wife and young daughter; or the physician whose career was prematurely abbreviated by the residual effects of what was considered a mild head injury; or the athletically and intellectually gifted college student whose youth and dreams were stolen by a ruptured aneurysm; or the buoyant and energetic lobbyist whose stumbling and imbalance presaged the degenerative neurologic condition that would

3

compromise her thinking and mobility and then claim her life; or the young teacher whose search for an etiology that could account for her disruptions in cognition and walking found herself lost in the borderlands of neurology and psychiatry, reliving yet again the familiar experience of not being understood. Each life set off its intended course by a condition affecting brain functioning; each person facing their unique expression of neuropsychological challenges; all "finding themselves astray in the dark wood where the straight road had been lost sight of."

NEUROPSYCHOLOGICAL CHALLENGES AND OPPORTUNITIES

How can we begin to think about neuropsychological challenges in a way that informs our treatment approaches? Perhaps it is best to begin with a clarification of terms. In our discussion, neuropsychological challenges will refer to the primary and secondary effects of neurological disorders on cognitive functioning and psychological status. Primary cognitive effects may include disruptions in any one of several cognitive domains—such as attention and concentration, language and verbal abilities, visual-analytic processing, learning and memory, or executive functions and conceptual problem-solving skills—that can be seen in a wide range of conditions affecting cortical or subcortical brain regions. Primary effects on psychological status and personality are equally widespread and can include disruptions in mood such as post–stroke depression, or problems with behavioral regulation like the disinhibition that can be seen when frontal brain regions are affected by traumatic brain injury. Recognizing secondary effects and emotional reactions is no less important for these lingering shock waves— often reflecting the complex interplay of longstanding personality dynamics with the adaptive challenges of dealing with compromised functioning, loss, and uncertainty—become the "dark wood" in which our patients find themselves after initial diagnosis has been made and acute medical care has been provided.

Adversity has a way of unmasking qualities that reveal the essence of who we are. No longer as facile in movement or quick to the hectic pace of this technological age, many people living with neuropsychological challenges nevertheless exemplify "grace under pressure," that expression of courage described by a Nobel laureate of literature, Ernest Hemingway. Their loss of function does not diminish the enduring determination and grit that are prerequisites for facing daily challenges and actively living with the truth of their experience. Such qualities are not bestowed by helping professions; rather they await discovery that can be prompted by illness. To work with such people, to as best we can *present* with their experience, is to be a witness to courage. Having the privilege of providing service, we are given opportunities to cultivate the wisdom and compassion that will enrich our own life experience and guide our efforts in providing a psychotherapeutic context within which healing and transformation can occur.

My patients have been and continue to be among my best teachers, and their stories inform the spirit and approaches offered in this book. Case vignettes and other clinical material are derived from a variety of professional and personal experiences including psychotherapy, neuropsychological assessment, supervision and consultation with trainees and colleagues, and other opportunities simply to talk with people living with neurological conditions along with their companions and family at support groups and conferences. When names are used in the text to refer to patients or family members, they are pseudonyms; and some accounts of neuropsychological challenges are composite pictures and interactions are condensed versions of what actually transpired. To further protect confidentiality and privacy, I have omitted or disguised information and situations hopefully while still doing justice to the lessons being taught by these many teachers and not losing the essence of their experiences.

PSYCHOTHERAPY GOALS

What are the goals of psychotherapy, or perhaps in today's vernacular—what constitutes effective psychological treatment? The aims and methods can be as diverse as the schools of thought that claim to have demonstrated either empirically or experientially how to address the maladies of the human condition, be they generalized anxiety disorder or existential angst. And what about those people living with neuropsychological challenges? How might we think about psychotherapy perspectives or treatment methods that address symptomatic expressions of suffering, without losing sight of the person whose experiences—sometimes irrevocably changed by a neurological condition—give rise to the sorrows and joys that color their lives?

Ultimately, our approaches—regardless of theoretical orientation—are not value free, so it would be best to acknowledge at the outset the predilections and attitudes that inform this book. If the aims of psychological treatments are to target specific psychopathologies (Barlow 2004) then the goals of psychotherapy are more encompassing, for the experiences of the patient that may contribute to the very psychopathologies being targeted are no less a focus of our attention. Let me amplify this point, because it is an organizing principle for the therapy perspective we will be discussing. Our approach in working with neuropsychological challenges recognizes the usefulness of specific strategies aimed at ameliorating psychological symptoms. Our methods include mindfulness-based meditation and stress reduction approaches that have roots in ancient traditions and recently have informed cognitive-behavioral therapies (Linehan 1993; Segal, Williams, and Teas-dale 2002). However our interventions are offered within the context of a relationship, *a psychotherapy*, in which the person of the therapist, the person of the patient whose experiences may include but are not restricted to symptoms or psychopathologies, and interaction of therapist and patient are critical variables in treatment and not an afterthought. In this view, psychotherapy is not relegated to some generic status with the second-rate connotations that such a designation may suggest. Psychotherapy is not the handmaiden for technique; it is the essential context for technique to be successful.

Among the factors contributing to successful outcomes in psychological treatments, the primacy held by the therapeutic relationship has long been known (Strupp 1989), yet in the climate of "empirically demonstrated treatments," we should not risk this essential ingredient for positive treatment outcome or personal transformation (depending on one's perspective of change) being marginalized to the appendices of a treatment manual. We might expect clinicians with a psychodynamic perspective to share similar views about the primacy of the therapy relationship, but it is equally important to note that empirical support is now forthcoming from research on cognitive-behavioral therapy (CBT). In a large-scale clinical trial (Vocisano et al. 2004) that investigated cognitive-behavioral analysis system of psychotherapy (CBASP), medication, and the effects of both on chronic depression, it was found that the single best predictor of outcome was the emphasis therapists placed on discussing the patient-therapist relationship. Emphases placed on other treatment variables including techniques (i.e., remediations of cognitions and behaviors) and desired outcomes were not associated with symptom reduction. And so we continue to rediscover that the core feature of psychotherapy makes the difference after all, even with psychological treatments aimed at specific psychopathologies.

> And the end of all our exploring
> Will be to arrive where we started
> And know the place for the first time.
>
> —T. S. Eliot, "Little Gidding" (1942)

PSYCHOTHERAPY FOR NEUROPSYCHOLOGICAL CHALLENGES

How shall we consider psychotherapy goals when working with neuropsychological challenges? To begin with a broad brushstroke, our goals are probably not very different from other psychotherapies; our efforts are aimed at reducing psychological/emotional suffering and promoting an active engagement in life as it is now and as it continues to unfold. Addressing the psychological manifestations of human suffering is nothing new for psychotherapy nor is it the exclusive province of a particular school of thought. The psychoanalyst Polly Young-Eisendrath (2003) recently has commented on the nature of human suffering and the transformative potential of psychotherapy. On the other side of the spectrum, cognitive-behavior therapists are promoting empirically supported treatments for anxiety and depression—manifestations of human suffering but perhaps packaged more neatly in the categorical classifications of DSM-IV-TR.

Reducing or at least easing psychological suffering certainly can help in approaching our second psychotherapy goal—promoting a more active engagement with life. Our work with neuropsychological challenges does not minimize the importance of addressing psychological/emotional pain, but when considering suffering and engagement with life, our orientation is more reciprocal than unidirectional. Let me explain. Recent developments in psychology have called for expanding the scope of our inquiry from a focus on pathology to factors that make life worth living (Seligman and Csikszentmihalyi 2000). This "positive psychology" with its focus on joy, hope, spirituality, and wisdom reminds us that an active engagement in life places illness and loss within a larger life context that may not eradicate symptoms, but changes our relationship to suffering in such a way that our experience is transformed and, as a by-product, suffering may be reduced. For our patients living with neuropsychological challenges, an active engagement in life may no longer be skiing in Aspen but instead the simple act of watering the houseplant on the kitchen counter with enough care and attention to notice the leaf that wasn't there last week; or maybe listening, really listening, to Mozart's *Ave Verum Corpus* as twilight descends; or perhaps seeing the maple at the end of the drive that seems to be bowing after another stunning autumn performance. Describing the experience of reading Marcel Proust's grand novel *In Search of Lost Time*, Alain de Botton reminds us to notice "such faint yet vital tremors" (2004, 43) for they are nothing less than the moments of our lives. In this light our second psychotherapy goal is less a destination and more an attitude of mind, a sensitivity to the moments we may have remembered with regret for not having been there, a gratitude for awakening to a new life—even if prompted by illness—that may temper the loss of the one we once knew.

Psychological research has demonstrated the powerful impact such shifts in life perspective can have, not only on the psychological well-being of people living with chronic medical conditions but also on the very physiology that underlies the conditions. Writing in an issue of *American Psychologist* featuring articles on positive psychology, Shelley Taylor and colleagues (2000) comment on a study (Bower et al. 1998) that showed recently bereaved HIV-seropositive men who found *meaning* in their experience of loss showed a lower level of CD4 T helper cell decline, and were less likely to die during the follow-up period than men who did not engage in such perspective-shifting reorientation. Meaning was defined as "a major shift in values, priorities, or perspective in response to the loss" and reflected such attitudes as living in the moment, and recognizing the fragility and preciousness of life.

While psychological research can elucidate the realities we suspect may exist, the stark essence of these realities is no better described than by those who live the experience—by those who know the transformative potential that lies within suffering and loss. This invitation to a new—and for some what may be a better—way of living is eloquently offered by distinguished writer and James B. Duke Professor of English at Duke University, Reynolds Price, in his book *A Whole New Life*. With the wisdom and compassion born of his own struggles with a spinal cord tumor, paralysis, and pain; his bracing advice carries the hope and reality of transformation: "Next find your way to be somebody else, the next viable you—a stripped-down whole other clear-eyed person, realistic as a sawed-off shotgun and thankful for the air, not to speak of the human kindness you'll meet if you get normal luck" (Price 1994, 183).

May we be of some assistance to our patients in finding their way out of a "dark wood" to be somebody else? May we as psychotherapists accept Reynolds Price's challenge—within an article, a book, a psychotherapy session—to offer "useful instruction in how to absorb the staggering but not-quite-lethal blow of a fist that ends your former life and offers nothing by way of a new life that you can begin to think of wanting" (Price 1994, 181).

A STARTING POINT

As a starting point, it is useful to maintain the open mind of a beginner and invite, listen to, and consider the experiences and opinions of those we intend to help. And so to begin, let us consider a research study that was aimed at identifying the needs of people living with multiple sclerosis that might be addressed by psychologists. Eklund and MacDonald (1991) found that those struggling with this neurological condition expressed the need for help in two primary areas: accepting the reality of the disease, and learning how to best live with it. Now consider the need for *useful instruction* underscored by Reynolds Price with the needs identified in this research study of patients whose lives have been irrevocably changed by multiple sclerosis; the parallel themes begin to resonate, and we may begin to hear more clearly their echoes in the stories of our own patients living with the losses and adaptive challenges of neurological conditions—to accept and go on living.

There is little doubt that neuropsychological challenges are daunting for our patients, their families, and even for us as psychotherapists, for more often than not a "return to baseline functioning"—that place which managed care may deem a successful treatment outcome—is an illusory concept that does not match the reality of our patients' lives. The baseline has shifted and the idea of returning to what was too often provokes more suffering and forestalls the engagement with the truth of what is now—accepting the reality of the condition and learning how to best live with it, which ultimately become the cornerstones for transformation.

If we are to assist our patients with the challenges of this transformation, we should know something about the neurological conditions they are living with, and we should develop psychotherapeutic approaches that address the unique expression of neuropsychological challenges in the person for whom the condition has become a part but not all of life. The intention of this book is to consider this twofold task by reviewing the nature of the neuropsychological challenges that can be associated with particular neurological conditions, and by offering ways of addressing these challenges in psychotherapy.

A SIMPLE TWIST OF FATE

It was 2:30 on a rainy April afternoon when my friend and colleague Dr. Joe Pernicone stepped away from the MRI monitor where his experienced eyes had been scanning yet another set of images whose shadows held a verdict. Radiology staff members who had been milling about just moments before had returned to their workstations and to awaiting patients, leaving the scanning area empty and strangely silent. As Joe approached, his concerned eyes now foretold the truth of a reality I had been trying to silence, but with his every step that truth seemed to grow louder, drowning any illusions that remained of certainty and control. In retrospect it was probably one last attempt to wrest control from a situation that just wasn't cooperating with my view of how that day was to turn out. I would say it before he could. I remember blurting out something like, "Does it look like MS?" With the clarity of a skilled physician couched in the kindness of a long friendship, Joe offered me the simple truth, "Yes Al, it does."

Linn and I had met several years earlier when she was the project manager for a research study several graduate students and I were doing that investigated the relationship between MRI findings and cognitive dysfunction in multiple sclerosis. Driving home that rainy afternoon a decade later, I remembered our once working together in that very place where hours earlier she had been the patient in the MRI scanner, and in a few moments I was going to tell my wife that she probably had the condition she once helped me study.

So what was this all about? A bad dream, a strange irony, maybe a complex interplay of karmic forces. The motivation to know is powerful if only because it tempers, albeit temporarily, that groundless feeling of uncertainty. But ultimately Linn's diagnosis with multiple sclerosis was nothing more complicated than "a simple twist of fate" in the immortal words of Bob Dylan—her crash with fate that would throw us off course to a new and unintended path whose challenges held different opportunities and teachings.

Maybe I was better prepared for this journey because I knew something about the condition. That thought was comforting at the beginning, and the knowledge has been helpful, but knowing about the condition is not living with the condition. I have come to learn that perspectives on both—what to know and how to live with what is known—are essential, and Linn has been a teacher in the art of living domain. Being with a wise and loving companion who embraces life with a challenging condition is both humbling and instructive. But whatever lessons were to be learned from her experiences would require—at least for me—a shift in attitude, a letting go of self-absorbed preoccupation to be gradually replaced by an attitude of mind open to the truth of what is.

Somewhere along this journey, I came across neurologist James H. Austin's exploration of consciousness, *Zen and the Brain* (1998) and his wonderfully insightful description of *I-Me-Mine* consciousness—those cherished beliefs about ourselves whose unmasking, while discomfiting, are the openings for liberation and the beginnings of true wisdom and compassion. In my case it was the *I* who knew something about neuropsychology and psychotherapy, and multiple sclerosis in particular; the *Me* who was assaulted when my wife was diagnosed with a neurological illness, the *Mine* whose desires, plans, concepts of what was supposed to be were forever altered and not by *my* choosing. Permanently eradicating *I-Me-Mine* consciousness is no longer the goal, although I must admit it was something *I* did strive for. Now just loosening up a bit to be aware of *I-Me-Mine* rearing its head seems to be enough to create a space, some breathing room for the lessons that come from outside the constricted realm of the self.

What have these lessons taught? Psychotherapy has much to offer to alleviate the suffering of our patients living with neuropsychological challenges if we can translate what we know into interventions that are guided by whatever degree of wisdom and compassion we can muster. Lessons in the art of living—even if that means living with neuropsychological challenges—are not the sole province of psychology. Positive psychology is a step in expanding our view, but we will benefit by opening our minds to sources outside our discipline to inform our work with patients whose lives have been irrevocably changed by neurological trauma or illness. The teachings of nature, poetry, art, music, the simple but challenging practice of mindful living offer rich lessons in the art of living that may complement our scientifically informed efforts to reduce suffering and cure illness.

PLANS AND INTENTIONS

The material in this book is offered with the intention that it be faithful to the lessons of the many teachers and sources that informed its contents, and that it be presented in a manner that is accessible and ultimately helpful to clinicians who work with people living with neuropsychological challenges. The perspectives of the book represent *a way* and not necessarily *the way* for approaching living with neuropsychological challenges. As we honor the unfolding process of our patients' experiences—as well as our own—we recognize that our treatment methods also continue to evolve, reflecting an openness that invites many possibilities. For people living with neuropsychological challenges and for the psychotherapists who join them on this part of their journey, may the possibilities in this book be a helpful guide.

> My guide and I set out on that hidden path
> to make our way into the bright world again,
> and so we climbed with no thought of rest—
> He first and I second—until we reached ground
> where I could see through a rounded opening
> the night sky with the beautiful things it carries;
> And we came out and looked up at the stars.
>
> —Dante, *Inferno*, canto XXXIV
> (quoted in Halpern, 1993)

REFERENCES AND READINGS

Austin, James H. 1998. *Zen and the brain.* Cambridge: MIT Press.

Barlow, David. 2004. Psychological treatments. *American Psychologist* 59 (9): 869–878.

Bower, Julienne E., Margaret E. Kemeny, Shelley E. Taylor, and John L. Fahey. 1998. Cognitive processing, discovery of meaning, CD4 decline, and AIDS-related mortality among bereaved HIV-seropositive men. *Journal of Consulting and Clinical Psychology* 66 (6): 979–986.

de Botton, Alain. 2004. My fine, scarlet, ever-changing morning. In *The Proust project*, edited by A. Aciman. New York: Farrar, Straus & Giroux.

Dylan, Bob. 2004. *Bob Dylan lyrics 1962–2001.* New York: Simon & Schuster.

Eklund, Victoria-Anne, and Marian L. MacDonald. 1991. Descriptions of persons with multiple sclerosis, with an emphasis on what is needed from psychologists. *Professional Psychology: Research and Practice* 22 (4): 277–284.

Eliot, T. S. 1942. *Four quartets.* New York: Harcourt.

Halpern, Daniel, ed. 1993. *Dante's inferno: Translations by 20 contemporary poets.* Hopewell, NJ: Ecco Press.

Linehan, Marsha. 1993. *Cognitive-behavioral treatment of borderline personality disorder.* New York: Guilford Press.

Price, Reynolds. 1994. *A whole new life: An illness and a healing.* New York: Scribner.

Segal, Zindel V., J. Mark G. Williams, and John D. Teasdale. 2002. *Mindfulness-based cognitive therapy for depression: A new approach for preventing relapse.* New York: Guilford Press.

Seligman, Martin, and Mihaly Csikszentmihalyi. 2000. Positive psychology: An introduction. *American Psychologist* 55 (1): 5–14.

Strupp, H. 1989. Can the practitioner learn from the researcher? *Psychotherapy* 44:717–724.

Styron, William. 1990. *Darkness visible: A memoir of madness.* New York: Vintage Books.

Taylor, Shelley, M. E. Kemeny, J. E. Bower, T. L. Gruenewald, and G. M. Reed. 2000. Psychological resources, positive illusions, and health. *American Psychologist* 55 (1): 99–109.

Vocisano, Carina, Daniel N. Klein, Bruce Arnow, Caridad Rivera, Janice A. Blalock, Barbara Rothbaum, Dina Vivian, John C. Markowitz, James H. Kocsis, Rachel Manber, Louis Castonguay, A. John Rush, Frances E. Borian, James P. McCullough, Susan G. Kornstein, Lawrence P. Riso, and Michael E. Thase. 2004. Therapist variables that predict symptom change in psychotherapy with chronically depressed outpatients. *Psychotherapy: Theory, Research, Practice, Training* 41 (3): 255–265.

Young-Eisendrath, Polly. 2003. Transference and transformation in Buddhism and psychoanalysis. In *Psychoanalysis and Buddhism: An unfolding dialogue,* edited by J. D. Safran. Somerville, MA: Wisdom Publications.

1

Sources and Teachers

In the beginner's mind there are many possibilities, but in the expert's there are few.

—Shunryu Suzuki (1997)

POSSIBILITIES AND HOPE

A mind that is open can see many possibilities, but so often our preconceived notions about illness, approaches to treatment, and what it means to live with life-altering conditions narrow our view such that we see only limited options with diminishing hope. Unfortunately we tend to become increasingly rigid when threatened, especially when our lives have been thrown off course by illness and loss. Caught in the dizzying disequilibrium of uncertainty, we flail about hoping to grab on to something if only to catch our breath. We tighten our hold, trying to maintain some semblance of the person who was, but that illusion of permanence slips through our grip like sand. We are left with something we recognize, but it is not who we were, and it is not what we want. We try to steady ourselves by predicting the future—"It's going to turn out this way or that"—but this illusion of certainty comes with the expense of more anxiety and fear. We feel our life slipping away because it is, as moments of living in the present are sacrificed to longings for the past and fears of the future. Our doctors and loved ones exhort us to maintain hope, and in our confusion and pain we grasp again, hoping to get what we want and avoid what we don't. Even with "hope" then, why do we remain so shaken? Perhaps because our idea of hope is just that, a concept that reflects an attitude of mind stuck

13

in wanting what was and avoiding what is. Might we be hopeful in a different way, not so much as a promise of return—"I hope to get something from this"—but more so as an openness to possibilities that hold the easing of suffering and a reengagement with life? With this shift in perspective hope is something we live, not just believe; it is no longer a static concept we hold on to waiting for it to deliver us someplace other than where we are. Hope is something dynamic and alive, something we do that powers the momentum of treatment and reengagement with life. With hope there are possibilities for healing and transformation; and with possibilities we maintain hope.

If we are encouraging our patients with neuropsychological challenges to make adaptations and adjustments to their life situation, we are implicitly asking them to have the openness and flexibility to consider new and different ways of going about their lives, and to maintain the hope that what they do will make a difference. Likewise if our therapy is to be infused with the hope that our efforts will be helpful, then an open mind and flexible attitude may allow us to see possibilities, especially when hope has been shaken. Such possibilities are available both within and outside our discipline.

My thinking about the possibilities of psychotherapy for neuropsychological challenges has been informed by many and varied sources ranging from the professional literature of neurology and psychology to the language of poetry; from the teachings of my patients, mentors, and colleagues to the lessons that are a part of our daily lives. Dealing with the complexity and uncertainty of neuropsychological challenges calls for the openness to consider different perspectives, and the flexibility to adjust to the changing nature of our patients' experiences. Dogmatic adherence to preconceived notions despite evidence to the contrary does not advance science, nor do rigidly held beliefs of how to approach neuropsychological challenges in psychotherapy provide helpful perspectives on living with change and uncertainty. Openness and flexibility do not mean "anything goes," which ultimately is desperation's invitation for the charlatan, but more so a willingness to consider options and possibilities with a discernment born of experience and tempered by balance. We may make the wrong turn here and there, and a dead-end will stop our journey of discovery if self-criticism for having taken a path rigidifies into a paralyzing fear about taking another step into uncertainty. Might it be more fruitful to have self-judgment replaced by the question of the wise teacher who asks, "What was the lesson at this point along the way, and how can we transform what seems a wrong turn into a right learning experience?"

So as not to confuse an open mind and flexible attitude with lack of rigor, let's consider the lessons of science. The debris of false starts and unproven hunches would only be litter on the pathways to scientific discovery if our focus were narrowed solely on the end-products of scientific endeavor. However, from a different perspective, such wrong turns are not simply failed end-products but essential learning experiences within a larger unfolding process of Science from which evolve refinements in thinking and method that allow a closer glimpse at Nature's truths. An attitude that has propelled the discoveries of science is no less applicable to the discoveries that await our patients and us in the unfolding process of psychotherapy. So often it is not the rightness or wrongness of our interventions in psychotherapy that make a difference, but our patients' responses to our interventions, and our capacity to be sufficiently open and flexible to attend to those responses that deepens our exploration and draws us closer to the truth of our patients' experiences, their inner lives. As Rilke advised in *Letters to a Young Poet,* "if it turns out that you are wrong, then the natural growth of your inner life will eventually guide you to other insights" (Letter 3).

KNOWING AND LIVING: SCIENCE AND ART

In the current climate of evidence-based practice, psychotherapy has been increasingly called upon to demonstrate its usefulness and scientific basis, and the promotion of empirically supported psychological treatments has been one response to this challenge. While such treatments certainly can be effective, their empirically demonstrated efficacy does not negate the usefulness of other approaches (e.g., psychodynamic), nor the reality that there are aspects of the human condition—which our patients bring with them to their therapy sessions—that have not yet been captured by scientific method or for that matter may remain outside the purview of science. This stark reality is no more evident than in the experiences of our patients who, having been diagnosed with a neurological condition and having received evidence-based medical and psychological treatments, are left with their unanswered questions: "What now?"; "How do I go on from here?" I think we can be helpful to our patients in living their way to an answer by not getting caught in the dead-end of dualistic thinking. In acknowledging the contributions of science to our methods, we also recognize that the practice of psychotherapy is no less an art. Both perspectives—art and science—are complementary and essential in appreciating the world and our experience in it.

From the vantage point of having lived in both worlds as a novelist and physicist, Alan Lightman (2005) provides a helpful perspective on the complementary relationship of art and science. In his collection of essays *A Sense of the Mysterious,* he beautifully describes the quest of Science in seeking the answers to questions, finding the results that already exist, discovering the truths of nature. Stepping away for a moment from physics and shifting our focus to health care, we see parallel themes in the efforts of medical science to find cures for the illnesses that plague us. Lightman, however, also recognizes the power of Art where unanswerable questions that hold the passions and mysteries of living find expression in music, literature, and visual arts. Perhaps while waiting for *cures* to be found by Science, living with the questions yet to be answered may begin a process of *healing* assisted by Art, a process of reengagement with life. In saying the unsayable, expressing the inexpressible, Art touches our emotions and "by doing so each of us finds a secret, private conduit to an inner life that is not just our *new* life but our true life" (Aciman 2004, 101).

A POSITIVE PSYCHOLOGY

Developments in positive psychology, while rooted in science, provide a bridge to those areas of our patients' experiences that are about the art of living. Psychological research and practice has a long history of focusing on pathology, abnormal behavior, "a preoccupation only with repairing the worst things in life" (Seligman and Csikszentmihalyi 2000). Positive psychology calls for expanding the focus psychological inquiry to include those factors that make life worth living: "hope, wisdom, creativity, future mindedness, courage, responsibility, and perseverance" (Seligman and Csikszentmihalyi 2000). Research in this area is now providing a promising scientific foundation for expanding the scope of psychotherapy and thereby increasing the possibilities for our patients with neuropsychological challenges. We already have seen how finding meaning in loss can have positive effects not only on psychological well-being but also on the underlying pathophysiology of illness. Researchers also are investigating the realms of emotions and their relationships to cognition and coping—areas that are equally relevant to our patients living with neuropsychological challenges. Consider the Broaden–and–Build Theory of Positive Emotions (Fredrickson 2001), which states that positive emotions—such as joy, interest, contentment, pride, and love—have the ability to broaden thought-action repertoires and build enduring personal resources ranging from physical and intellectual resources to social and psychological resources. The results of studies based on this theory have significant implications for developing psychotherapy approaches for people living with neuropsychological challenges. Cultivating positive emotions may help people place the events in their lives in a broader context, thus lessening the resonance of any particular negative event; and further positive emotions may fuel psychological resilience and in doing so increase capacities to deal with current and future stress (Frederickson 2001).

AWAKENINGS: LESSONS OF ILLNESS

Illness can be a bracing wake-up call that sharpens our awareness and focuses our attention on the deeper currents of life experience—the impermanence of all that we know and love, the preciousness of the present moment, the simple and ordinary joys of life we may have been too preoccupied and too busy to notice.

> Since the heart attack, I come up the stairs
> and say to myself, "Now I'm opening
> the door, now I'm hanging up my coat, now I hear
> someone yell 'Daddy!' in my extra life."
> It's like having seconds after Thanksgiving dinner,
> savoring my favorite things, but not quite.
> It's as if I now feast on turnips and cranberry sauce,
> the mundane side dishes I used to push aside
> for more stuffing and gravy, more flamboyant breast.
> I count the hops out loud ad infinitum
> as my daughter jumps rope in the living room.
> In my regular life, I would
> have had thoughts in my head.
> In my extra life, I don't.
>
> —Doug Dorph, "Second Helping" (1999)

Our patients living with neurological conditions have many lessons to teach if we are open to learning from their experience. From a lawyer and mother who prided herself on being a multi-taskmaster before her head injury: "Being forced to slow down has been terrifying because I've been running from me as long as I can remember, but I'm realizing more and more the life I've been missing—me included." From a teacher of autistic children who struggles with seizures and a movement disorder: "I still catch myself reacting to the old expectations to be productive, but I'm learning I can contribute in other ways, sometimes just being with another person, not judging them or myself is enough, maybe there can be a positive ripple effect." From an auto worker with a degenerative neurological condition arriving for his appointment with a quart of rocky road ice cream and two spoons: "Hey doc, time's running out, let's live it up a little."

Returning home one summer evening after a day of seeing patients, teaching medical students, and meeting in a weekly seminar with a group of psychiatry residents, I hadn't really noticed much of the drive from campus or the telltale signs of a thunderstorm having passed through town earlier that afternoon. As I approached the driveway to my home, my mind was still on campus, bouncing from thoughts about my last session with a patient, to revisions I might make for next week's seminar. And my preoccupation with the seeming accomplishments of the day just wasn't delivering the feeling of peace and contentment I hoped would greet me as I drove down the driveway, finally home after a long day. Instead I saw my wife sitting in a lawn chair in front of the garage looking down at the ground. My first thought of, what is she doing? was quickly followed by, what did she get done today? She seemed to anticipate my questions and gently smiling said, "I'm watching this puddle dry." It was time for this professor to be a student, for what started as a wave of incredulity at this seeming waste of time transformed into a much-needed slap on the side of my "head"—yet another one of Linn's teachings by being. With her simple, unadorned statement of noticing her world as it existed right in front of her, she prompted an awakening, although I must admit a rush of thoughts too—but this time about noticing, being present for life, lightening up on expectations, striving less for peace and contentment and allowing it to be here now. Meanwhile, she kept watching that puddle dry.

> So the wise soul
> doesn't go, but knows;
> doesn't look, but sees;
> doesn't do, but gets done.
>
> —*Tao Te Ching* (quoted in Le Guin, 1997)

TEACHINGS OF POETRY

Watching interviews with soldiers who have lost limbs while serving in Iraq is a humbling lesson in gratitude—as one young amputee said, "I'm still alive, that is something to be joyful about." My patients who have suffered life-changing losses have expressed similar feelings of gratitude. It's as if the awakenings to life prompted by loss and illness are sustained by gratitude for what remains; whereas those of us who have yet to have our crash with fate tend to forget, our awakenings fade into the busyness of getting someplace other than where we are.

We need reminders that stir awakenings, that surprise us, that help us feel something once known but long since forgotten, or maybe appreciate for the first time what has always been but remained unseen. In the simple act of reading a poem, in "saying the unsayable" (Hall 2003), we hear the sounds and feel the rhythms of something familiar, and we recognize that something as ourselves. From the poem *Love after Love*, by Derek Walcott (1986): "You will love again the stranger who was your self."

In his essay *The Unsayable Said*, poet Donald Hall (2003) offers us a reason as good as any for poetry to inform our psychology: "Poetry, on the other hand, wants to address *the whole matter of the human*—including fact and logic, but also the body with its senses, and above all the harsh and soft complexities of emotion." And perhaps there is no better example of a poem's power to "address the whole matter of the human" than *Otherwise*, Jane Kenyon's (1996) poignant reminder of life to be lived with gratitude.

> I got out of bed
> on two strong legs.
> It might have been
> otherwise. I ate
> cereal, sweet
> milk, ripe, flawless
> peach. It might
> have been otherwise.
> I took the dog uphill
> to the birch wood.
> All morning I did
> the work I love.
>
> At noon I lay down
> with my mate. It might
> have been otherwise.
> We ate dinner together
> at a table with silver
> candlesticks. It might
> have been otherwise.
> I slept in a bed
> in a room with paintings
> on the walls, and
> planned another day
> just like this day.
> But one day, I know,
> it will be otherwise.

TEACHINGS OF NATURE

Perhaps no teacher speaks as eloquently or simply of the truths of our existence as the natural world that surrounds us. Having grown up not far from the Jersey Shore, images of the ocean hold a special place in my memory even as these words are being typed in a university office, and outside the season's first snowstorm blankets a midwestern campus. Hopefully these images may resonate with your personal experiences and provide visual equivalents of different ideas and perspectives that may be useful in your work with patients living with neuropsychological challenges.

We are of water, as it constitutes about 60%–70% of our body weight; at the same time water, as manifested in the form of the great oceans, surrounds us. The qualities and forms of water provide us with metaphors that reflect the universal truths, be they the ever-changing flow of our lives, or perhaps that stillness that can be found beneath the surface turbulence of our daily frustrations. And yes, there is also the reminder of today's snowstorm—that life is happening now outside a fourth floor office window, if we just take the time to notice. Nature in all her forms can be a continuing source of wisdom offering lessons in our daily lives, if we can quiet the chatter in our minds and our preconceived notions of what ought to be and try to remain open to her teachings of what is.

> When anxious, uneasy and evil thoughts come I go to the sea,
> and the sea drowns them with its great wide murmurs,
> purifies me with its syllables and lays a rhythm in me
> upon all that is bewildered and confused.
>
> —Rainer Maria Rilke, *Selected Letters* (1947)

A SYNTHESIS: LESSONS FROM NEUROSCIENCE

Drawing upon sources such as poetry or nature, which at a superficial glance may seem outside the scientific or professional health care community offers perspectives in the art of living and thereby provides the right conditions for discussing the neuropsychological consequences of illness without getting lost in its symptoms. Ultimately, however, we may find that the boundaries among various disciplines are arbitrary distinctions that do not reflect the nature of mind and brain functioning as the wondrous synthesizing activities they are. Perhaps we may more easily see the relationships between seemingly disparate ideas or disciplines if we maintain an open mind that taps into the brain's natural organization and capacity to integrate information from multiple sources. In his book *Mozart's Brain and the Fighter Pilot*, the neurologist Richard Restak (2001, 31) comments on this phenomenon, "Today we know that the brain is naturally organized to attain synthetic overviews that draw on knowledge and information from the widest possible sources."

REFERENCES AND READINGS

Aciman, Andre. 2004. Upheaval of my entire being. In *The Proust project*, edited by A. Aciman. New York: Farrar, Straus & Giroux.

Dorph, Doug. 1999. Second helping. *The New Yorker*, July 12.

Fredrickson, Barbara. 2001. The role of positive emotions in positive psychology: The broaden-and-build theory of positive emotions. *American Psychologist* 56 (3): 218–226.

Hall, Donald. 2003. *Breakfast served any time all day: Essays on poetry new and selected.* Ann Arbor: University of Michigan Press.

Kenyon, Jane. 1996. *Otherwise: New and selected poems.* St. Paul, MN: Graywolf Press.

Le Guin, Ursula K. 1997. *Lao Tzu Tao Te Ching: A book about the way and the power of the way.* Boston: Shambhala Publications.

Lightman, Alan. 2005. *A sense of the mysterious: Science and the human spirit.* New York: Pantheon.

Restak, Richard. 2001. *Mozart's brain and the fighter pilot: Unleashing your brain's potential.* New York: Harmony Books.

Rilke, Rainer Maria. 1947. *Selected letters of Rainer Maria Rilke.* Translated by R. F. C. Hull. London: Macmillan & Co. Ltd.

———. 2001. *Letters to a young poet.* Translated by S. Mitchell. New York: Modern Library.

Seligman, Martin, and Mihaly Csikszentmihalyi. 2000. Positive psychology: An introduction. *American Psychologist* 55 (1): 5–14.

Suzuki, Shunryu. 1997. *Zen mind, beginner's mind.* New York: Weatherhill, Inc.

Walcott, Derek. 1986. *Collected poems, 1948–1984.* 1st ed. New York: Farrar, Straus & Giroux.

2

Uncertainty and Acceptance

FROM DIAGNOSIS TO LIVING

Beyond reducing uncertainty in identifying the conditions that give rise to neuropsychological challenges, continuing improvements in diagnosis and assessment advance our understanding of the neural networks and pathophysiology underlying our patients' symptoms, and thus open the way for early intervention that may affect the very course of a condition. But after diagnosis and treatment planning, our patients still may be left with questions, the lingering aftershocks of trauma, the challenges of a new and different life. The aloneness of this space can be frightening, but if we can be still with where we are and not fill the space reactively trying to reconstruct what was, then the space becomes an invitation to be *with* our life, as only we can live it.

Living with neuropsychological conditions is living with uncertainty, an experience that can provoke anxiety and fear about a future that is far from predictable despite the best efforts of medical science to map the course of a condition. Perhaps one constant in life upon which we can truly rely is that everything changes. Living with a neuropsychological condition magnifies that reality. The manifestations of change may differ but its inevitability remains the same.

For some of our patients the change is abrupt, as it was for a seventeen-year-old high school senior whose car was broadsided on her way home from a dance. Denise doesn't remember the dance at all; she vaguely remembers getting ready for what was to be a night of fun in a round of graduation parties. A planned future for many teenagers may extend as far as college; Denise's future included college in the fall and so much more that was to happen that summer before taking off for school. In a matter of moments, all that would change.

For other patients, change takes a fluctuating course. Symptoms may appear several months to, at times, years before a formal diagnosis is made. An unsteadiness of gait or periodic loss of balance may come and go. Initially it is not unusual to minimize these odd happenings because the first flush of anxiety that something isn't right is countered with the hope that this intrusion will go away, and relief is often at hand when the symptoms seem to disappear. But their untimely return sets into motion a series of consultations with medical specialists who seek to confirm a reality that ultimately disrupts the equilibrium of life. For some people a diagnosis of multiple sclerosis brings an initial sense of relief that finally something appears certain—there is a reason for these episodes of imbalance and fatigue. A young man recently diagnosed with the condition expressed the contradictory experience, "It was a strange sort of relief to finally have a diagnosis. People would now see I wasn't making it up, it wasn't all in my head, even though I guess it was."

For other patients the change may be slow but unrelentingly progressive. Consider the experience of the professor whose life-long struggles with dysthymia and anxiety were offered as reasons by his family and friends for his more recent preoccupations with forgetfulness and troubles expressing himself in ways to which he was accustomed, which for the professor meant with the precision and flair that had become his signature. A psychiatrist who had known him for many years suggested a neuropsychological evaluation—the first of many—which confirmed the professor's superior intellectual abilities, but also revealed relative weakness in cognitive areas including aspects of memory and language. There were follow-ups and second opinions with neurologists and neuropsychologists that either did not yield a clear diagnosis or attributed the professor's cognitive changes to anxiety, depression, or a combination of both. A couple years later the professor returned for another consultation. He talked about continuing with his academic work but also added, "but I'm not the same, it all takes so much more effort, it's not just anxiety." Another neuropsychological evaluation showed further declines in cognitive areas that had been relatively weak two years earlier and evidence of emerging problems in other areas of functioning, all suggesting a progressive dementia. The professor's cognitive status continued to worsen and several months later he gracefully retired and moved to another state to live with his son.

There is no right reaction to a diagnosis of a neuropsychological condition, but only an individual's personal response—neither good nor bad—at a particular moment in time, which is the accumulation of all that came before and the uncertainty of all that will follow. A middle-aged teacher remembers stepping into the sunshine with the words of his neurologist echoing in his mind, "It looks like MS." He recalled, "The neurologist spoke for several more minutes, but I guess I stopped listening. When I walked to my car the sun was still shining just as it was when I arrived for my appointment. I can remember thinking my life has been changed forever, and everything else will go on like nothing has happened." Looking back on his initial reaction many years later, the teacher would offer another perspective on change and uncertainty: "Life has changed but in different ways than I expected. I'd rather not have MS, but it's taught me that nothing was ever certain. It's still a challenge, but my focus has shifted a bit from *trying to control my life to trying to live it.*"

LOSING CONTROL AND REGAINING BALANCE

Remember learning to ride a bike. Our first attempts were wobbly at best, and we probably looked pretty stiff and rigid as our feeling of tipping to one side was overcorrected by a reaction that only made us fall the other way. We were simply trying to maintain our equilibrium and our first awkward attempts were a bit forced. But with the steadying hand of a parent on the back of our seat, we eventually would loosen our grip, let go into the flow of the ride, and find our balance. I doubt that we thought much about the process of learning to ride and now, so many years later, we can remember that scraped knees wouldn't dampen our determination, but fighting to control the bike only got in the way.

No, living with the losses and limitations of a neurological condition isn't the joy of learning to ride a bike but it is about balance, both physically and mentally, and perhaps even the lessons of childhood can help us develop an attitude of mind to deal with the challenges that have become a part of life. There is no doubt that these challenges can make a person feel that a brain trauma or neurological illness has taken control of his or her life, and an initial reaction might be to wrestle control back or *fight* the condition. Unfortunately, directing this determination into *fighting* can end in feelings of defeat and resignation when symptoms rear their head once again, despite the best efforts to combat them—yet another loss that can leave our patients feeling like *victims* of an illness that won't let go. Try as we may to regain our equilibrium, the *fight versus victim* dilemma only gets in the way. Might there be another way? An ancient teaching suggests there is, and offers a perspective of working with our attitudes, our beliefs, our mind.

> What we are today comes from our thoughts of yesterday,
> and our present thoughts build our life of tomorrow:
> our life is the creation of our mind.
>
> —*The Dhammapada* (quoted in Mascaró, 1973)

ACCEPTANCE AND DENIAL

A Patient's Story

Jennifer had been recently diagnosed with multiple sclerosis and was referred for psychotherapy by her neurologist to help her with the challenge of accepting and coping with the condition. She was the mother of two young boys, and she juggled a busy schedule that included an active involvement in her son's school programs and participation in a number of community organizations. She had begun treatment with one of the disease modifying injectables, but she was reluctant to follow through with her neurologist's recommendation that she also consider attending an MS support group.

Jennifer began her first therapy session by stating, "I guess I'm still in denial because I'm just not ready to go to an MS support group, not now." She tearfully continued, "I'm not ready to face what can happen to me." She talked about family members encouraging her to get all the help she could, and her feelings of guilt and frustration for not complying with their wishes. She would later say, "I've never been a wimp but now I'm afraid . . . I feel my family wants the old Jennifer back. . . . I can see the worry on their faces, and I don't want to cause them more pain. . . . I just don't know what to do next."

A Question of Denial

Was Jennifer "in denial"? If we accept that she believed herself to be, then yes she was in a mindset that could concretize a complex flow of feelings and perceptions into a concept—*denial*. This concept or idea offers the illusion of understanding—Jennifer is struggling with the diagnosis of MS and is denying the reality of the condition. This conceptualization may bring some comfort to the therapist, but it may not do much for Jennifer. If we stay at this level of thinking we run the risk of *denying* her experience as it manifests now, and in doing so we inadvertently reinforce her fear that her life is being consumed by an illness. Sometimes in focusing on the illness we miss the person who has the illness—something like diagnosing the condition but losing the patient.

A Here and Now Perspective

Let's try to refocus our attention and see if we can get a different perspective on Jennifer's situation. How can we help Jennifer accept the reality of living with MS if we don't acknowledge the reality of the condition as it manifests now in the present-moment experience of her life. It is often best to simply start where we are; and at that moment in her first therapy session, Jennifer was flooded by feelings of anxiety and fear of the unknown that threatened her sense of who she thought she was. Her idea of what might happen to her was just that—a mental image of the future that was the product of her anxiety and fear. Acknowledging where she was now in her life—rather than where she thought she was going to be—began a process of accepting the reality of her condition. Sometimes our attempts to impose certainty on an uncertain future—"This is what's going to happen to me"—only come back to haunt us and rob us of the only life we really have, which is now.

Acceptance as a Process

Since everything changes, acceptance isn't a particular point to get to, but an ongoing process of trying as best we can to be with the truth of our experience as it is now. Being with our experience as it is today doesn't mean we disregard tomorrow or "bury our heads in the sand" about the future consequences of our present actions. On the contrary, we are choosing not to be held hostage by the future that can't be known with certainty. Within the process of being with our experience as it is now—trying not to turn away from it nor get caught up in it—we recognize that the consequences of neurological conditions are a part of experience but not all of life. Being with life as it is now—our present-moment experience—provides a foundation for facing the challenges of the future. It allows for a shift in perspective from conquering fears about the future to becoming increasingly comfortable with the uncertainty of life as it continues to unfold today.

Postscript

A year had gone by since her last psychotherapy session, when Jennifer called her therapist to invite him to speak at an MS support group she had organized.

When spring comes, the grass grows by itself.

—A Zen saying (quoted in Hamill and Seaton, 2004)

UNCERTAINTY AS OPPORTUNITY: LIVING THE QUESTION

Our ideas about uncertainty become the lenses through which we view our futures, and sometimes our search for security fuels a quest for answers that are not to be found, at least not in the ways we have been seeking them. As a Sung Dynasty poet wrote, "Searching for spring all day, I never saw it. . . ."

For our patients whose foundations of security have been shaken by neurological conditions, uncertainty looms ever more ominous. But a shift in attitude can temper fear of the unknown and invite a return to life as it can only exist—now—and the feeling may be something like coming home.

> Coming home, I laughed, catching
> the plum blossom's scent:
> spring at each branch tip, already perfect.
>
> —anonymous Sung Dynasty nun

Deepak Chopra (1994, 86–87), a physician and leader in the field of mind-body medicine, invites us to consider a perspective of possibilities as we consider uncertainty: "The unknown is the field of all possibilities, ever fresh, ever new, always open to the creation of new manifestations. Without uncertainty and the unknown, life is just a stale repetition of outworn memories. You become the victim of the past, and your tormentor today is your self left over from yesterday."

With possibilities there is hope, and with hope we stay engaged in living rather than forcing solutions to questions that can't be answered—at least not now. In just the last ten years there have been significant advances in the health sciences in developing treatments that can affect the course of neurological conditions and improve the quality of life. These treatments presage the future developments of neuroprotective agents, and ultimately the discovery of possible cures. But until then, there are lives to be lived now as only our patients can live them.

> Don't search for answers, which could not be given to you now, because you would not be able to live them. And the point is, to live everything. Live the questions now. Perhaps then, someday far in the future, you will gradually, without even noticing it, live your way into the answer
>
> —Rainer Maria Rilke, Letter 4 (2001)

REFERENCES AND READINGS

Chopra, Deepak. 1994. *The seven spiritual laws of success: A practical guide to the fulfillment of your dreams.* Novato, CA: New World Library.

Hamill, Sam, and Jerome P. Seaton. 2004. *The poetry of Zen, Shambhala library.* Boston: Shambhala.

Mascaró, Juan, tr. 1973. *The Dhammapada.* London: Penguin Classics.

Rilke, Rainer Maria. 1960. *Selected letters of Rainer Maria Rilke.* Edited by H. T. Moore. Garden City, New York: Doubleday & Company, Inc.

———. 2001. *Letters to a young poet.* Translated by S. Mitchell. New York: Modern Library.

3

An Attitude of Mind

A SURFING STORY

Jon Kabat-Zinn and Jack Kornfield are among a group of influential teachers who helped introduce mindfulness and meditation to our Western minds. Clear and accessible, their writings have provided inspiration and guidance for many, including patients and psychotherapists alike. Interestingly, both tell a story about surfing that invites us to develop an "attitude of mind" for dealing with adversity, illness, and loss—the inevitable changes in life that will touch us all. The story goes something like this: There was a poster of a famous guru with gray hair and a flowing beard riding a large wave atop a surfboard. The caption on the poster read: "You can't stop the waves, but you can learn to surf." The spirit of this wonderful image resonated with themes that have been informing my work with patients living with neuropsychological challenges. We don't necessarily have to fight current realities nor do we have to fall victim to them. We can develop an attitude of mind that transcends dichotomous thinking—the victim versus fight dilemma. We need not be defeated by that which we cannot control, because we can *change our relationship* to the challenges of life that seem to rise unceasingly like ocean waves—we can "learn to surf."

Over the years I have used the surfing analogy in talks to different groups, and the humorous but empowering image of the surfing guru has drawn many a chuckle and seems to transfer—if only for a moment—a feeling of shared power to people who are feeling powerless in the face of their life circumstances. And a moment is enough to plant a seed of possibility that something can be done, and "that something" can be affected by the very

29

person who is suffering—a patient with neuropsychological challenges, a family member, and maybe even a psychotherapist. What was needed next was a way to nurture that seed, to keep that glimmer of possibility alive, to reconnect again and again with the power of that moment—to reengage with life by changing one's relationship to a neurological condition. It seemed that this "way" was an attitude of mind, but how could I help my patients to get there, and was it even someplace to get?

THE ELEMENTS OF A WAY

I began thinking more about surfing and the elements that might reflect the essence of that experience. What began to emerge were ways of experiencing that might serve as guideposts to, or maybe more accurately reminders of, an attitude of mind that could be helpful to my patients. Let's consider the possibilities.

A surfer approaches the ride with an *open mind*. No two waves are the same and therefore each ride is different. Holding firm to some preconceived notion about how to ride this particular wave, because that's the way it's always been done, just doesn't work when being with this wave, at this moment, is now the ride.

A surfer has an *active orientation*. Passively sitting on the surfboard may take you tumbling into the surf, but it's not surfing. On the other hand, fighting the wave, attempting to tame its power, will send you tumbling to shore yet again. A surfer realizes the ride is a continuous and active engagement with the wave.

There may be no better example of *present-moment awareness* than surfing. The challenge and beauty of the ride is to be with this wave at this moment, not thinking about yesterday's ride or tomorrow's waves, but here right now with an ever changing force of nature.

Closely related to present-moment awareness is the element of *process perspective*. The aim of riding a wave isn't to reach the beach but to be with the wave in its moment-to-moment unfolding. The surfer isn't trying to get anywhere other than where she is, and in being with the wave at each moment she gets to where she's going.

Like the other elements, *balance* is an active, continuous, and dynamic process. The surfer doesn't try to achieve a "once and for all" position on the surfboard. On the contrary, her *balance* is as fluid and ever changing as the waves themselves, because it reflects an open and flexible response to the circumstances of the moment. With each ride the surfer develops and deepens her sense of balance; not too tight, not too loose—in harmony with what is.

A PRACTICE TO COMPLEMENT THE ELEMENTS

If the five elements could serve as guideposts or reminders of an attitude of mind for my patients, something else still was needed: an active experience that would become their practice—their version of surfing—that would help change their relationship to neurological conditions and invite an engagement with life as it is. The practice didn't lie very far from the origins of the surfing story.

Through books, lectures, and retreats, Jon Kabat-Zinn (1994) and Jack Kornfield (1993)—along with a host of other wise and compassionate teachers—have invited many to consider the possibilities of transforming our relationship to our life experience by simply being present for the experience, or put another way, to be mindful of the moment-to-moment unfolding of our lives. Sounds simple, yet it can be quite challenging, because this awareness is always there but has been obscured. Our habits, conditionings, fixations, preconceived notions, attachments, aversions—all those factors that seem to define our lives—actually keep us steps removed from our experience, from being awake, from really living. Henry David Thoreau recognized this simple truth at Walden Pond, "Only that day dawns to which we are awake" (2004, 303). Mindfulness is attitude of mind that brings us back to the present moment; it's an awakened sensibility, a way of engaging in life as a surfer may dance with a wave, and mindful living can be cultivated with a regular practice of meditation.

With the "elements of a way" as guideposts reminding us of the potential for transformation—changing a relationship to illness and loss—and the practice of "mindfulness meditation" to cultivate an awareness of life and its possibilities, we have the foundations of an approach that may be useful to people living with neuropsychological challenges. Let's now consider some applications for our patients.

CLINICAL APPLICATIONS

People living with the consequences of neurological illness or trauma are dealing with complex challenges that reflect the primary effects of the condition and their reactions to the condition. These psychological and emotional reactions—the secondary effects of illness or trauma—are significant factors because they not only have a direct bearing on the quality of our patients' lives, but also can affect the very course of their illness. Such complexity calls for multilevel treatment approaches that include medical and rehabilitation specialists. It is not unusual for a patient's treatment team, at one time or another, to include a primary care physician, neurologist, physiatrist, psychiatrist, speech therapist, physical therapist, occupational therapist, cognitive remediation specialist, and a psychotherapist. Among these specialists, it is frequently the psychotherapist who has the most regular and consistent contact with the patient over time. From this privileged and challenging position in the overall treatment scheme, the psychotherapist has the opportunities to address suffering as manifested in a patient's depression, anxieties, and fears, and to promote a patient's active engagement with life as it is now and as it continues to unfold.

The Attitude of Mind Perspective and Research on Positive Psychology

If we are to offer our patients treatment approaches that expand possibilities and foster hope, then it is best to start with an *open mind* that can consider possibilities. Harkening back to the words of Shunryu Suzuki, "In the beginner's mind there are many possibilities, but in the expert's there are few," the perspectives of "experts" are too frequently the self-absorbed manifestations of ego, *I-Me-Mine consciousness*, that leave little room for appreciating sources that may threaten valued opinions and hard-earned turf. In the best of circumstances, however, clinical experience and scientific effort inform each other for the ultimate benefit of patients.

In reviewing her broaden-and-build theory of positive emotions, Fredrickson (2001) notes that narrowed thought-action patterns that may have been adaptive in an immediate life-threatening crisis situation—the fight or flight reaction—are not necessarily beneficial over the long haul. Actively changing one's relationship to a stressful event and its aftershocks may be more helpful, and is likely to become increasingly adaptive over time.

The importance of such shifts in perspective in response to life stress was demonstrated in a study by Taylor et al. (2000). The researchers found that finding meaning in a traumatic event like bereavement, which is known to have adverse effects on the immune system (Kemeny 1994; Kemeny and Dean 1995), had positive effects on quality of life and pathophysiology of the bereaved's illness (HIV). In this case, *meaning* was defined as "a major shift in values, priorities, or perspective in response to the loss." Statements reflecting meaning indicated such changes as "a greater appreciation for the loved one, an enhanced sense of living in the present, a perception of life as fragile and precious, or a commitment to enjoying life" (Taylor et al. 2000).

Shifting perspectives in response to trauma and loss—be it the death of a loved one or the onset of a neurological condition—calls for an open mind, and research based on the broaden-and-build theory of positive emotions underscores this element. The theory suggests that "positive emotions—including joy, interest, contentment, pride, and love—although phenomenologically distinct, all share the ability to broaden people's momentary thought-action repertoires and build their enduring personal resources, ranging from physical and intellectual resources to social and psychological resources" (Fredrickson 2001). Studies have shown that people experiencing positive emotions show patterns of thought that are flexible and open to new information, and positive affect may expand attention so that people "see" and accept a broader array of behavioral options (Isen 2000; Fredrickson 2001). If positive emotions help people place the events of their lives in a broader context, lessening the resonance of any particular negative event (Fredrickson 2001), then the question arises: Can these positive, resilience-building emotions be cultivated? Our clinical experience would suggest positive emotions and resilience are the positive by-products of an attitude of mind that reflects the elements of a way and mindful living. Research in positive psychology has suggested a similar possibility by demonstrating positive affect can be generated and sustained in the context of chronic stress. Studies have shown three kinds of coping related to positive affect: positive reappraisal, problem-focused coping, and infusing ordinary events with positive meaning (Folkman and Moskowitz 2000).

Positive reappraisal is characterized by reframing a stressful or perceived negative situation in a positive light. Such reframing can be something like a neurological condition being experienced as a "wake-up call" to moments in life that had been passing by unnoticed. Consider the busy executive whose mild traumatic brain injury was sufficient to slow him down enough to get to know the person who had become the man in the gray flannel suit, that "him" with whom he had lost touch somewhere back in college. Or recall the factory worker with a degenerative neurological condition who reminded his therapist about the preciousness of the *present moment* with some ice cream and two spoons.

Problem-focused coping is characterized by taking action to address the problem that is causing distress. This strategy is akin to the *active orientation* element in our attitude of mind approach. Taking action doesn't mean fighting a current reality, but instead changing one's perspective in a situation that appears uncontrollable. Consider a young mother dealing with MS fatigue, which is a fact of life for most patients with MS and viewed by 50%–60% as the worse symptom of the condition (Ben-Zacharia and Lublin 2001). Gathering information about MS fatigue, discussing symptom management with her neurologist, participating in a regular exercise program, and taking medication to address the symptoms, all reflected her *active orientation* and were efforts in problem-focused coping. She began to feel less sluggish and the weight of MS fatigue seemed to have lifted a bit; yet there were days when its presence was again felt. Perhaps she overdid it getting the house ready for a family reunion; or the heat of a midsummer's day has zapped her energy; or maybe she just can't find a reason because it seems as though she has done everything right, but still the fatigue is there.

Does it mean she has failed at problem-focused coping and should abandon the strategy? No, because we realize the active orientation that underlies problem-focused coping can manifest in different ways, and the elements of an active orientation and balanced view still offer a perspective for living with fatigue. With awareness cultivated by our practice of mindfulness, we heed the call of our body and spirit asking to be restored. We don't fight the fatigue, but we allow our active orientation to manifest as the effortless action of "going with the flow." We recognize that our balanced view isn't rigid, but dynamic and fluid—and renewal is a process. We are not trying to get it right once and for all; but we are trying to be open to what is now—and today is a day of rest.

The third coping strategy of infusing ordinary events with positive meaning shares features with our practice of living mindfully with gratitude—present-moment awareness. Such moments need not be extravagant; in fact, striving for something memorable only serves to obscure the very specialness that can make the moment memorable. Awakening to watch a sunrise, coffee with a friend, a Bob Dylan concert with a daughter, rocky road ice cream with a patient—all can be infused with positive meaning if we are there to live them. Recall Jane Kenyon's poem *Otherwise* for a poignant reminder of infusing ordinary events with positive meaning. Positive meaning is in large measure a function of gratitude, and "touching the positive" with gratitude can provide a foundation for dealing with the challenges of life. I remember hearing the phrase "touching the positive" at a retreat with Thich Nhat Hanh, a Zen master, poet, and peace activist. Thay, as he is affectionately known, was telling a story about the pain of having a toothache and how relieved and grateful we feel when the pain subsides. He then reminded us that many days, including today, are "non-toothache" days for which to be grateful. Unfortunately we tend to forget that we may be in the midst of a "non-toothache day." Can we appreciate what we have—infuse the ordinary with positive meaning—without the reminder of pain? Mindful living is a way.

Although arising from multiple sources, we sometimes find parallel themes converging with a common lesson—an attitude of mind teaching—for dealing with adversity. The sources may be as different as a Zen master, a stroke patient, and positive psychology. At his retreat, Thich Nhat Hanh went on to discuss how actively "touching the positive"—being grateful for the blue sky, the laughter of your granddaughter, your breathing—provides a helpful foundation for attending to painful emotions. His message brought to mind a patient I had seen several years earlier. My patient's illustrious career and active involvement in athletics were compromised by a stroke that placed him in a wheelchair. His losses were painfully obvious yet he arrived for his psychotherapy sessions, which were intended to help him "come to terms with my new status," with an attitude of good cheer and optimism. Many of our early encounters were spent with his talking about seemingly irrelevant topics—including his love of Chinese food, his granddaughters' activities, or the results of the latest sporting event at the university—all of which, at least in my initial view, seemed to reflect an avoidance of his painful situation. My efforts to redirect him to the topic at hand, my agenda—his losses and presumed associated painful emotion—were steadfastly met with his agenda that seemed all too positive given his circumstances. Finally one session, probably feeling outdone by my patient's persistence, I decided simply to be quiet and listen. We started as usual with an update of the positive events of the week, and then there was a silence when I usually would have made some attempt to redirect my patient to what ultimately proved to be just a concept of what we were supposed to be doing, which was my idea of how to deal with his pain. Preconceived notions of what's to happen in therapy frequently narrow our view to the content of a session, which may support our concepts but do little to advance our understanding, because from this limited perspective we miss the process of a session where the real message lies. Remaining silent for a few more moments my patient then looked at me with a rueful smile and said, "I just have to remember the good before I take on the bad." He then went on to talk about a painful conversation he had had with his wife about the effects of his disability on their relationship. Echoing the teachings of Thich Nhat Hanh for "touching the positive," my patient's process also resonated with the findings of positive psychology, which suggest that positive emotions not only help people feel good in the moment, but also may expand awareness, undo the aftereffects of negative emotions, and build resilience needed to cope with future stress.

Research on Mindfulness-Based Psychological Interventions

There are now almost two decades of research demonstrating that mindfulness-based acceptance and intervention approaches are effective in treating chronic pain (Kabat-Zinn et al. 1986), anxiety (Kabat-Zinn et al. 1992), borderline personality disorder (Linehan 1993), symptoms of stress in cancer patients (Speca et al. 2000), and depression (Segal, Williams, and Teasdale 2002). Recent reviews of mindfulness and acceptance based approaches in treating substance abuse (Breslin, Zack, and McMain 2002), and generalized anxiety disorders (Roemer and Orsillo 2002) point to the growing recognition of these perspectives and their incorporation into mainstream clinical psychology. Within the field of psychiatry, the writings of Epstein (1995) and Magid (2002) provide lucid explorations of meditative traditions informing modern psychotherapy. And the titles of recently edited volumes show that the appeal of mindfulness-meditative traditions for contemporary psychotherapy transcends the boundaries of different schools of thought: *Psychoanalysis and Buddhism: An Unfolding Dialogue* (Safran 2003); *Mindfulness and Acceptance: Expanding the Cognitive-Behavioral Tradition* (Hayes, Follette, and Linehan 2004).

The linkage between mindfulness and positive psychology has been noted in *Defining an Agenda for Future Research on the Clinical Application of Mindfulness Practice* (Dimidjian and Linehan 2003). The authors comment that "research on mindfulness may work in parallel with recent efforts to establish a 'positive psychology.'" While the parallel tracks of mindfulness research and positive psychology may be relatively new, the meditative and contemplative traditions that inform mindfulness practices have ancient roots. We need be respectfully cautious about appropriating methods steeped in traditions outside of Western psychology and laying claim to having formulated yet another new psychological treatment. The lessons of the wisdom traditions are timeless and therefore will always have a contemporary ring, as they do now in resonating with recent developments in psychotherapy; but it serves us well to remember where it all began. Dimidjian and Linehan (2003) stress the importance of maintaining an ongoing dialogue with spiritual teachers of mindfulness as these methods evolve in Western psychology. Commenting on his work with Jon Kabat-Zinn in developing mindfulness-based stress reduction (MBSR), Larry Horwitz (Boyce 2005) emphasizes the importance of a solid grounding and commitment to mindfulness practice for those who teach the approach. By maintaining an abiding respect for traditions informing our psychology and with the steadiness of ongoing practice, our approaches may be developed with a sound foundation.

MINDFULNESS MEDITATION

Let's begin with our definition: mindfulness is an attitude of mind that brings us back to the present moment; it's an awakened sensibility, a way of engaging in life as a surfer may dance with a wave, and mindful living can be cultivated with a regular practice of meditation. Jon Kabat-Zinn (1994, 4) notes, "Mindfulness means paying attention in a particular way: on purpose, in the present moment, and nonjudgmentally." Living mindfully does not entail complicated procedures; if anything, mindfulness is the essence of simplicity, and by bringing careful attention to the ordinary we are able to touch the extraordinary—the immediacy of life. Mindful living beautifully incorporates our five elements, and provides us an experiential lesson in changing our relationship to the activities of daily living. These lessons develop the foundation for changing our relationship to adversity and engaging in life as it is.

Let's try an example informed by a traditional Zen story that goes something like this. A student approached a Zen master for instruction. The teacher asked, "Have you had your rice?" The student answered, "Yes." The Zen master replied, "Then go wash your bowl." Even in this age of dishwashers, this lesson still can be powerfully instructive and enjoyable. Perhaps we still have some pots and pans to scrub before we can "relax." Facing this pile of grease-encrusted cookware we may be thinking, "What a mess; this is going to be real drudgery." And so we approach the job with an attitude of mind that the task itself is negative and to be gotten through as quickly as possible. An interesting phenomenon then begins to emerge— the faster we scrub, the more resistantly those lasagna remnants cling to the pan, and the pile of greasy pots yet remaining seems to be growing larger. So let's change our relationship to the task and try a different approach. We will consider bringing a careful, nonjudgmental, attention to the moment-to-moment activity of pot-scrubbing. With an *open mind* we suspend judgment that the task will be drudgery, and instead simply view it as pot-scrubbing, open to what the experience might be. We take an *active orientation* and as we lift each pot and pan to place it in the sudsy hot water, we are mindful of the heft and feel of the metal in our hands, mindful of our movements with the scouring pad as the grease loosens its grip on the pan. We get closer and closer to the *present moment* of activity, one pot at a time, one movement at a time, opening our senses to the touch, sound, sight, smell of pot-scrubbing. Our attention isn't with the pile of pots remaining to be washed, but only with the one in our hand right now. We are involved in the *process perspective*, and one by one the pile of dirty pots and pans is getting smaller. We've approached the task with a *balanced view*, neither rushing nor dawdling, neither forcing nor slacking; we put enough elbow grease into our scrubbing to remove the stains and get the job done. Before we know it, the pots and pans are clean and neatly stacked, and we are feeling curiously contented and peaceful.

Let's transfer an attitude of mindfulness to some challenges that can accompany neurological conditions. It is not unusual for our patients to struggle with tasks that were once automatic behaviors, the routines of daily life—bathing, dressing, and getting to an appointment on time. Compromised mobility, slowed processing, difficulties with multitasking—the ubiquitous expectations of modern life—are magnified by the sensory and information overload of a culture preoccupied with speed. Like us, our patients are products of this culture, and for many the expectation "to keep up" remains while their abilities to do so have diminished. Perhaps our patients' experiences foreshadow our own in becoming lost in the rapidity of time, the surrealistic landscape of cell phones, fax machines, and e-mail.

We begin by asking our patients to maintain an open mind and consider a perspective of "slowing down and getting there faster." In getting dressed or putting on a leg brace, we encourage patients to approach each step of the task with a mindful attitude giving careful attention to the activity of the present moment—pulling up a sock, reaching for a shoe. Frustrations may mount as a shoe stubbornly refuses to cooperate, or buttons challenge fingers that have lost their nimbleness. Rather than fight through the frustration by trying harder, which only serves to exacerbate the problem, we encourage patients to pause, note their feelings, and bring their attention to their breath, following its flow as they regain their equilibrium. Back in the driver's seat, having interrupted the momentum of reactivity, they may reengage with the task at hand, maintaining a balanced view of mindful self-directed activity and allowing others to help when needed. Their focus has shifted from where they have to go, to being where they are; and in being in the present moment with mindfulness they get to where they are going with far less frustration and maybe even more speedily. This mindfulness approach obviously isn't a once and for all, one size fits all, fix-it solution; it is a practice that reflects a way of living and not a means to an end.

We cultivate mindfulness by living in the here and now, and our senses are openings to the present moment. Consider pausing in the midst of a busy day, if only for a moment, to bring your attention to your breathing and noticing the aliveness of your body. Allow yourself to be openly receptive to the sounds that surround you—the ticking of the clock, the humming of the air conditioner, the clicking of the computer keys, the gurgling in your stomach. Look with care and attention at the items on your desk— a pile of books, a photograph of your daughter, the dust motes landing on a lampshade. Feel the doorknob in your hand, the heft of the paperweight, and the warmth of a hot cup of coffee. Try eating mindfully, slowing down and bringing awareness to the aromas, tastes, and textures of breakfast—sizzling bacon, warm toast, sweet peaches, fresh cream, hot coffee. Awaken to all these "faint yet vital tremors" that make our lives.

We also cultivate mindfulness by setting aside some time each day for "formal" meditation practice in contrast to the "informal practice" of living mindfully. Formal practice can take different forms such as sitting or walking meditation, and there are variations in approach (different sitting positions; eyes closed, eyes open) that reflect different traditions. We also consider two basic categories of meditation: focused concentration and receptive or insight meditation. In focused concentration, we bring our attention to a focus such as our breathing as it shows itself in the flow of breath in and out of our nostrils, or in the rising and falling of our belly. With receptive meditation our awareness is open in a nonjudgmental way to whatever the experience is at the moment—a body sensation, sound, thought, or perhaps a feeling. We neither push away these experiences nor do they carry us away. We simply note them for what they are—a tension in the neck, a thought of unfinished business at work, a feeling of frustration and anxiety, developing a storyline to justify or excuse whatever we think we should or should have not done—and we let them pass. In our practice we can make a transition from focused meditation to an openly receptive form, creating a bridge by focusing first on our breath, then progressively and deliberately shifting our focus to our body sense, then sound, then thoughts, then feelings, then to an open and receptive awareness.

Our approach with mindfulness meditation must be flexible to accommodate personal styles, different needs, and the changing conditions of our patients. One approach to mindfulness or style of meditation doesn't take precedence over another. For many of our patients the formal practice of sitting meditation is a helpful adjunct to treatment; for others walking meditation, yoga, or perhaps mindfully sorting stamps and placing them in an album are openings to the present moment and the immediacy of life.

Practicing mindfulness meditation within the context of a psychotherapy relationship allows for the opportunity to monitor patients' experiences over time, discuss their reactions to the practice, and address emerging feelings. For example, such feelings may include affect associated with past trauma. Painful emotions may reemerge in the present, as when a neurological condition places a patient again in a vulnerable and dependent position that is reminiscent of past traumatic experiences. The reawakening of such feelings can be fraught with anxiety, but their being experienced in the here and now also offers the opportunity for transformation. Mindfulness meditation provides a way to deal with painful emotions and increase a patient's stability in tolerating feelings that previously had been defended against. The psychotherapy relationship provides the essential context for transformation as the dynamics of trust and vulnerability with their associated affects manifest in the present moment interaction with therapist, thus permitting the chance for working through.

Basic Instructions for Mindfulness Meditation

As a starting point, mindfulness of breathing is a helpful place to begin a meditation practice, and Jon Kabat-Zinn (1990, 58) has offered useful instructions. For our patients living with neurological conditions, specific aspects of the instructions (e.g., posture, length of time for meditation) are adapted to fit their unique needs and circumstances.

1. Assume a comfortable posture lying on your back or sitting. If you are sitting, keep the spine straight and let the shoulders drop.
2. Close your eyes if it feels comfortable.
3. Bring your attention to your belly, feeling it rise or expand gently on the in-breath and fall or recede on the out-breath.
4. Keep the focus on your breathing, "being with" each in-breath for its full duration and with each out-breath for its full duration, as if you were riding the waves of your own breathing.

5. Every time you notice that your mind has wandered off the breath, notice what it was that took you away and then gently bring your attention back to your belly and the feeling of the breath coming in and out.
6. If your mind wanders away from the breath a thousand times, then your "job" is simply to bring it back to the breath every time, no matter what it becomes preoccupied with.
7. Practice this exercise for fifteen minutes at a convenient time every day, whether you feel like it or not, for one week and see how it feels to incorporate a disciplined meditation practice into your life. Be aware of how it feels to spend some time each day just being with your breath without having to *do* anything.

A RECAP OF THE APPROACH

- Psychotherapy for neuropsychological challenges aims to reduce suffering and promote a reengagement with life. These goals are reciprocal processes that build upon each other, and are realized by changing our relationship to adversity. This change promotes an active and ongoing process of accepting the truth of what is and placing neuropsychological challenges within the context of a larger life to be lived.
- The five elements of a way guide our efforts in changing our relationship to adversity, and they inform our treatment approaches and reengagement in living.
  —With an *open mind* there are possibilities and with possibilities there is hope. We encourage patients to maintain an open, flexible, and nonjudgmental attitude that will allow them to consider a broad array of options for living with neuropsychological challenges.
  —We invite patients to have an *active orientation* in their treatments and in living, neither fighting the truth of what is nor falling victim to it.
  —We cultivate *present-moment awareness* to counter reactive patterns of being attached to the past with regret or yearning, or projecting a future filled with anxiety and fear.
  —By not trying so hard to get someplace other than where we are, we maintain a *process perspective* and recognize that everything changes. Bringing careful attention to where we are now—be it in psychotherapy or living—we are better able to realize our goals, and sometimes even get there more speedily.
  —With a *balanced view* we accept uncertainty but change our relationship to adversity. Neither forcing solutions nor giving up, we loosen our grip on trying to control the circumstances of our lives and open ourselves to the possibilities of living.

- With mindfulness meditation we develop the stability to deal with adversity and uncertainty. And we are better able to interrupt the momentum of reactive psychological tendencies that can fuel depression, anxiety, and interpersonal conflict. With *mindfulness* we bring careful attention to the ordinary moments of living that yield extraordinary gifts, if we are there to receive them.

- The attitude of mind perspective develops the type of coping resources that cultivate positive emotions, which in turn may undo the aftereffects of negative emotions and build resilience to deal with current and future stress.

REFERENCES AND READINGS

Ben-Zacharia, A. B., and F. D. Lublin. 2001. Palliative care in patients with multiple sclerosis. *Neurologic Clinics* 19 (4): 801–827.

Boyce, Barry. 2005. The man who prescribes the medicine of the moment. *Shambhala Sun,* May 28.

Breslin, F. Curtis, Martin Zack, and Shelley McMain. 2002. An information-processing analysis of mindfulness: Implications for relapse prevention in the treatment of substance abuse. *Clinical Psychology: Science and Practice* 9 (3): 275–299.

Dimidjian, Sona, and Marsha M. Linehan. 2003. Defining an agenda for future research on the clinical application of mindfulness practice. *Clinical Psychology: Science and Practice* 10 (2): 166–171.

Epstein, Mark. 1995. *Thoughts without a thinker: Psychotherapy from a Buddhist perspective.* New York: Basic Books Inc.

Folkman, Susan, and Judith Tedlie Moskowitz. 2000. Positive affect and the other side of coping. *American Psychologist* 55 (6): 647–654.

Fredrickson, Barbara. 2001. The role of positive emotions in positive psychology: The broaden-and-build theory of positive emotions. *American Psychologist* 56 (3): 218–226.

Hayes, Steven C., Victoria M. Follette, and Marsha Linehan. 2004. *Mindfulness and acceptance: Expanding the cognitive-behavioral tradition.* New York: Guilford Press.

Isen, A. M. 2000. Positive affect and decision making. In *Handbook of emotions,* edited by M. L. M. Haviland-Jones. New York: Guilford Press.

Kabat-Zinn, Jon. 1990. *Full catastrophe living: Using the wisdom of your body and mind to face stress, pain and illness.* New York: Dell Publishing.

———. 1994. *Wherever you go, there you are: Mindfulness meditation in everyday life.* New York: Hyperion.

Kabat-Zinn, Jon, L. Lipworth, R. Burney, and W. Sellers. 1986. Four-year follow-up of a meditation-based program for self-regulation of chronic pain: Treatment outcomes and compliance. *Clinical Journal of Pain* 2:159–173.

Kabat-Zinn, Jon, Ann O. Massion, Jean Kristeller, Linda G. Peterson, et al. 1992. Effectiveness of a meditation-based stress reduction program in the treatment of anxiety disorders. *American Journal of Psychiatry* 149 (7): 936–943.

Kemeny, M. E. 1994. Stressful events, psychological responses, and progression of HIV infection. In *Handbook of human stress and immunity*, edited by R. Glaser and J. Kiecolt-Glaser. New York: Academic Press.

Kemeny, M. E., and L. Dean. 1995. Effects of AIDS-related bereavement on HIV progression among gay men in New York City. *AIDS Education and Prevention* 7:36–47.

Kornfield, Jack. 1993. *A path with heart: A guide through the perils and promises of spiritual life*. New York: Bantam Books.

Linehan, Marsha. 1993. *Cognitive-behavioral treatment of borderline personality disorder*. New York: Guilford Press.

Magid, Barry. 2002. *Ordinary mind: exploring the common ground of Zen and psychotherapy*. Boston: Wisdom Publications.

Roemer, L., and S. M. Orsillo. 2002. Expanding our conceptualization of and treatment for generalized anxiety disorder: Integrating mindfulness/acceptance-based approaches with existing cognitive-behavioral models. *Clinical Psychology: Science and Practice* 9 (1): 54–68.

Safran, Jeremy D., ed. 2003. *Psychoanalysis and Buddhism: An unfolding dialogue*. 1st ed. Boston: Wisdom Publications.

Segal, Zindel V., J. Mark G. Williams, and J.D. Teasdale. 2002. *Mindfulness-based cognitive therapy for depression: A new approach for preventing relapse*. New York: Guilford Press.

Speca, M., L. E. Carlson, E. Goodey, and M. Angen. 2000. A randomized, wait-list controlled clinical trial: The effect of a mindfulness meditation-based stress reduction program on mood and symptoms of stress in cancer outpatients. *Psychosomatic Medicine* 62 (5): 613–622.

Taylor, S., M. E. Kemeny, J. E. Bower, T. L. Gruenewald, and G. M. Reed. 2000. Psychological resources, positive illusions, and health. *American Psychologist* 55 (1): 99–109.

Thoreau, Henry David. 2004. *Walden: Or, life in the woods*. Boston: Shambhala.

Part II

NEUROPSYCHOLOGICAL CHALLENGES

4

Conditions and the Neuropsychological Domains

My review of the conditions that can give rise to neuropsychological challenges is by no means exhaustive. We will be considering multiple sclerosis, traumatic brain injury and post concussion syndrome, cerebrovascular disorders, degenerative dementias, and elusive diagnoses. The variability of neuropsychological problems even within these selected conditions is wide, and when we consider the complex interplay of long-standing personality dynamics with the adaptive challenges of dealing with compromised functioning, loss, and uncertainty—a one size fits all treatment approach just doesn't apply. Also, we cannot discount the constraints each condition can place on our traditional treatment methods because cognitive-processing weaknesses, depleted energy, and the sheer exhaustion that can diminish hope—so often a part of our patients' daily life experiences—will challenge our creativity and will require the flexibility to modify and adapt our approaches to fit our patients' changing abilities and needs. The selection of the conditions reviewed simply reflects that all can be accompanied by neuropsychological challenges—some much more so than others—and equally relevant, people living with these challenges have given me the privilege of working with them, and in doing so have shaped my views of what psychotherapy may offer. In allowing me the opportunity to provide service—inviting me into their life experience—my patients also have been my teachers. Their lessons continue to be instructive, and if I can do them justice in my translation, perhaps these lessons can be useful to other psychotherapists.

The lessons of the young man with HIV encephalitis who hopes to start his own business, or those of the high school football player who sat in front of me in a wheelchair following the resection of a cerebellar tumor, are no less instructive than the experiences reflected in the conditions I have chosen to highlight. Their stories also inform the spirit of the book, but we have to start somewhere, and any selection is just that—a selection.

Acknowledging the variability in the expression of neuropsychological problems found within each condition, we start our review with those in which the patient's status allows a more active engagement in psychotherapy and progress to those in which intervention approaches necessarily must be more modified. Our discussion begins with multiple sclerosis, a paradigmatic condition of neuropsychological consequences, which also provides a historical nexus between dominant influences in the development of clinical neurology and psychology. Credited with being "the father of clinical neurology," the 19th-century French neurologist Jean-Martin Charcot did the first major clinical studies and advanced anatomical correlations of multiple sclerosis (Goetz, Bonduelle, and Gelfand 1995). Charcot also had an inspirational impact on Sigmund Freud, whose eloquent eulogy of this teacher he considered "positively fascinating" acknowledged the great success of Charcot's anatomical-clinical methods with organic nervous diseases such as multiple sclerosis, and among other accomplishments, being the first to elucidate hysteria and its psychological mechanisms. With his own studies of hysteria, Freud would launch the explorations of the psyche that would become the foundation for psychotherapy—"the talking cure." Our review concludes with a chapter on elusive diagnoses, those conditions that inhabit the borderlands of neurology and psychology but stubbornly refuse to fit neatly into either-or conceptual schemas. These conditions continue to challenge diagnostic and treatment efforts, and Freud's recollection of Charcot's method remains instructive for clinicians today.

> He himself told us the following about his method of working: he was accustomed to look again and again at things that were incomprehensible to him, to deepen his impression of them day by day, until suddenly understanding of them dawned upon him (1893, 10).

REVIEWING NEUROPSYCHOLOGICAL CHALLENGES

The psychotherapist who sees patients with neurological conditions will often be in the position to review a report of a neuropsychological evaluation during the course of treatment. A neuropsychological evaluation may accompany the initial referral for psychotherapy, or may be ordered by psychotherapists themselves to assist with treatment planning. Neuropsychological assessment is essentially a study of behavior samples obtained with standardized psychological tests from which inferences are made about the integrity of brain functioning. The assessment of cognitive functions and personality (or psychological and emotional dimensions) is integrated with a review of a patient's current status and background history to constitute a neuropsychological evaluation. Historically, the neuropsychological evaluation has had a role in the diagnosis and treatment planning of patients with neurological conditions, although the emphasis of its contribution has shifted over time. Sophisticated neuroimaging is now the vanguard for diagnostic accuracy, but the diagnostic contributions of neuropsychological assessment remain important in cases such as the evaluation of mild traumatic brain injury, or of mild cognitive impairment that may reflect the early stages of dementia. However, the role of neuropsychological assessment in providing a functional analysis of brain-behavior relationships has not been eclipsed for informing rehabilitation treatment strategies and adaptations for daily living for people living with neuropsychological challenges. Its strength lies in its ability to provide a comprehensive, in-depth, standardized review of cognitive and psychological strengths and weaknesses—a neuropsychological profile.

Neuropsychological assessment approaches have been broadly characterized as fixed battery or flexible battery procedures. The Halstead-Reitan battery is an example of the "fixed" approach in which a predetermined set of tests (i.e., the battery) is given to each patient. In their consideration of fixed and flexible battery approaches, Armengol and Jamieson (2001) note that an argument advanced to support fixed battery approaches (Kane, Goldstein, and Parsons 1989) is "that a fixed battery ensures that functions are routinely assessed which otherwise might be neglected due to incorrect clinical assumptions." The contributions of Reitan and his colleagues have had an enduring impact on the development of clinical neuropsychology, however a majority of neuropsychologists now use flexible as opposed to fixed battery approaches (Sweet, Moberg, and Westergaard 1996). Flexible batteries also provide a comprehensive review of essential neuropsychological functional domains; but test selection may be tailored for a specific condition (e.g., assessment of dementia in the elderly vs. assessment of traumatic brain injury in a young adult), and there is sufficient "flexibility" to accommodate a patient's particular needs and circumstances. Flexible batteries also are associated with a process interpretation approach (Kaplan 1988) in which qualitative features of test performance (i.e., how a patient arrived at an answer) are as relevant as quantitative aspects (i.e., specific test score).

In elucidating strengths and weaknesses in adaptive functioning, the neuropsychological evaluation provides a useful organizational framework for a psychotherapist in considering "what needs to be known" about the cognitive and psychological challenges that will affect a patient's participation in treatment and reengagement in life. The format of a neuropsychological evaluation also will be helpful in providing an organizational framework for our review of the functional domains that may be affected by neurological conditions. Neuropsychological test selection may vary as a function of a patient's condition and specific needs, and the preferences and orientation of the examiner. However most flexible test batteries will address several core domains of cognitive functioning that often include: general intellectual ability, attention and concentration, language and verbal skills, visuoanalysis, learning and memory, conceptual problem solving, and executive functioning. In the following chapters, we will be reviewing the impact of specific neurological conditions on cognitive and psychological status. Let us first begin by considering the cognitive domains that may be affected by a neurological condition and some methods that may be used to assess the nature and extent of dysfunction.

General Intellectual Status

Just what constitutes intelligence and how it should be measured are beyond the scope of our review, but for clinical purposes psychologists frequently rely on a version of the Wechsler Intelligence Scales (Wechsler 1997) for an assessment of general intellectual ability. The Wechsler Scales have a long history in psychology and their construction incorporates two fundamental perspectives on the nature of intelligence. The multidimensional aspect of intelligence is reflected by the Wechsler Scales including a number of composite tests that are intended to assess specific intellectual or cognitive abilities, such as the Similarities subtest being a measure of verbal concept formation. The Wechsler Scales also yield composite IQ scores, which reflect the tradition of there being a global factor of intelligence. Despite their psychometric rigor and respected position in the history of psychology as being the "gold standard" in intelligence testing, neither the Wechsler Scales nor any other standardized measure of intelligence can capture the depth and range of adaptive and creative abilities of which humans are capable. Parenthetically, the Wechsler Scales also do not lay claim to having accomplished such a feat. With this caveat, the Wechsler Scales nevertheless remain among the most widely used instruments in neuropsychological assessment.

An IQ score, as may be derived from the Wechsler Scales, has become part of our vernacular, a catchword for intelligence. However, from a clinical perspective—particularly in working with neuropsychological challenges—the concept of IQ as an index of a patient's intellectual capacity to support a return to the competitive job market or perhaps to participate meaningfully in a treatment program has questionable utility. In a standard and well-regarded text, *Neuropsychological Assessment*, the authors conclude: "In sum, 'IQ' as a score is inherently meaningless and not infrequently misleading as well. 'IQ'—whether concept, score, or catchword—has outlived whatever usefulness it may once have had and should be discarded" (Lezak et al. 2004, 22). The problem, at least in part, lies in the fact that composite IQ scores can obscure the variability in cognitive functioning resulting from the initial impact, and the progression or resolution of a neurological condition. While test score variability may reflect a patient's current neurocognitive status, an accurate estimate of premorbid intellectual ability—which frequently may be expressed as an estimated IQ—remains an important component of a neuropsychological evaluation because it provides a context within which to consider variations in a patient's cognitive abilities, as well as being a "proxy" of a patient's *cognitive reserve*—that factor which can influence the clinical expression of a neurological condition.

Let's explore the issues of intellectual context and cognitive reserve in more depth with some clinical examples. Consider the cases of a physician and factory line worker, both of whom sustained a mild traumatic brain injury in a motor vehicle accident. Both obtained low average "normal range" scores on Wechsler Scale measures of working memory and processing speed. The physician obtained scores within the above average to superior range on other Wechsler Scale subtests, whereas the line worker's remaining scores were within the average range. Although their test scores were identical for abilities that can be compromised following brain trauma, might the "clinical significance" for each patient be different? Addressing the question requires an estimate of premorbid ability, which will provide a context for comparing a patient's current neuropsychological status with that which preceded the onset of the neurological condition. While an IQ score is one index of a person's general intellectual ability, it may not provide an accurate estimate of premorbid intellectual ability in a patient who has suffered neuropsychological compromise. Because test scores reflecting specific abilities (e.g., working memory, processing speed), which may be compromised by a neurological condition, contribute to the derivation of a composite IQ value, the IQ value itself may not be an accurate estimate of a patient's premorbid intellectual status. Neuropsychologists have addressed this issue by proposing various estimates of premorbid ability that include use of demographic information (e.g., education, occupation) and measures of abilities that are considered relatively resilient to the effects of brain dysfunction (reading level, vocabulary). See Lezak et al. (2004) for a comprehensive review of this topic. Performance on the Vocabulary subtest of the Wechsler Scales is one variable that can contribute to an estimate of premorbid intellectual ability. Among the Wechsler Scale subtests, Vocabulary correlates most highly with Full Scale IQ and with education, which also is a good indicator of premorbid functioning (Lezak et al. 2004). When we consider our two cases, the physician's Vocabulary score was at the 99th percentile, whereas the line worker's score was at the 37th percentile; and these scores provide one perspective on premorbid intellectual functioning. Ultimately, however, an estimate of premorbid ability is not just based on one test score but on clinical judgment that takes into account multiple variables including test scores and demographic information. Considering available information from multiple sources, we can estimate that the physician's premorbid ability was likely within the superior range, and the line worker's ability was closer to the average range. Therefore low average scores on measures of working memory and processing speed likely reflected a greater decline from "normal expectations" for the physician than they were for the line worker. In similar fashion, the estimate of premorbid ability also serves as a comparison standard for performance levels on other measures within the neuropsychological test battery (e.g., memory, conceptual problem solving).

There is a wide variability in how people adapt to the neuropsychological consequences associated with a neurological condition, and there are individual differences in the expression of symptoms, even in those conditions that may be thought to be similar in terms of underlying pathophysiology and severity. Studies have shown that there is not necessarily a direct relationship between brain pathology and the behavioral manifestation of that pathology (Katzman et al. 1988). There are individuals who, upon autopsy, may show evidence of Alzheimer's disease pathology, yet have shown no clinical manifestations of the disease during their lifetimes. This individual difference in clinical symptom expression can be a function of at least two factors, which have come to be known as *brain reserve capacity* (Satz 1993) and *cognitive reserve* (Stern 2002).

Brain reserve capacity (BRC) as a hypothetical construct may be represented in anatomic features such as brain size, head circumference, synaptic count, and dendritic branching (Stern 2002). IQ and educational level represent "indirect and probably less precise measures of the construct BRC" (Satz 1993). The BRC construct is expressed within a threshold model wherein a lesion of a particular size may result in clinical symptoms in a person with less BRC because it is beyond the threshold of brain damage sufficient to produce the symptom. Conversely the same lesion in a person with more BRC may not be beyond threshold to produce clinical symptoms. Stern (2002) characterizes BRC as a *passive model* in contrast to the *active model* of cognitive reserve, which is defined as "the ability to optimize or maximize performance through differential recruitment of brain networks, which perhaps reflect the use of alternate cognitive strategies." Essentially a person with more cognitive reserve has the cognitive resilience to use alternative processing paradigms when previously used approaches are no longer effective due to brain damage. Contrasting *active* cognitive reserve with *passive* brain reserve, two patients theoretically may have the same BRC, but the patient with more cognitive reserve will be able to tolerate a greater degree of brain damage before functional impairment is evident. Stern (2002) put the difference nicely: "The threshold approach supposes that the person with more BRC has more to lose before they reach some clinical cut-point. The cognitive reserve hypothesis focuses less on what is lost and more on what is left." With an *active* reserve model, premorbid IQ can be a "powerful" measure of reserve in some cases (Stern 2002). Returning to our cases of the physician and the line worker, we may hypothesize that the physician has more cognitive reserve than the line worker, and therefore has more adaptive capacity (i.e., ability to develop alternate cognitive strategies) to cope with functional limitations secondary to brain trauma. Moreover, the reserve models would suggest that brain trauma may have decreased BRC for both patients, but the physician's greater cognitive reserve may impart more resilience against symptom expression that may be associated with diseases of later life (e.g., Alzheimer's disease).

Attention, Concentration, and Processing Speed

Attention and concentration can be compromised in a wide range of neurological conditions, and also may be affected by associated symptoms like depression and fatigue. Deficits in attention and poor concentration also can compromise performance efficiency in other cognitive domains (e.g., learning and memory). Attention is not a unitary factor and is best conceptualized as a system with multiple components. Although there are different models of the attention system (Van Zomeren and Brouwer 1994) several component factors are common to many descriptions and are relevant for clinical assessment.

Immediate Attention Span is a part of the capacity/encoding aspect of the attention system, and is defined by the amount of information that can be handled at once. In contrast to other components of the attention system, immediate attention span is relatively resilient to the effects of brain dysfunction. Digit Span Forward is a frequently used measure of auditory-verbal attention span.

Focused or Selective Attention is the capacity to attend to relevant information while ignoring irrelevant or distracting stimuli. This component of attention is susceptible to disruption by brain dysfunction, and can be measured by a number of tests including the Digit Symbol subtest of the Wechsler Scales (Wechsler 1997), the Symbol Digit Modalities Test (Smith 1982), the Trail Making Test (Reitan 1979), and the Stroop Test (Golden 1978).

Sustained Attention or Vigilance is the capacity to maintain attention over time. Like focused or selective attention, sustained attention reflects a deployment function of the attention system that can be compromised by neurological conditions. Sustained attention can be measured by Continuous Performance Tests, and also is operative on measures of attention that are multifactorial and reflect more than one aspect of the system. For example, performance on the Symbol Digit Modalities Test requires focused attention, sustained attention, and processing speed.

Divided Attention is the capacity to respond to more than one task at a time—the ubiquitous "multitasking" of a hectic and fast-paced society—or the ability to attend to different operations within the same task. Part B of the Trail Making Test (Trails-B) and the Paced Auditory Serial Addition Test (Gronwall 1977) place demands on divided attention. Tasks of divided attention call upon the second component of the capacity/encoding aspect of the attention system—*working memory*, which is the capacity to hold information in mind while performing a mental manipulation. Measures of working memory can include such tests as Digit Span Backwards, the Letter-Number Sequencing subtest of the Wechsler Scales, and the Paced Auditory Serial Addition Test.

With some neurological conditions (e.g., multiple sclerosis, traumatic brain injury), the efficient functioning of the attention system may be compromised by reduced *processing speed*. Patients may feel overwhelmed by the information processing demands associated with daily functioning and complain of memory problems. For some patients with MS, what may appear as a deficit in memory retrieval actually may reflect disruptions in the acquisition stage of learning that are associated with slowed processing (DeLuca, Barbieri-Berger, and Johnson 1994). A processing speed component is incorporated into several measures of focused attention, sustained attention, and working memory (e.g., Trail Making Test, Symbol Digit Modalities Test, Paced Auditory Serial Addition Test).

Language and Verbal Abilities

A comprehensive assessment of speech and language—such as that offered by an aphasia battery like the Boston Diagnostic Aphasia Examination (Goodglass, Kaplan, and Barresi 2000)—will consider a range of functions that can be compromised by neurological conditions. These areas may include: spontaneous speech, auditory comprehension, repetition of words and sentences, confrontation naming and verbal associative fluency, writing, and reading. Neuropsychological test batteries often will include an aphasia screening such as the Aphasia Screening Test (Reitan 1979) or a combination of measures that assess different aspects of language ability that can be disrupted by brain dysfunction.

Verbal expressive and reasoning abilities may be assessed by Wechsler Scale subtests: Comprehension (verbal reasoning), Similarities (verbal concept formation), and Vocabulary (expressive vocabulary). These measures have a differential sensitivity to brain dysfunction. For some conditions, these tests—notably Vocabulary—may serve as indicators of premorbid ability, but all may be affected by left hemisphere involvement.

Neuropsychological test batteries also will include measures of language ability that are particularly sensitive to brain dysfunction such as the Boston Naming Test (Goodglass and Kaplan 2000) for confrontation naming, or Controlled Oral Word Association Tests (Delis, Kaplan, and Kramer 2001) for verbal associative fluency. Patients often will complain of that "tip of the tongue" phenomenon of not being able to find the word they want to say, and measures of naming and fluency provide objective evidence of this frustrating experience. Disruptions in confrontation naming can be seen in a wide range of neurological conditions that have left hemisphere involvement. Edith Kaplan also has noted that what may appear as linguistically based errors on measures of confrontation naming actually may reflect a visual-perceptual deficit—"perceptual fragmentation"—associated with right frontal involvement. Lezak et al. (2004) cite the example of misinterpreting the mouthpiece of a harmonica (Boston Naming Test item) as the line of windows on a bus. Other examples of perceptual fragmentation may be elicited by test stimuli of the Hooper Visual Organization Test (Hooper 1983).

Disruptions in the speed and facility of verbal expression (i.e., verbal fluency) can be seen in all the neurological conditions in our review. Tests of verbal fluency are among the most sensitive measures of dementia, as was reflected in the title of a recent editorial in the journal *Neurology,* "The One-Minute Mental Status Examination" (Cummings 2004). Canning et al. (2004) demonstrated the utility of a one-minute semantic fluency test (Animal Naming) for the early detection of dementia in a memory clinic setting, and furthermore showed that the differential sensitivity of fluency measures might help discriminate dementia of Alzheimer's Disease (AD) from a "subcortical" dementing process (e.g., vascular dementia). A score less than 15 for producing the names of as many animals as possible in one-minute (category fluency) was twenty times more likely to occur in a person with AD as opposed to a person without AD. An optimal cutoff score of 13 for letter fluency (number of words produced in one-minute beginning with F) was approximately three times as likely to occur with a person with AD. Animal fluency also was the best measure to discriminate between vascular dementia and normal elderly controls, but the addition of a letter fluency test to a battery was suggested as helpful in discriminating AD from vascular dementia because scores less than 4 on F fluency may be more indicative of a vascular etiology.

Visuoanalytic Functions

Visuoanalytic functioning can be affected by disruption in a complex array of abilities that can include visual attention, spatial judgment, visual detail analysis, perceptual integration, and visual organization and planning. Subtle deficits in visuospatial information processing can become significant when trying to negotiate the stimulus complexity of a metropolitan highway system in rush hour traffic. Other visuoanalytic deficits can manifest in extraordinary syndromes that challenge our phenomenological experience. In his book *The Man Who Mistook His Wife for a Hat* (1985, 13) Oliver Sacks provides a poignant description of visual agnosia as experienced by Dr P. People with visual agnosia may be able to "see" a rose but not recognize it as such until they smell its perfume. They can see a hammer but not know its identity until they come to feel its weight and contours by touch.

Reviews of visuospatial functioning in neurological conditions often include the consideration of visuoperceptual and visuoconstruction abilities. Although disruptions in specific visuoanalytic abilities frequently involve right hemisphere lesions, qualitative analysis of test performances also may reveal features that implicate the left hemisphere. Some commonly used tests will illustrate these points. The Judgment of Line Orientation Test is a visuoperceptual measure of spatial orientation that yields a quantitative score that is particularly sensitive to right hemisphere lesions (Benton, Sivan, and Hamsher 1994). In contrast, the Hooper Visual Organization Test (Hooper 1983)—a measure of visuoperceptual integration—is open to more interpretive possibilities. Rathbun and Smith (1982) noted that defective performances on this test usually reflected damage to the right hemisphere and persisting impairment in some cases with right-posterior lesions. Nadler et al. (1996) found that laterality differences could be demonstrated by quantitative scores as well as by analysis of qualitative errors. Higher rates of part and unformed/unassociated responses (poor visuospatial processing) were found with right hemisphere involvement, and more language-based errors were associated with left hemisphere involvement.

Examinations of visuoconstruction abilities are typically done with assembly and drawing tasks. Perhaps the best known assembly task is the Block Design subtest of the Wechsler Scales. Block Design is sensitive to visuospatial deficiencies associated with right hemisphere dysfunction, particularly in the parietal region (Warrington, James, and Maciejewski 1986). Performances can be affected by multiple factors (e.g., manual motor deficiencies, processing speed, executive abilities) such that disruptions in Block Design constructions can be seen in a range of neurological conditions. Drawing tasks require little in the way of equipment yet provide another rich source of information about visuospatial functioning. While quantitative scoring methods are available for drawing tasks such as the Rey-Osterrieth Complex Figure and Clock Drawing (Spreen and Strauss 1991), qualitative analyses of error patterns can provide useful information on laterality and specific functional deficiencies (e.g., inattention, organization and planning weaknesses, sequencing problems).

Memory

Complaints about faulty memory are among the most common cognitive problems reported by people living with neurological conditions. Memory, however, is not a unitary phenomenon, and disruption in efficient memory processing can reflect deficiencies in specific components of the memory system, as well as problems in other cognitive domains (e.g., attention, executive abilities) or functional status (e.g., depression, fatigue). There are numerous models describing the components and stages of memory processing (Squire 1986; Tulving and Craik 2000), and inconsistencies in the use of descriptive terms (e.g., short-term memory versus long-term memory) can cause confusion in discussing an already complex system. For purposes of clinical assessment, however, several key areas are frequently addressed.

Short-term memory is a capacity-limited system that includes immediate memory span, which is independent of the medial temporal, and diencephalic regions damaged in amnesia syndromes (Squire 1986). Immediate memory span generally can manage seven bits of information plus or minus two (Miller 1956). Besides having capacity limitations, immediate memory is susceptible to disruption by distraction (i.e., rehearsal prevented by turning one's attention away from the task to be remembered). Working memory, which also was considered the section on attention above, is considered another component of the *short-term memory system* (Baddeley 2000). Working memory can be considered the workspace in which information is being held in mind while it is being worked on. Immediate memory span can be assessed by Digit Span Forward, and working memory can be assessed by Digit Span Backward.

Long-term memory requires the integrity of the medial temporal and diencephalic regions (Squire 1986) and comes into play when the capacity of immediate memory span is exceeded or when material is to be "remembered" after distraction (i.e., prevention of rehearsal). The components of *long-term memory* include the acquisition (i.e., learning), storage, and retrieval of new information; and disruptions in specific areas can be seen in all the neurological conditions in our review. In many clinical situations, a combination of the Wechsler Memory Scale III–Abbreviated (Wechsler 1997) and the California Verbal Learning Test–II (Delis et al. 2000) offers an economical and comprehensive review of different aspects of *long-term memory* including auditory-verbal and visual memory processing, performance differences in dealing with organized versus unorganized verbal material, learning strategy and efficiency, susceptibility to interference, retrieval abilities, capacity to benefit from retrieval strategies, and distinctions between retrieval deficits and memory storage problems (free recall versus recognition memory). Such information may contribute to diagnostic clarification (e.g., differentiation of dementia syndromes), and also provide a functional analysis of memory processing strengths and weaknesses that can inform adaptation and rehabilitation strategies.

Remote memory is a reference for "older memories" which confusingly also may be referred to as "long-term memory" depending on one's semantic framework. In contrast to recent memory, which is disrupted by an amnesic episode or state, remote memory is recall of information stored prior to disruption (Lezak et al. 2004). This clinical distinction is illustrated by patients frequently commenting on being able to recall events from the distant past (remote memory), but not being able to remember what happened yesterday (recent memory).

Executive Functions, Conceptual Problem Solving, and Reasoning

Higher-order cognitive abilities such as organization, planning, strategy development and implementation, responsiveness to feedback, decision making and judgment, and mental flexibility are all part of a system of operations collectively known as executive functions. Thinking about the range of abilities that are subsumed by the term executive function can conjure the image of a corporate CEO, or perhaps closer to home, the daily work of a busy mother as she organizes, plans, and manages the activities of her family household. The integrity of this system allows for effective interaction with our world and ongoing adaptation to changing life circumstances. Disruptions in executive functions, which may be associated with a wide range of neurological conditions and with frontal system involvement in particular, can have broad behavioral implications. Decision making, judgment, and behavioral regulation can be compromised to the extent that a patient is unable to manage financial affairs or interact in a manner that conforms to social expectations. Less obvious deficiencies in executive functioning may compromise the ability to adapt to changing life circumstances, especially those that are accompanied by new challenges and problem-solving demands. For some people, the capacity to independently develop organizational and problem-solving strategies has been weakened by disruptions in the executive system; nevertheless they may be able to continue working effectively if given a structure or schema to focus their efforts. Such deficiencies in executive ability and subsequent responsiveness to intervention may be illustrated by performances on measures of learning and memory like the California Verbal Learning Test–II. This measure places demands on the independent organization of an encoding and retrieval strategy to deal with a large amount of unorganized verbal material. Test performances can be examined for evidence on how a patient organizes encoding and retrieval strategies (a function of the executive system) to facilitate memory processing. If memory retrieval has been deficient—perhaps as a function of executive ability weaknesses—we also may assess whether a patient's memory processing benefits from organizational cues (i.e., executive system supports). Executive abilities are involved in other cognitive domains as well (e.g., graphomotor organization and planning in the drawing of the Rey-Osterrieth Complex Figure), and frequently are assessed by measures that place demands on conceptual problem solving, reasoning, and mental flexibility. Developing a problem-solving strategy based on abstract reasoning and trial and error learning, maintaining a mental set to successfully deploy the strategy, and having the mental flexibility to alter strategy in response to corrective feedback all involve executive functioning, and are required by tests of conceptual problem solving like the Category Test (Reitan and Wolfson 1993) and the Wisconsin Card Sorting Test (Heaton 1981). Mental flexibility is a key component for efficient performances on Trails-B, which involves visual spatial tracking, and also on verbal fluency tests, which place demands on rapid processing and organizing retrieval strategies. Abstract reasoning is a factor in Wechsler Scale subtests: Similarities for verbal concept formation, and nonverbal analogous reasoning for Matrix Reasoning. There also are comprehensive batteries such as the Delis-Kaplan Executive Function Scale that have been designed to assess a broad range of abilities that may be compromised by disruption in the executive system (Delis, Kaplan, and Kramer 2001).

NEXT STEPS: RATIONALE FOR CHAPTER FORMAT

With a review of the neuropsychological domains serving as a foundation, let's now move on to consider the neurological conditions and their neuropsychological consequences. The remaining chapters in Part II will begin with a basic orientation to the epidemiological and pathophysiological features of the conditions followed by a review of associated neuropsychological challenges. The chapters will conclude with summary points for psychological intervention which will serve as a transition from diagnosis and assessment to treatment and more in-depth discussions of psychotherapy in Part III. Essentially, the chapter organization parallels the unfolding diagnostic process that takes us from knowledge of the condition a patient has and its effect on neuropsychological status, to a deepening appreciation of a patient's experience with the condition and its impact on quality of life.

A NOTE ON SUMMARY POINTS
FOR PSYCHOLOGICAL INTERVENTION

The summary points for psychological intervention, which conclude the chapters, are offered to highlight the neuropsychological challenges associated with the conditions as well as the more generic quality of life issues that may be a focus for psychological intervention. This emphasis reflects our reciprocal psychotherapy goals of reducing suffering associated with neuropsychological challenges, and promoting an engagement in life as it is now and as it continues to unfold. Psychotherapy plays an important role in addressing the psychological/emotional symptoms that accompany neurological conditions (e.g., delayed onset depression with traumatic brain injury), however I am not proposing condition-specific psychological interventions.

Knowledge of the conditions and their neuropsychological consequences is essential information if we are to develop a comprehensive understanding of the complexity of our patients' experiences. However the neuropsychological heterogeneity both within conditions and over the course of an illness, and patients' unique responses to these challenges, do not lend themselves easily to condition-specific psychological interventions; this is no more evident than when considering quality of life issues for patients and caregivers. We will consider quality of life challenges in greater depth in chapter 12, but for now let's adopt a person-centered perspective that views quality of life as a person's perception or subjective assessment of the impact of a condition on one's personal experience that may include physical, psychological/emotional, social, spiritual dimensions. From a clinical viewpoint, my patients continue to offer the lesson that attitude and how a person relates to, or copes with, the challenges of a neurological condition are significant factors influencing quality of life; and this attitudinal perspective does not appear to be condition-specific nor necessarily tied to the severity of a condition. This impression also has been supported in the reflections of authors who are living with the after-effects of life-changing neurological conditions (see Price [1994] and Dass [2000]), and in the psychological/rehabilitation research literature. In studying patients who had suffered a stroke, Niemi et al. (1988) concluded that the most important variable affecting quality of life seemed to be the patient's "subjective experience of disability and insufficiency." Similarly Glozman (2004) suggested that the quality of life of caregivers may be affected less by the actual symptoms of the carereceiver (patients with Parkinson's disease) than by the caregiver's perception and attitude toward the carereceiver's symptoms and their own coping adequacy. Glozman (2004) also suggested that caregiving for a family member with a chronic debilitating condition should be considered a generic phenomenon such that results of a study on Parkinson's disease may be applicable to other neurological conditions. In examining patients coping with different neurological illnesses including malignant brain tumors, stroke, Parkinson's disease, and traumatic brain injury, Hermann et al. (2000) concluded that coping with brain disease is only minorly influenced by illness-specific variables, and instead coping behavior may reflect premorbid personality traits rather than different psychological reactions to the illness.

To set the stage for our discussions of psychotherapy, the summary points will note neuropsychological features commonly seen within each condition, as well as more generic quality of life themes common across neurological conditions that involve significant losses, limitations, and adaptive challenges.

REFERENCES AND READINGS

Armengol, C. G. and W. Jamieson. 2001. Screening versus comprehensive neuropsychological examinations. In *The consumer-oriented neuropsychological report*, edited by C. G. Armengol, E. Caplan, and E. J. Moes. Futz, FL: Psychological Assessment Resources, 61–81.

Baddeley, A. 2000. Short-term and working memory. In *The Oxford handbook of memory*, edited by E. Tulving and F. I. M. Craik. Oxford: Oxford University Press.

Benton, A. L., A. B. Sivan, and K. Hamsher. 1994. *Contributions to neuropsychological assessment. A clinical manual*. 2nd ed. New York: Oxford University Press.

Canning, S. J., L. Leach, et al. 2004. Diagnostic utility of abbreviated fluency measures in Alzheimer disease and vascular dementia. *Neurology* 62 (4): 556–562.

Cummings, J. L. 2004. The one-minute mental status examination. *Neurology* 62 (4): 534–535.

Dass, Ram. 2000. *Still here: Embracing aging, changing, and dying*. New York: Riverhead Books.

Delis, D., E. Kaplan, and J. Kramer. 2001. *Delis-Kaplan Executive Function Scale*. San Antonio, TX: Psychological Corporation.

Delis, D., J. H. Kramer, E. Kaplan, and B. A. Ober. 2000. *California Verbal Learning Test–Second Edition (CVLT–II)*. San Antonio, TX: Psychological Corporation.

DeLuca, J., S. Barbieri-Berger, and S. K. Johnson. 1994. The nature of memory impairments in multiple sclerosis: Acquisition versus retrieval. *Journal of Clinical and Experimental Neuropsychology* 16 (2): 183–189.

Freud, Sigmund. 1893. Charcot. In *Sigmund Freud: Collected papers*, edited by J. Riviere. New York: Basic Books.

Glozman, J. M. 2004. Quality of life of caregivers. *Neuropsychology Review* 14 (4): 183–196.

Goetz, C. G., M. Bonduelle, and T. Gelfand. 1995. *Charcot*. New York: Oxford University Press.

Golden, C. J. 1978. *Stroop Color and Word Test*. Chicago: Stoelting.

Goodglass, H., and E. Kaplan. 2000. *Boston Naming Test*. Philadelphia: Lippincott Williams & Wilkins.

Goodglass, H., E. Kaplan, and B. Barresi. 2000. *The Boston Diagnostic Aphasia Examination (BDAE-3)*. 3rd ed. Philadelphia: Lippincott.

Gronwall, D. M. 1977. Paced auditory serial-addition task: A measure of recovery from concussion. *Perceptual and Motor Skills* 44 (2): 367–373.

Heaton, R. K. 1981. *Wisconsin Card Sorting Test*. Odessa, FL: Psychological Assessment Resources.

Herrmann, M., N. Curio, T. Petz, H. Synowitz, S. Wagner, C. Bartels, and C.W. Wallesch. 2000. Coping with illness after brain diseases—a comparison between patients with malignant brain tumors, stroke, Parkinson's disease, and traumatic brain injury. *Disability and Rehabilitation* 22 (12): 539–546.

Hooper, H. E. 1983. *Hooper Visual Organization Test Manual*. Los Angeles: Western Psychological Services.

Kane, R. L., G. Goldstein, and O. A. Parsons. 1989. A response to R. L. Mapou. *Journal of Clinical and Experimental Neuropsychology* 11 (4): 589–595.

Kaplan, E. 1988. A process approach to neuropsychological assessment. In *Clinical neuropsychology and brain function: Research, measurement, and practice.* edited by T. J. Bolls and B. Bryant. Washington, D.C.: American Psychological Association.

Katzman, R., R. Terry, R. DeTeresa, T. Brown, P. Davies, P. Fuld, X. Renbing, and A. Peck. 1988. Clinical, pathological, and neurochemical changes in dementia: A subgroup with preserved mental status and numerous neocortical plaques. *Annals of Neurology* 23 (2): 138–144.

Lezak, M. D., D. B. Howieson, D. W. Loring, H. Julia Hannay, and J. S. Fischer. 2004. *Neuropsychological Assessment*. 4th ed. New York: Oxford University Press.

Miller, G. A. 1956. The magical number seven, plus or minus two: Some limits on our capacity for processing information. *Psychological Review* 63:81–97.

Nadler, J. D., J. Grace, et al. 1996. Laterality differences in quantitative and qualitative Hooper performance. *Archives of Clinical Neuropsychology* 11(3): 223–29.

Niemi, M. L., R. Laaksonen, M. Kotila, and O. Waltimo. 1988. Quality of life 4 years after stroke. *Stroke* 19:1101–1107.

Price, R. 1994. *A whole new life: An illness and a healing*. New York: Scribner.

Rathbun, J., and A. Smith. 1982. Comment on the validity of Boyd's Validation Study of the Hooper Visual Organization Test. *Journal of Counseling and Clinical Psychology* 50 (2): 281–283.

Reitan, R. M. 1979. *Manual for administration of neuropsychological test batteries for adults and children*. Tucson, AZ: Reitan Neuropsychological Laboratory.

Reitan, R. M., and D. Wolfson. 1993. *The Halstead-Reitan neuropsychological test battery: Theory and clinical interpretation*. Tucson, AZ: Neuropsychology Press.

Sacks, Oliver W. 1985. *The man who mistook his wife for a hat and other clinical tales.* New York: Summit Books.

Satz, Paul. 1993. Brain reserve capacity on symptom onset after brain injury: A formulation and review of evidence for threshold theory. *Neuropsychology* 7 (3): 273–295.

Smith, A. 1982. *Symbol Digit Modalities Test. Manual (revised)*. Los Angeles: Western Psychological Services.

Spreen, O., and E. Strauss. 1991. *A compendium of neuropsychological tests*. New York: Oxford University Press.

Squire, L. R. 1986. Mechanisms of memory. *Science* 232:1612–1619.

Stern, Y. 2002. What is cognitive reserve? Theory and research application of the reserve concept. *Journal of the International Neuropsychological Society* 8 (3): 448–460.

Sweet, J. J, P .J. Moberg, and C. K. Westergaard. 1996. Five-year follow-up survey of practices and beliefs in clinical neuropsychologists. *Clinical Neuropsychologist* 10: 202–221.

Tulving, E., and F. I. M. Craik, eds. 2000. *The Oxford handbook of memory.* New York: Oxford University Press.

Van Zomeren, A. H., and W. H. Brouwer. 1994. *Clinical neuropsychology of attention.* New York: Oxford University Press.

Warrington, E. K., M. James, and C. Maciejewski. 1986. The WAIS as a lateralizing and localizing diagnostic instrument. *Neuropsychologia* 24: 223–239.

Wechsler, D. 1997. *Wechsler Adult Intelligence Scale–III.* San Antonio, TX: Psychological Corporation.

Wechsler, D. 1997. *Wechsler Memory Scale–Third Edition Abbreviated.* San Antonio, TX: Psychological Corporation.

5

Multiple Sclerosis

Multiple sclerosis (MS) is the most common nontraumatic neurological illness of young adults (Staffen et al. 2002). The nature of the condition and why its symptoms manifest in any one person at a particular time in their lives is a mystery that continues to be unraveled by medical science. Evidence points to MS being an autoimmune mediated inflammatory disorder that affects the central nervous system, but its specific cause or etiology and the onset of clinical symptoms may reflect a complex and not yet fully understood interaction of genetic, environmental, and immunologic factors. MS is thought to be acquired before puberty, but its onset in terms of clinical symptoms typically does not occur until early adulthood (Poser 1994). In addition to the cognitive and psychological challenges that we will review in greater detail, MS can result in a wide range of physical symptoms that include sensory and motor dysfunction, visual disturbance, dysarthria, dysphagia, fatigue, pain, spasticity/decreased coordination, loss of bladder and bowel control, and sexual dysfunction (Ben-Zacharia and Lublin 2001).

EPIDEMIOLOGY

MS is considered to be a condition of young adulthood. Seventy to eighty percent of MS patients are between the ages of 20 to 40 years. Another 15%–25% are more than 41 years old, and 5%–10% are less than 20 years old (Bashir and Whitaker 2002). The risk of MS is 1.5 to 2.0 times higher in women than men; women tend to present at an earlier age than men, and men are more likely to have a progressive course and accumulate disability (Bashir and Whitaker 2002). MS most commonly occurs in Caucasians of northern European background. The risk for MS in African-Americans is about half that for whites living in the same geographic area. The risk is progressively less for Native Americans, Asians, and residents of Hawaii (Bashir and Whitaker 2002). MS prevalence has a geographic variation with higher risk in the temperate regions than in the tropics. Immigration from high- to low-risk areas decreases the risk of developing MS, especially if the immigration occurs before the age of 15. Immigration from low- to high-risk areas increases the risk of MS in genetically susceptible individuals, however the susceptibility decreases with age (Bashir and Whitaker 2002). Genetic factors affect susceptibility to MS. There is a familial recurrence rate of about 15% (Compston and Coles 2002), and for first-degree relatives the risk of developing the disease is 10 to 20 times that in the general population (Bashir and Whitaker 2002).

PATHOPHYSIOLOGY

MS is an autoimmune mediated inflammatory disorder affecting the central nervous system (Feinstein et al. 1999). The two phases in MS are inflammatory demyelination and degeneration with axonal loss (Ben-Zacharia and Lublin 2001). Demyelination compromises nerve conduction and transmission of impulses and explains many of the clinical and laboratory features of MS (Compston and Coles 2002).

MS is classified into several subtypes (Lublin and Reingold 1996). The majority of patients initially presenting with the disease (85%) have the relapsing-remitting form, which is characterized by periods of neurologic symptoms followed by remissions (Frohman 2003). For many, the condition evolves into a secondary progressive form with or without occasional relapses or remissions. Primary progressive MS is defined as disease progression from onset with occasional plateaus and temporary minor improvements (Lublin and Reingold 1996), and it represents about 10% of the MS population (Frohman 2003). A less frequently seen progressive relapsing form of the condition also has been defined and is characterized by progressive disease at onset with periods of disease exacerbation and continuing progression between relapses (Lublin and Reingold 1996). Besides the above classifications of clinical course, severity definitions for benign MS and malignant MS also have been suggested, although the terms may be more appropriate in a research context than in a clinical setting (Lublin and Reingold 1996).

ASSOCIATED CLINICAL FEATURES

Fatigue

Fatigue is one of the most common and disabling symptoms of MS. It can affect up to 87% of patients with the condition, and as many as 40%

of patients regard fatigue to be their most disabling symptom (Racke, Hawker, and Frohman 2004). Multiple factors can contribute to MS-related fatigue including co-existing conditions (e.g., depression), medication effects, sleep disorders, elevations in core body temperature, and associated symptoms (e.g., weakness, ataxia) that increase the amount of exertion needed to carry out daily activities. There remains, however, "primary MS fatigue" which is thought to be related to the underlying pathophysiology of the disease itself (Racke, Hawker, and Frohman 2004). Combinations of pharmacologic and nonpharmacologic strategies (e.g., rest-activity balance, assistive devices and environmental modifications to conserve energy, cooling strategies, appropriate exercise, and stress management) are used to address this common and disabling symptom. Despite patients engaging in these treatment efforts, however, it still is not unusual to hear complaints about fatigue compromising cognitive processing and contributing to inconsistencies in performance efficiency, especially as a day wears on. Increased efforts to manage job demands or household chores in the face of accumulating fatigue may further drain cognitive reserve creating a vicious negative cycle of increasing fatigue, decreasing cognitive efficiency, more frustration, and increased susceptibility to depression. This issue was addressed in a study (Krupp and Elkins 2000) that showed a sample of patients with MS did not differ significantly from healthy controls on baseline measures of cognitive functioning but, in contrast to the healthy controls, the MS participants showed significant declines on measures of memory and conceptual planning following a continuous effortful cognitive task. The importance of this study for understanding the implications of fatigue for daily functioning was commented upon in *Lancet* (Senior 2000), "The results suggest that patients who don't show overt cognitive dysfunction are probably at risk of developing it during their daily lives. This may become a problem much earlier in the disease process than is commonly accepted."

Heat Reactivity

Managing heat becomes especially challenging for people living with MS because "temperature increases of 0.5C will slow and ultimately block nerve impulse conduction in demyelinated fibers, resulting in temporary clinical worsening" (Petajan and White 1999). Recognition of this phenomenon can be traced back to the 1890s when exercise-induced visual symptoms in MS patients were described (Uhthoff 1890), although the connection between heat exposure (i.e., rise in body temperature) and symptoms expression was not appreciated at that time. The accumulated results of subsequent research studies, however, would later demonstrate the connection between heat and the visual loss of Uhthoff's syndrome (Guthrie and Nelson 1995).

The temporary exacerbation of MS symptoms in reaction to heat became the basis for "heating reaction" procedures (e.g., hot bath test) that were employed diagnostically until the 1980s when their use declined due to lack of diagnostic specificity and the risk of permanent deficits in some MS patients. About 80% of patients with MS deteriorate when heated, and 60% have signs not previously recognized (Guthrie and Nelson 1995). This heating reaction may deter some patients with MS from activities (e.g., exercise) that otherwise could have a beneficial effect on their condition. However it has been shown that well-balanced exercise programs can be designed to activate working muscles but avoid overload that can result in conduction block and symptom exacerbation (Petajan and White 1999).

Stress

Many people with MS believe that psychological stress may be related to disease activity (Mohr et al. 2002), and considerations that stressful life factors may be related to onset of MS can be traced to Charcot's lectures on the condition (Charcot 1962). However there remains controversy as to the specific relationship between stress and MS disease activity. Goodin (2004) has offered the opinion that "the validity of any association between MS exacerbation and stress has been very difficult to establish with certainty." Ackerman (2004) has proposed that clinicians and researchers move beyond "all-or-none thinking" regarding the relationship between stress and MS disease activity and "begin to identify individual risk factors, mediators, and moderators of this relationship." A large-scale meta-analysis of the association between stressful life events and exacerbations in multiple sclerosis (Mohr et al. 2004) concluded: "There is a consistent association between stressful life events and subsequent exacerbation in multiple sclerosis. However these data do not allow the linking of specific stressors to exacerbations nor should they be used to infer that patients are responsible for their exacerbations." In the same year, the results of a nationwide cohort study in Denmark (Li et al. 2004) reported a higher MS risk in parents who lost a child than in parents who did not experience this tragedy, suggesting that the psychological stress induced by the death of a child may play a role in both the disease development and disease progression.

It has been suggested that the negative effects of stress on MS are at least as great as the positive effects of a class of disease-modifying drugs (interferon beta) widely considered to produce clinically meaningful results (Mohr et al. 2004). Reducing distress (i.e., depression) associated with MS not only improves quality of life but also can have a positive effect on the underlying pathophysiology of the disease (Mohr et al. 2001). Research also has suggested that effective coping can moderate the relationship between stress and MS disease activity (Mohr et al. 2002). While these studies do not purport to offer conclusive evidence for the relationship between clinical interventions and moderations of disease activity, they do offer possibilities and with possibilities there is hope.

COGNITIVE CHALLENGES

Descriptions of what have come to be known as the neuropsychological consequences of MS can be found in the 19th-century lectures of Charcot, yet it wasn't until the later part of the 20th century that these features gained more widespread acceptance in the medical community. A number of institutional and cultural forces may have contributed to the delay in recognizing this very real aspect of MS (Peyser and Poser 1986).

Disruption in mental abilities traditionally had been associated with dementia, and Alzheimer's disease was the prototype for the dementia syndrome. However the nature and extent of neurocognitive difficulty demonstrated by people with MS differed from the more pervasive cognitive disruption and decline found with dementia of the Alzheimer's type, and this very difference may have contributed to the minimization of a distinct yet different neuropsychological profile. Some theorists have suggested that the pattern of cognitive difficulty seen with MS is characteristic of what have been described as the *subcortical dementias,* however other researchers have cautioned that there may not be any single pattern of cognitive difficulty associated with MS but a variety of problems that may manifest in one or more cognitive domains with other functions remaining normal (Ryan et al. 1996).

Controversy in science is not unusual, and early 20th-century researchers provided differing perspectives on the neuropsychological aspects of MS with some emphasizing the emotional components, and others more thoroughly making note of the cognitive aspects. However, views tending to minimize the disruption in cognition associated with MS held sway in parts of the neurological community for some time, as reflected in proceedings from professional meetings and in editions of standard neurology texts (Peyser and Poser 1986).

The appreciation of the cognitive challenges that can confront people with MS was advanced significantly with the development of psychometric assessment procedures that could accurately quantify and describe even subtle disruptions in cognitive functioning. In the early 1970s, a pioneering figure in American neuropsychology, Ralph Reitan, and his colleagues were demonstrating that cognitive disruption could be a frequent occurrence with MS (Reitan, Reed, and Dyken 1971). An important turning point was reached in 1986 when comprehensive reviews of the neuropsychological aspects of MS appeared in the professional literature (Peyser and Poser 1986;

Rao 1986). These reviews would herald an explosion of research activity on the neurobehavioral correlates of MS that would call upon the collaborative efforts of several disciplines and provide empirical validation for the clinical observations made by Charcot over a century ago.

Estimates of the prevalence of cognitive dysfunction in people with MS have varied, but generally a figure between 40%–50% emerges as an approximation (Brassington and Marsh 1998). The heterogeneity of the MS groups studied and differences in cognitive assessment procedures used in the studies probably contributed to variations in prevalence estimates. It generally has been reported that cognitive impairment in people with MS seems to be unrelated to duration of the condition or neurological disability status (Rao et al. 1991). Duration of the condition is not necessarily related to disease activity, and physical disability status may reflect areas of nervous system involvement that are not related to cognitive functioning. However when considering disease activity, it has been shown that cognitive functioning can be adversely affected during periods of exacerbation, and in most cases cognitive functioning could be expected to return to baseline following an exacerbation (Foong et al. 1998). Studies also have suggested that disease course may be more closely related to cognitive dysfunction, with greater problems seen in people with chronic-progressive MS in contrast to the relapsing-remitting type (Heaton et al. 1985). Additional research, however, has led to some modification of this interpretation by noting that it may not be disease course per se, but what has been described as *lesion load* in the brain (i.e., number and size of areas of demyelination in the brain as visualized by neuroimaging procedures like magnetic resonance imaging) that is the primary factor related to cognitive difficulty in people with MS (Feinstein 1999).

Attention, Concentration, and Processing Speed

Disruptions in the attention and concentration of people with MS tend to become increasingly evident as demands on the attention system become more complex. Immediate attention span, as assessed by the Digit Span test, has been reported to be normal in some studies (Rao, Leo, and Aubin-Faubert 1989), but deficient relative to control subjects in other studies (Beatty et al. 1996). However when performances on forward and backward spans were distinguished, patients with MS had more difficulty on the more complex backward span task (Rao et al. 1991; Feinstein et al. 1997) Weaknesses in working memory, as implicated by difficulties in digit backward span performances, also have been found on other studies suggesting dysfunction within the central executive system (D'Esposito et al. 1996). Problems with complex attention deployment can challenge many patients with MS, who often complain of having difficulty with "multitasking," especially under time pressures. These deficits in focused and divided attention can be revealed by measures like the Symbol Digit Modalities Test, Trails-B, and the Paced Auditory Serial Addition Test. These tests also have in common one of the more vexing challenges for people with MS—a processing speed demand. People with MS often describe some slowing in their thinking. This reduction in processing speed and efficiency may be experienced as not being able to solve problems quickly or perform tasks as fast as had once been possible. Patients may not have difficulty actually hearing what is being said, but there can be the sense of feeling overwhelmed if the information they are trying to process is coming too fast or from multiple sources. Reductions in processing speed in people with MS have been shown in numerous studies using a variety of measures (Demaree et al. 1999). Deficient processing speed also may be a significant contributory factor to problems in other cognitive domains such as memory (DeLuca, Barbieri-Berger, and Johnson 1994) and executive functioning (Denney et al. 2004).

Language and Verbal Abilities

Although language functions may be largely unaffected by MS, patients can have subtle deficiencies in language that can obstruct communication. Word finding can be challenging. Studies have demonstrated that patients with MS may have difficulties with confrontation naming (Friend et al. 1999), but deficiencies in verbal fluency may be more common (Beatty et al. 1989). Perhaps better known as the "tip-of-the-tongue" phenomenon, these interruptions to the flow of speech can be especially exasperating for people with MS because, unlike the difficulty of retrieving from memory something recently learned, the problem is in retrieving something that is experienced as familiar and well known—but the harder one tries to find the word the more elusive it seems to be.

Visuoanalytic Functions

MS can cause disruptions in vision that are primarily sensory in nature (e.g., optic neuritis), but other problems in "seeing" may reflect visuoperceptual processing difficulties (Beatty et al. 1989; Rao et al. 1991). Tests of visuoconstruction (e.g., Block Design, Rey-Osterrieth Complex Figure Drawing) also may elicit subpar performances but the multifactorial nature of these measures may also be tapping MS-related deficiencies in other areas (e.g., organization and planning, processing speed, manual motor control).

Memory

Problems in memory processing can be seen in 40%–60% of people with MS (Brassington and Marsh 1998). But memory is a complex neuropsychological system, and some areas are more susceptible to disruption by MS while others remain relatively unaffected.

Recent memory (i.e., new learning and retention) has been a major focus of study, and one aspect of recent memory that has been implicated as being affected by MS is retrieval, that is, the ability to recall information that has been recently learned (Rao, Leo, and Aubin-Faubert 1989). Deficit in retrieval may be demonstrated by poor performances on recall measures in contrast to relatively intact abilities in recognition memory. However researchers also have considered that problems in the beginning stages of learning or acquisition—which also can include aspects of working memory—may be responsible for the difficulties with information recall that can be seen with MS (DeLuca, Barbieri-Berger, and Johnson 1994). We know that MS can have an impact on processing speed and efficiency. If processing capacity is overwhelmed, patients may not actually be able to "get" all the information that they are trying to remember, and the information they are able to process may not be encoded efficiently enough into long-term storage to permit recall at a later time. It is as if one caught a glimpse of something flying by—we can remember and recall some of it, but perhaps not all of it.

Remote memory also has been investigated in people with MS, but the results here are again equivocal, with some researchers identifying problems (Beatty et al. 1989) whereas others have not (Rao et al. 1991). Perhaps we ultimately may discover that the memory processing difficulties experienced by people living with MS are heterogeneous, and the overall results of studies—while helpful in advancing our knowledge of the impact of MS on different parts of the memory system—may not fully describe the experience of any one person who has the condition (Beatty et al. 1996).

Executive Functions and Conceptual Problem Solving

Executive functions can be affected in people living with MS (Foong et al. 1997), and disruptions in this complex system can manifest in problems with organization, planning, and mental flexibility. Deficits may be identified on tests of concept formation (Beatty and Monson 1996), sequencing and planning (Arnett et al. 1997), and verbal fluency (Foong et al. 1997). To the extent that deficiencies in this cognitive domain may manifest behaviorally as "stubbornness" or "disorganization," they may be erroneously attributed to personality factors that obscure the neurological basis of the problem (Lezak et al. 2004).

PSYCHOLOGICAL AND EMOTIONAL CHALLENGES

The psychological and emotional challenges associated with MS can reflect the primary effects of the disease such as structural brain abnormalities and disease characteristics, as well as the secondary effects of the complex interplay of long-standing personality dynamics with the adaptive demands of dealing with compromised functioning, loss, and uncertainty. Depression in its various forms has been considered the most common mental state change associated with MS, as evidenced by a review conducted by Feinstein (1999) that found 80% of 100 consecutive referrals to a neuropsychiatry clinic had mood disorders with the majority being major depression. Anxiety, although less well studied, can be a frequent accompaniment to depression and add to the morbidity of MS (Feinstein et al. 1999).

The lifetime prevalence of major depression in MS ranges from 25%–50% (Feinstein et al. 2004). The causes for depression are multifactorial and can reflect structural brain abnormalities (Feinstein et al. 2004), disease exacerbations and course (Feinstein 1999), and secondary psychosocial adaptive challenges. Fatigue and physical disability can contribute to depressed mood, and depression also may be mediated by the ability to participate in recreational activities (Voss et al. 2002).

Emotional dyscontrol in MS may manifest in pathological laughing and crying (PLC) that is defined "as sudden, involuntary displays of laughing or crying or both, without subjective feelings of pronounced sadness or euphoria" (Feinstein and Feinstein 2001). The phenomenon was demonstrated in 10% of community-based MS patients (Feinstein et al. 1997). Difficulty with emotional control, as manifested by irritability, sadness, and tearfulness, also may be experienced by a substantial group of MS patients (almost 50%) and is thought to be indicative of generalized psychological distress that warrants clinical attention (Feinstein and Feinstein 2001).

Appreciating the interaction between depression and cognitive challenges is important for the clinician working with MS patients. Research has suggested that cognitive dysfunction is a major factor in determining the quality of life of people with MS, and cognitively impaired patients are more likely to be unemployed, divorced, and depressed (Brassington and Marsh 1998). Depression also can have an impact on cognitive functioning in patients with MS, and researchers have suggested "that a true understanding of the nature of cognitive dysfunction in MS would be incomplete without considering the important role that depression plays" (Arnett, Higginson, and Randolph 2001).

SUMMARY POINTS FOR PSYCHOLOGICAL INTERVENTION

- Cognitive dysfunction can affect up to half of people living with MS, and it is a major factor determining quality of life. Reduction in processing speed is a common feature in the cognitive profile of MS patients.

- Depression is the most common mental state change associated with MS, and the lifetime prevalence for major depression can approach 50%. Patients with MS also may experience generalized psychological distress that does not meet criteria for a formal psychiatric diagnosis but nevertheless affects their quality of life.
- Fatigue is one of the most common and disabling symptoms of MS, affecting up to 87% of people with the condition. Patients who do not show overt cognitive dysfunction may be at risk—as a result of fatigue—for having cognitive difficulties during their daily lives leading to problems at the workplace or other aspects of daily functioning.
- Heat can result in a temporary exacerbation of MS symptoms.
- A consistent association has been found between stressful life events and subsequent exacerbations of MS.

A Closing Note

Uncertainty is one of the hallmark characteristics of MS. For many patients, an initial diagnosis may have been elusive with initial vague and fleeting symptoms being attributed to stress or worrisome somatic preoccupation. However once a diagnosis is made, uncertainty doesn't necessarily recede; if anything it continues to rear its head, leaving patients with fears of the worst and the anxiety not knowing the specific course their MS will take. A neuropsychological informed psychotherapy approach can be an important component in our patients' treatment regimens as they cope with the losses in adaptive functioning, inefficiencies in cognitive processing, and the compromising effects of heat, stress, and fatigue on neuropsychological status and quality of life. The attitude of mind perspective for psychotherapy was developed to assist patients in developing a foundation for living with the losses and uncertainties that accompany a condition such as multiple sclerosis. With the five elements of a way serving as guideposts for accepting and living with the reality of the condition, and with mindfulness meditation approaches supporting efforts to address symptoms and promote a continuing engagement in life, our patients develop the coping resources to deal with current stressors and future uncertainties.

REFERENCES AND READINGS

Ackerman, K. 2004. Relationship between multiple sclerosis exacerbations and stress: Response. *Psychosomatic Medicine* 66 (2): 288–289.

Arnett, P. A., C. I. Higginson, and J. J. Randolph. 2001. Depression in multiple sclerosis: Relationship to planning ability. *Journal of the International Neuropsychological Society* 7 (6): 665–674.

Arnett, P. A., S. M. Rao, J. Grafman, L. Bernardin, T. Luchetta, J. R. Binder, and L. Lobeck. 1997. Executive functions in multiple sclerosis: an analysis of temporal ordering, semantic encoding, and planning abilities. *Neuropsychology* 11 (4): 535–544.

Bashir, K., and J. N. Whitaker. 2002. *Handbook of multiple sclerosis*. Philadelphia: Lippincott Williams & Wilkins.

Beatty, W. W., D. E. Goodkin, N. Monson, and P. A. Beatty. 1989. Cognitive disturbances in patients with relapsing remitting multiple sclerosis. *Archives of Neurology* 46 (10): 1113–1119.

Beatty, W. W., and N. Monson. 1996. Problem solving by patients with multiple sclerosis: Comparison on the Wisconsin and California Card Sorting Tests. *Journal of the International Neuropsychological Society* 2:134–140.

Beatty, W. W., S. L. Wilbanks, C. R. Blanco, K. A. Hames, R. Tivis, and R. H. Paul. 1996. Memory disturbance in multiple sclerosis: Reconsideration of patterns of performance on the selective reminding test. *Journal of Clinical and Experimental Neuropsychology* 18 (1): 56–62.

Ben-Zacharia, A. B., and F. D. Lublin. 2001. Palliative care in patients with multiple sclerosis. *Neurologic Clinics* 19 (4): 801–827.

Brassington, J. C., and N. V. Marsh. 1998. Neuropsychological aspects of multiple sclerosis. *Neuropsychology Review* 8 (2): 43–77.

Charcot, J. M. 1962. *Lectures on the diseases of the nervous system. Second series*. Translated by G. Sigerson. New York: Hafner Publishing Co.

Compston, A., and A. Coles. 2002. Multiple sclerosis. *Lancet*. 359 (9313): 1221–1231.

D'Esposito, M., K. Onishi, H. Thompson., K. Robinson, C. Armstrong, and M. Grossman. 1996. Working memory impairments in multiple sclerosis: Evidence from a dual-task paradigm. *Neuropsychology* 10:51–56.

DeLuca, J., S. Barbieri-Berger, and S. K. Johnson. 1994. The nature of memory impairments in multiple sclerosis: Acquisition versus retrieval. *Journal of Clinical and Experimental Neuropsychology* 16 (2): 183–189.

Demaree, H. A., J. DeLuca, E. A. Gaudino, and B. J. Diamond. 1999. Speed of information processing as a key deficit in multiple sclerosis: Implications for rehabilitation. *Journal of Neurology, Neurosurgery, and Psychiatry* 67 (5): 661–663.

Denney, D. R., S. G. Lynch, B. A. Parmenter, and N. Horne. 2004. Cognitive impairment in relapsing and primary progressive multiple sclerosis: Mostly a matter of speed. *Journal of the International Neuropsychological Society* 10 (7): 948–956.

Feinstein, A., and K. Feinstein. 2001. Depression associated with multiple sclerosis. Looking beyond diagnosis to symptom expression. *Journal of Affective Disorders* 66 (2–3): 193–198.

Feinstein, A., K. Feinstein, T. Gray, and P. O'Connor. 1997. Prevalence and neurobehavioral correlates of pathological laughing and crying in multiple sclerosis. *Archives of Neurology* 54 (9): 1116–1121.

Feinstein, A., P. O'Connor, T. Gray, and K. Feinstein. 1999. The effects of anxiety on psychiatric morbidity in patients with multiple sclerosis. *Multiple Sclerosis (Houndmills, Basingstoke, England)* 5 (5): 323–326.

Feinstein, A., P. Roy, N. Lobaugh, K. Feinstein, P. O'Connor, and S. Black. 2004. Structural brain abnormalities in multiple sclerosis patients with major depression. *Neurology* 62 (4): 586–590.

Feinstein, Anthony. 1999. *The clinical neuropsychiatry of multiple sclerosis.* New York: Cambridge University Press.

Foong, J., L. Rozewicz, G. Quaghebeur, C. A. Davie, L. D. Kartsounis, A. J. Thompson, D. H. Miller, and M. A. Ron. 1997. Executive function in multiple sclerosis. The role of frontal lobe pathology. *Brain: A Journal of Neurology* 120:15–26.

Foong, J., L. Rozewicz, G. Quaghebeur, A. J. Thompson, D. H. Miller, and M. A. Ron. 1998. Neuropsychological deficits in multiple sclerosis after acute relapse. *Journal of Neurology, Neurosurgery, and Psychiatry* 64 (4): 529–532.

Friend, K. B., B. M. Rabin, L. Groninger, R. H. Deluty, C. Bever, and L. Grattan. 1999. Language functions in patients with multiple sclerosis. *Clinical Neuropsychologist* 13 (1): 78–94.

Frohman, E. M. 2003. Multiple sclerosis. *Medical Clinics of North America* 87 (4): 867–897, viii–ix.

Goodin, D. S. 2004. Relationship between multiple sclerosis exacerbations and stress. *Psychosomatic Medicine* 66(2): 287–289; author reply 287–289.

Guthrie, T. C., and D. A. Nelson. 1995. Influence of temperature changes on multiple sclerosis: Critical review of mechanisms and research potential. *Journal of the Neurological Sciences* 129 (1): 1–8.

Heaton, Robert K., et al. 1985. Neuropsychological findings in relapsing-remitting and chronic-progressive multiple sclerosis. *Journal of Consulting and Clinical Psychology* 53 (1): 103–110.

Krupp, L. B., and L. E. Elkins. 2000. Fatigue and declines in cognitive functioning in multiple sclerosis. *Neurology* 55 (7): 934–939.

Lezak, M. D., D. B. Howieson, D. W. Loring, H. J. Hannay, and J. S. Fischer. 2004. *Neuropsychological assessment.* 4th ed. New York: Oxford University Press.

Li, J., C. Johansen, H. Bronnum-Hansen, E. Stenager, N. Koch-Henriksen, and J. Olsen. 2004. The risk of multiple sclerosis in bereaved patients: A nationwide cohort study in Denmark. *Neurology* 62 (5): 726–729.

Lublin, F. D., and S. C. Reingold. 1996. Defining the clinical course of multiple sclerosis: Results of an international survey. National Multiple Sclerosis Society (USA) Advisory Committee on Clinical Trials of New Agents in Multiple Sclerosis. *Neurology* 46 (4): 907–911.

Mohr, D. C., D. E. Goodkin, J. Islar, S. L. Hauser, and C. P. Genain. 2001. Treatment of depression is associated with suppression of nonspecific and antigen-specific T (H) 1 responses in multiple sclerosis. *Archives of Neurology* 58 (7): 1081–1086.

Mohr, D. C., D. E. Goodkin, S. Nelson, D. Cox, and M. Weiner. 2002. Moderating effects of coping on the relationship between stress and the development of new brain lesions in multiple sclerosis. *Psychosomatic Medicine* 64 (5): 803–809.

Mohr, D. C., S. L. Hart, L. Julian, D. Cox, and D. Pelletier. 2004. Association between stressful life events and exacerbation in multiple sclerosis: a meta-analysis. *BMJ (Clinical research ed.)* 328 (7442): 731.

Petajan, J. H., and A. T. White. 1999. Recommendations for physical activity in patients with multiple sclerosis. *Sports medicine (Auckland, N.Z.)* 27 (3): 179–191.

Peyser, J. M., and C. M. Poser. 1986. Neuropsychological correlates of multiple sclerosis. In *Handbook of clinical neuropsychology,* edited by S. B. Filskov and T. J. Boll. New York: Wiley-Interscience.

Poser, C. M. 1994. The epidemiology of multiple sclerosis: A general overview. *Annals of Neurology* 36:S180–S193.

Racke, M. K., K. Hawker, and E. M. Frohman. 2004. Fatigue in multiple sclerosis: is the picture getting simpler or more complex? *Archives of Neurology* 61 (2): 176–177.

Rao, S. M., G. J. Leo, and P. St. Aubin-Faubert. 1989. On the nature of memory disturbance in multiple sclerosis. *Journal of Clinical and Experimental Neuropsychology* 11:699–712.

Rao, S. M., G. J. Leo, L. Bernardin, and F. Unverzagt. 1991. Cognitive dysfunction in multiple sclerosis. I. Frequency, patterns and predictions. *Neurology* 41:685–691.

Rao, S. M. 1986. Neuropsychology of multiple sclerosis: A critical review. *Journal of Clinical and Experimental Neuropsychology* 8 (5): 503–542.

Reitan, R. M., J. C. Reed, and M. L. Dyken. 1971. Cognitive, psychomotor, and motor correlates of multiple sclerosis. *Journal of Nervous and Mental Disease* 153 (3): 218–224.

Ryan, L., C. Clark, H. Klonoff, D. Li, and D. Paty. 1996. Patterns of cognitive impairment in relapsing-remitting multiple sclerosis and their relationship to neuropathology on magnetic resonance images. *Neuropsychology* 10 (2): 176–193.

Senior, K. 2000. Mental fatigue problems in multiple sclerosis. *Lancet* 356 (9238): 1332.

Staffen, W., A. Mair, H. Zauner, J. Unterrainer, H. Niederhofer, A. Kutzelnigg, S. Ritter, S. Golaszewski, B. Iglseder, and G. Ladurner. 2002. Cognitive function and fMRI in patients with multiple sclerosis: Evidence for compensatory cortical activation during an attention task. *Brain: A Journal of Neurology* 125:1275–1282.

Uhthoff, W. 1890. Untersuchungen über die bei der multiplen Herdsklerose vorkommenden Augenstörungen. *Archiv für Psychiatrie und Nervenkrankheiten* 21:55–116 and 303–410.

Voss, W. D., P. A. Arnett, C. I. Higginson, J. J. Randolph, M. D. Campos, and D. G. Dyck. 2002. Contributing factors to depressed mood in multiple sclerosis. *Archives of Clinical Neuropsychology* 17 (2): 103–115.

6

Traumatic Brain Injury and Postconcussion Syndrome

Traumatic brain injury (TBI) can be defined as brain injury from externally inflicted trauma that may result in significant impairment in a person's physical, cognitive, and psychosocial functioning. TBI affects people of all ages, and it is the leading cause of long-term disability among children and young adults (National Institutes of Health 1998). The neuropsychological sequelae of TBI can compromise academic endeavor, occupational pursuit, and interpersonal relationships. There are approximately 300,000 hospital admissions annually for persons with mild or moderate TBI, and an additional unknown number of traumatic brain injuries that are not diagnosed but which may result in long-term disability (NIH 1998).

EPIDEMIOLOGY

The annual incidence rate for TBI in the United States and most industrialized countries is 200 per 100,000 population, with rates up to 400 per 100,000 in urban areas (Cummings and Mega 2003). Males are twice as likely as females to have a TBI, and the highest incidence occurs between the ages of 15 to 24, and 75 and older, with another peak for children age 5 and younger. Alcohol is associated with half of all TBIs (NIH 1998). Motor vehicle accidents are the most common cause of TBI, approximately 50%; followed by falls generally among the frail elderly and very young, 21%; violence, 12%; and injuries from sports and recreational activities, 10% (NIH 1998; Rao and Lyketsos 2000). Head injuries typically are classified by the nature of trauma and severity of the initial impairment. In open head injuries or penetrating head wounds, the integrity of the skull and dura are

77

breached or penetrated (e.g., missile wounds). With a closed head injury, the skull remains relatively intact and the brain is not exposed. Duration of coma and post-traumatic amnesia (PTA) frequently are used to estimate severity of injury, and duration of PTA has been shown to be more accurate than coma in predicting cognitive status two years after injury (Brooks et al. 1980; Lezak et al. 2004). Broadly speaking, the period of time from head injury to when a patient "wakes up" is referred to as PTA. Refinements of this definition have evolved to include "the length of the interval during which current events have not been stored" (Russell and Smith 1961). Patients may appear to have "regained consciousness" following head trauma, yet have little or only patchy recollections of the time spent in the emergency room or in initial diagnostic studies. This period of "anterograde amnesia," including coma, defines PTA (Brooks 1989). PTA ends when a patient begins to register experience again, but only when registration is continuous, that is, resumption of continuous memory (Lezak et al. 2004). Estimates of severity of head injury based on PTA are: "very mild," less than 5 minutes; "mild," 5–60 minutes; "moderate," 1–24 hours; "severe," 1–7 days; "very severe," 1–4 weeks; and "extremely severe," more than 4 weeks (Lezak et al. 2004).

PATHOPHYSIOLOGY

We will be focusing our review on closed head injuries, where TBI is the result of mechanical forces applied to the skull and transmitted to the brain by *direct impact* and/or through *acceleration/deceleration forces*. The immediate disturbance in neurologic function or mental status created by the mechanical forces of rapid acceleration/deceleration defines *concussion*. Concussion does not require a direct blow to the head; "the rapid angular acceleration in itself is sufficient to set these forces into motion" (Lezak et al. 2004, 166).

TBI can result in focal damage in the form of contusions (i.e., bruising) at the area of impact (coup), and countercoup lesions in which damage is sustained opposite the site of impact. The orbital-frontal areas and temporal tips are common sites of contusions with TBI (Rao and Lyketsos 2000). Diffuse damage results from acceleration forces that cause shearing effects on blood vessels and nerve fibers throughout the brain, with the stretching or tearing of axons referred to as diffuse axonal injury (DAI). Microscopic white matter lesions due to DAI, which probably account for much of the cognitive dysfunction associated with concussion, may not be visualized by neuroimaging techniques such as MRI (Lezak et al. 2004). Whiplash injuries often resulting from rear-end collisions also result from acceleration/deceleration forces that cause strain or sprain of the cervical region (Cummings and Mega 2003), but whether such injuries (without loss of consciousness or blow to the head) can cause TBI and associated neuropsychological problems is more controversial. Nevertheless, studies have demonstrated that patients with whiplash injury can have residual symptom patterns similar to those evidenced by patients with mild TBI resulting from rapid acceleration/deceleration and impact to the head. See Lezak et al. (2004) for a comprehensive review.

TBI also can damage larger blood vessels of the brain causing hemorrhage and hematoma (collections of blood within the skull) that displace brain tissue. In the elderly, the effects of a subdural hematoma may emerge several weeks after what has been considered a "trivial" head injury because already existing brain atrophy allows for the slow expansion and distortion of the brain (Lezak et al. 2004). Other later or secondary effects of TBI, which can have a significant effect on a patient's status, include hypoxia, anemia, metabolic abnormalities, hydrocephalus, intracranial hypertension, fat embolism, along with a cascade of biochemical changes (Rao and Lyketsos 2000).

RECOVERY AND POSTCONCUSSION SYNDROME

Residual deficits can occur in 10% of individuals with mild TBI, 67% with moderate TBI, and 100% with severe injuries (Cummings and Mega 2003). Primary recovery of simple functions occurs mainly in the first six months after injury with secondary recovery, involving psychosocial adaptation, being a longer process (Bond 1986). Dikmen and Reitan (1976) have noted that most neuropsychological recovery takes place in the first year after injury, and that greater recovery is seen in patients with more severe initial deficits although such patients show greater deficits 18 months after injury. Studies have suggested that recovery from mild TBI generally is favorable, with more than two-thirds of people returning to premorbid activities, yet such optimism is tempered by the fact that many patients show mild yet persisting neuropsychological problems that compromise functioning and may not be diagnosed until appropriate and sensitive testing (i.e., neuropsychological evaluation) is undertaken. See Lezak et al. (2004) for a comprehensive review.

The majority of head injured patients fall into the mild TBI classification with estimates ranging from 70% of all TBIs (Busch and Alpern 1998) to 50%–90% of all cases (Cummings and Mega 2003). The consequences of a mild TBI can include a range of symptoms collectively known as Postconcussion Syndrome (PCS). These symptoms reflect physical, cognitive, and psychological factors; and include difficulties in attention and memory, becoming easily fatigued, disordered sleep, headache, vertigo or dizziness, irritability or aggression on little provocation, anxiety, depression, affective lability, changes in personality (e.g., social or sexual inappropriateness), and apathy or lack of spontaneity (American Psychiatric Association and American Psychiatric Association Task Force on DSM-IV 2000). PCS symptoms are common within the first three months following mild TBI (Busch and Alpern 1998) and gradually resolve in most patients after one year, with 85%–90% of patients having largely recovered (Cummings and Mega 2003). For some patients, however, PCS symptoms may persist, with 10%–15% developing what has been termed "chronic postconcussion disorder." The legitimacy of this syndrome is not without controversy. It has been suggested that desires for compensation and involvement in litigation strongly influence chronic postconcussion symptoms. On the other hand, alternative explanations for the persistent neuropsychological consequences associated with mild TBI are suggested by studies demonstrating an increased vulnerability to cognitive deficits following a second concussion, and by the emergence of cognitive inefficiency in seemingly "recovered" mild TBI patients in response to stress. See Gasquoine (1997) for a comprehensive review.

Ultimately, the messiness of our lives does not always abide with facile either-or categorizations, and the multiplicity of factors that influence our behavior is no more evident than after a neurological insult, even a "mild" one. Such complex interactions as those responsible for the after-effects of mild TBI were aptly summed up by Ponsford et al. (2000): "Functional outcome following mild TBI is determined by the complex interaction of neurological, physical, and psychological factors, the injured individual's premorbid personality and coping style, environmental demands and expectations and support of others."

COGNITIVE CHALLENGES

Depending on the nature and extent of injury, TBI can result in disruption in any of the major cognitive domains we have been reviewing. Rao and Lyketsos (2000) note that TBI is associated with "a plethora of cognitive deficits" that can include impairment of arousal, attention, concentration, memory, language, and executive function. Lucas (1998) further notes that the high incidence of orbitofrontal and anterior temporal lobe contusions associated with moderate to severe closed head injuries typically produce attention deficits and distractibility, slowed cognitive processing and behavioral responding, impaired learning and retrieval of new information, deficits in auditory and visual processing, and frontal lobe signs. Disruptions in executive functioning (i.e., "frontal lobe signs") are especially problematic with moderate to severe head injuries because impairments in self-awareness and behavioral regulation significantly challenge rehabilitative efforts and adaptive functioning (Lezak et al. 2004; Prigatano 1991).

Mild TBI can be characterized by considerable interindividual variability in cognitive deficit patterns. Despite such variability, however, some relatively common cognitive deficits do emerge. Disruptions in the attentional domain and problems with verbal retrieval are frequently cited challenges (Lezak et al. 2004; Lucas 1998). Attentional deficits may manifest in slowed mental processing, distractibility, susceptibility to information overload, and difficulties with mental tracking or working memory. Complaints of memory problems may more accurately reflect difficulties with attention and verbal retrieval than a memory deficit per se. Disruptions in verbal retrieval may be demonstrated by problems with confrontation naming and inefficiencies in verbal fluency. So-called memory retention problems may be unmasked to be deficits in retrieval when defective performances on measures of free recall are compared to normal performances on measures of cued recall and recognition memory on tests like the California Verbal Learning Test–II. For many patients, information processing demands that were once handled in an automatic and routine fashion (e.g., planning an itinerary for a trip and packing a suitcase) now require greater effort, which depletes already compromised energy reserves and sets into motion a vicious cycle of decreased cognitive efficiency, increased frustration and irritability, and ultimately, a greater susceptibility to depression.

PSYCHOLOGICAL AND EMOTIONAL CHALLENGES

It has been estimated that depression occurs in approximately 25% of patients in the immediate post-traumatic period following head injury and the symptoms are thought to reflect a combination of neurobiological and situational factors (Cummings and Mega 2003; Moldover, Goldberg, and Prout 2004; Rao and Lyketsos 2000). Late onset depression also is common, as patients with moderate to severe injuries confront the reality of chronic disabilities, or when the initial optimism about "complete recovery" following a mild head injury is eroded by persistent postconcussion symptoms. The consequences of a mild head injury are anything but trivial for people who continue to be challenged by cognitive inefficiency, headache, lowered frustration tolerance, easy fatigability, and susceptibility to sensory overload—especially when such symptoms collide with recovery expectations either from oneself or others to resume preinjury levels of functioning. Given the multiplicity of factors that can affect mood after traumatic brain injury, it can be well appreciated that depression is considered a major source of disability with prevalence estimates ranging over 50% in this population (Moldover, Goldberg, and Prout 2004).

It has been estimated that anxiety can occur in approximately 20% of patients following head trauma (Cummings and Mega 2003), and persistent anxiety often co-occurs with symptoms of depression, fatigue, and lowered frustration tolerance in PCS. Anxiety disorders are considered common in TBI with prevalence estimates ranging from 11%–70%, and different subtypes including generalized anxiety disorder, panic disorder, phobic disorders, post-traumatic stress disorder, and obsessive-compulsive disorder (Rao and Lyketsos 2000).

Family members may report personality changes in relatives who have suffered TBI. Such alterations may range from apathetic disengagement to symptoms of behavioral dyscontrol that can include problems with disinhibition, impulsivity, and temper outburst. The exaggeration of pre-existing personality features and/or the emergence of unfamiliar behaviors can represent a complex interaction between underlying neurological disruption (e.g., frontal lobe involvement) and the interplay of long-standing personality dynamics with the adaptive challenges of dealing with compromised functioning, loss, and uncertainty.

Alterations in psychological functioning following TBI also may include disruptions in awareness that can manifest in "denial" of deficit. The term *anosognosia* was introduced by Babinski to describe lack of awareness of hemiplegia, however disorders in self-awareness following brain injury can manifest in a variety of forms that can change over time, and are thought to reflect neurological and psychological mechanisms (Prigatano 1986, 1999). Disruptions in awareness can be especially challenging for family members and health care providers who "see" the significant impact of a patient's disability on daily functioning while the patient tends to minimize or deny neuropsychological deficits. Prigatano (1986, 1999) has contributed extensively to our understanding of impaired self-awareness following brain injury and his writings contain instructive clinical examples of this disruption in consciousness.

In our discussion of multiple sclerosis we considered the impact of fatigue on neuropsychological status. Increasing attention is now being directed to studying the relationship between fatigue and TBI. Fatigue is among the most common symptoms of TBI with prevalence ratings ranging from 32.4%–73% at 5 years postinjury (Masson et al. 1996; Olver, Ponsford, and Curran 1996; Ziino and Ponsford 2005). A recent study by Ziino and Ponsford (2005) revealed a number of relationships between fatigue and TBI that are relevant for the clinician working with TBI patients. Among the key findings, TBI patients reported that physical and mental exertion were more frequent causes of fatigue relative to controls; the impact of fatigue on lifestyle may increase with time since injury as patients become more engaged in preinjury activities or become increasingly aware of the reality of residual deficits which may contribute to distress that exacerbates fatigue; higher level of education was associated with greater self-reported fatigue, suggesting that greater personal expectations for "productivity" after

TBI may push some patients beyond realistic limits of physical and mental exertion, thus contributing to fatigue and the cascade of negative effects that may follow (e.g., increased frustration, decreased cognitive efficiency, increased susceptibility to depression and anxiety). The relationships between fatigue and TBI revealed in this study are yet other examples of the complex interactions that influence the neuropsychological status and adaptive challenges of people following TBI such that the consequences of even "mild" TBI may be variable from person to person but are anything but trivial for the individual living with these new challenges.

SUMMARY POINTS FOR PSYCHOLOGICAL INTERVENTION

- Moderate to severe TBIs result in a broad range of neuropsychological deficits, with disruption in executive functioning (i.e., self awareness, control and regulation of affect and behavior) being especially problematic.
- Mild TBI represents the majority of head injured patients, and residual sequelae can include a combination of physical, cognitive, and psychological symptoms—known as PCS—that have a negative impact on quality of life.
- Depression is a major cause of disability following TBI and can co-occur with persisting symptoms of anxiety, fatigue, and lowered frustration tolerance in PCS.
- Alternations in psychological functioning following TBI also can include disorders of awareness that reflect both neurological and psychological mechanisms.
- Fatigue is among the most common symptoms of TBI. Expectations to resume formal levels of productivity can exacerbate fatigue and lead to a negative cascade of decreasing cognitive efficiency, increasing frustration, and a lowering of the threshold for the emergence of anxiety and depression.

A Closing Note

The effects of moderate and severe TBIs can be both devastating and obvious in terms of their impact on patients' physical status (e.g., seizure disorders, residual speech, and motor dysfunction), cognitive functioning (disruptions in memory and executive functions), and personality (e.g., affective lability, disinhibition, and impaired judgment). The adaptive challenges associated with moderate to severe TBIs are daunting and call for the multilevel involvement of a treatment team that often will include a psychotherapist.

The adaptive challenges of patients who have suffered a "mild TBI" are more complex than can be gauged by a quantitative dimension of injury and symptom severity that the term "mild" may connote. In contrast to patients with moderate to severe TBIs, patients with mild TBIs may have limited or less obvious residual physical symptoms (e.g., perhaps an increased susceptibility to fatigue and headache), and the nature and extent of their persisting cognitive impairment may be sufficiently subtle to escape notice on casual observation although it can be detected by sensitive neuropsychological testing. They may be successfully engaged in or perhaps even have completed a neurorehabilitative treatment program where they learned accommodation procedures and developed compensatory cognitive strategies to support their recovery and facilitate, at least for some, a return to work. However for many such patients an ongoing adaptive challenge will remain, which is dealing with the performance expectations of self and others when residual symptoms are mild or largely invisible. These expectations may manifest in the resumption of family responsibilities, in the workplace, and in social encounters that once provided relaxation and now feel like an overload. As one patient put the situation, "I look and speak as if I am perfectly fine, and it is hard enough for me to understand, let alone explain to others why it is still difficult to do all the things the way I once could." When such patients have completed other neurorehabilitative treatments, psychotherapy may continue to play an important role in addressing expectations and the continuing adaptive challenges of remaining actively engaged in life but in a different and more balanced way.

REFERENCES AND READINGS

American Psychiatric Association and American Psychiatric Association Task Force on DSM–IV. 2000. *Diagnostic and statistical manual of mental disorders: DSM–IV–TR.* 4th ed. Washington, D.C.: American Psychiatric Association.

Bond, M. R. 1986. Neurobehavioral sequelae of closed head injury. In *Neuropsychological assessment of neuropsychiatric disorders,* edited by Igor Grant and K. M. Adams. New York: Oxford University Press.

Brooks, D. N., M. E. Aughton, M. R. Bond, P. Jones, and S. Rizvi. 1980. Cognitive sequelae in relationship to early indices of severity of brain damage after severe blunt head injury. *Journal of Neurology, Neurosurgery, and Psychiatry* 43 (6): 529–534.

Brooks, N. 1989. Closed head trauma: Assessing the common cognitive problems. In *Assessment of the behavioral consequences of head trauma,* edited by M. D. Lezak. New York: Alan R. Liss.

Busch, C. R., and H. P. Alpern. 1998. Depression after mild traumatic brain injury: A review of current research. *Neuropsychology Review* 8 (2): 95–108.

Cummings, J. L., and M. S. Mega. 2003. *Neuropsychiatry and behavioral neuroscience.* New York: Oxford University Press.

Dikmen, S., and R. M. Reitan. 1976. Psychological deficits and recovery of functions after head injury. *Transactions of the American Neurological Association* 101: 72–77.

Gasquoine, P. G. 1997. Postconcussion symptoms. *Neuropsychology Review* 7 (2): 77–85.

Lezak, M. D., D. B. Howieson, D. W. Loring, H. J. Hannay, and J. S. Fischer. 2004. *Neuropsychological assessment.* 4th ed. New York: Oxford University Press.

Lucas, J. A. 1998. Traumatic brain injury and postconcussive syndrome. In *Clinical neuropsychology: A pocket handbook for assessment,* edited by P. Snyder and P. Nussbaum. Washington, D.C.: American Psychological Association.

Masson, F., P. Maurette, L. R. Salmi, J. F. Dartigues, J. Vecsey, J. M. Destaillats, and P. Erny. 1996. Prevalence of impairments 5 years after a head injury, and their relationship with disabilities and outcome. *Brain Injury: [BI].* 10 (7): 487–497.

Moldover, J. E., K. B. Goldberg, and M. F. Prout. 2004. Depression after traumatic brain injury: A review of evidence for clinical heterogeneity. *Neuropsychology Review* 14 (3): 143–154.

National Institutes of Health (NIH). 1998. Rehabilitation of persons with traumatic brain injury. *NIH Consensus Statement* 16 (1): 1–41.

Olver, J. H., J. L. Ponsford, and C. A. Curran. 1996. Outcome following traumatic brain injury: A comparison between 2 and 5 years after injury. *Brain Injury: [BI].* 10 (11): 841–848.

Ponsford, J., C. Willmont, A. Rothwell, P. Cameron, A-M. Kelly, R. Nelms, C. Curran, and K. Ng. 2000. Factors influencing outcome following mild traumatic brain injury in adults. *Journal of the International Neuropsychological Society* 6 (5): 568–579.

Prigatano, G. P. 1991. Disturbances of self-awareness of deficit after traumatic brain injury. In *Awareness of deficit after brain injury: Clinical and theoretical issues,* edited by G. P. Prigatano and D. L. Schacter. New York: Oxford University Press.

———. 1986. *Neuropsychological rehabilitation after brain injury.* Baltimore, MD: Johns Hopkins University Press.

———. 1999. *Principles of neuropsychological rehabilitation.* New York: Oxford University Press.

Rao, V., and C. Lyketsos. 2000. Neuropsychiatric sequelae of traumatic brain injury. *Psychosomatics* 41:95–103.

Russell, W. R., and A. Smith. 1961. Post-traumatic amnesia in closed head injury. *Archives of Neurology* 5: 4–17.

Ziino, C., and J. Ponsford. 2005. Measurement and prediction of subjective fatigue following traumatic brain injury. *Journal of the International Neuropsychological Society* 11 (4): 416–425.

7

Progressive Dementias

Many neurological conditions are characterized by a progressive deterioration in brain tissue resulting in multiple acquired cognitive deficits that can result in a dementia syndrome. Dementia generally refers to a chronic, progressive, and irreversible condition as opposed to delirium, which is characterized by an acute and transient disturbance in consciousness and cognition. Dementia is frequently a condition of the elderly and the cognitive deficits that are its hallmark features must be in excess of "the normal decline in cognitive functioning that occurs with aging" (American Psychiatric Association and American Psychiatric Association Task Force on DSM-IV 2000). Despite some degree of consensus on the global nature of cognitive deficits that constitute dementia, there are variations in the criteria for neuropsychological impairments that define the syndrome. Let's consider some examples. Cummings, Benson, and LoVerme (1980) offer a definition of dementia that reflects the global nature of acquired impairment: "Dementia is a syndrome of acquired intellectual impairment characterized by persistent deficits in at least three of the following areas of mental activity: memory, language, visuospatial skills, personality or emotional state, and cognition (abstraction, mathematics, judgment)." In contrast, the definition of dementia proposed by DSM-IV-TR (2000) is more restricted because memory impairment is an essential component: "The essential feature of dementia is the development of multiple cognitive deficits that include memory impairment and at least one of the following cognitive disturbances: aphasia, apraxia, agnosia, or a disturbance in executive functioning." In reviewing practice parameters for the diagnosis of dementia, the

American Academy of Neurology recommends that memory disorder not be a required part of the definition of dementia because disturbance in memory is not necessarily a part of the initial presentation of some forms of vascular dementia, dementia with Lewy bodies (DLB), and frontotemporal dementia (FTD)—all conditions which then could be better integrated into the definition of dementia (Knopman et al. 2001).

Dementia is largely a disorder of the elderly with estimates of 10% of people over age 65 having the syndrome (Knopman et al. 2001). With baby boomers approaching their seventh decade of life, the aged are becoming a rapidly growing segment of our population. It is estimated that by the year 2030, people over the age of 65 will represent 20% of the U.S. population (Cummings and Mega 2003). The concomitant demands on the health care system will challenge the resources needed to provide care and treatment for the large group of our population that will be affected by a dementia syndrome either directly as a patient or indirectly as a family member or caregiver. By end stage, the neuropsychological profiles of dementias associated with different degenerative neurological diseases may be virtually indistinguishable, but variability in the initial stages of these conditions helps differentiate one from another. Appreciating this neuropsychological variability has advanced our understanding of brain-behavior relationships and guided research in developing specific treatments for symptom management. Such scientific efforts led to the development of cholinesterase inhibitors now commonly used to treat the neurobehavioral symptoms of Alzheimer's disease (AD). However for psychotherapists working today with patients and families who are dealing with a dementia syndrome, or perhaps seeing patients who have a variant of mild cognitive impairment (MCI) that may convert to dementia, having knowledge of the neuropsychological consequences of different conditions can inform treatment adaptations and the guidance offered to patients and their families facing present-day challenges and future planning needs.

DEMENTIA CLASSIFICATIONS AND REVIEWS

There are numerous comprehensive and brief informative reviews of the broad range of progressive neurological conditions that can result in a dementia syndrome. The authors of these reviews by no means claim to provide exhaustive treatments of the subject, and their selections of conditions discussed often reflect the different ways dementia syndromes may be classified and understood. Some reviews address the most prevalent or "major" progressive dementias. As an example, Rosenstein's (1998) paper in *Neuropsychology Review* is an excellent resource on the differential diagnosis of the major progressive dementias that include AD, vascular dementias, Parkinson's disease (PD), Lewy body dementia, Huntington's disease, and frontal lobe dementia; depression is also addressed. The American Academy of Neurology practice parameter for the diagnosis of dementia considers the "prevalent" dementias of the elderly: AD, vascular dementia, DLB, FTD, and prion diseases (Knopman et al. 2001). Other reviews are organized around a classification schema based on the distinction between "cortical dementia" and "subcortical dementia." AD can be considered the prototypic cortical dementia with brain pathology primarily seen in the hippocampus, cortex association areas, and medial temporal lobes (Arango-Lasprilla et al. 2006). The neuropsychological features of cortical dementias are reflected in the very definitions of dementia we have been considering, and include deficits in memory, executive functioning and problem solving, aphasia, apraxia, and agnosia. In contrast, the dementia associated with PD is an example of the subcortical type where pathology involves subcortical brain structures such as the basal ganglia, thalamus, and brain stem (Albert, Feldman, and Willis 1974). Such dementias are characterized by the absence of aphasia, apraxia, and agnosia; but do include disturbances in motivation, mood, attention/concentration, cognitive processing speed, and executive functioning (Arango-Lasprilla et al. 2006; Cummings 1986). Although of some heuristic value, the cortical–subcortical dementia distinction is not universally accepted (Lezak et al. 2004), and a recent study has suggested the distinction may not be clinically meaningful based on results showing that people with familial AD (prototypic cortical disease) and Huntington's disease (prototypic subcortical disease) have similar neuropsychological profiles (Arango-Lasprilla et al. 2006). Bearing in mind its limitations, the cortical–subcortical distinction nevertheless provides a helpful organizational framework for discussing the neuropsychological characteristics of progressive diseases that affect primarily cortical structures versus those conditions whose clinical features include movement disorders and neuropsychological disturbance associated with subcortical involvement. See reviews by Cummings and Mega (2003) and Lezak et al. (2004).

Our review is broadly organized around the cortical–subcortical dimension with emphasis placed on the most prevalent prototypic examples of AD, the most common dementia of the elderly; and PD, the most common movement disorder of the elderly. We will consider the core clinical characteristics of dementia with Lewy bodies, which has features of AD and PD (Cummings and Mega 2003) and therefore does not fall neatly into a dichotomous cortical–subcortical classification scheme. We will conclude with the main neuropsychological characteristics of FTD as another example of a cortical dementia.

ALZHEIMER'S DISEASE

Epidemiology

It is estimated that 65%–72% of dementia cases are attributed to AD (Kokmen et al. 1993; Rosenstein 1998). The typical age of onset is after 50 years (Cummings and Mega 2003), with an age range from 40 to 90 (McKhann et al. 1984; Rosenstein 1998). The incidence of AD rises with age, affecting 11% of males and 14% of females at age 85 (DSM-IV-TR 2000). People with specific autosomal dominant genetic mutations will develop a familial form of AD (FAD), which represents approximately 5% of total cases, and has an earlier age of onset (between 40 and 60) compared to the sporadic type (Arango-Lasprilla et al. 2006).

Pathophysiology

AD is a neurodegenerative condition that is characterized by progressive atrophy, neuron and synapse loss, and abnormal accumulation of senile plaques and neurofibrillary tangles in the limbic region and neocortical association areas (Salmon and Lange 2001). The temporal and parietal lobes are likely to be disproportionately involved, which accounts for the impairments in memory, naming, and visuoconstruction often seen in the early stages of the disease (Rosenstein 1998). AD has a progressive deteriorating course, with the duration of illness from onset of symptoms to death generally being 8 to 10 years (APA and APA Task Force on DSM-IV 2000), however for some patients the time between diagnosis and death can be as long as 15 to 20 years (Mesulam 2000).

Cognitive Features

Disruption in multiple areas of cognitive functioning is the core feature of the dementia syndrome; and dementia of the Alzheimer's type (DAT) is the prototypic example of a "cortical" dementia, and it constitutes the "clinical" diagnosis of AD. Although there can be some degree of variability in the cognitive profiles of patients in the initial stages of the disease, a pattern of disruption including memory deficits, anomia, and visuoconstruction impairment is often obtained (Rosenstein 1998). Our review will emphasize disruptions in cognitive abilities that are likely to be present in the beginning stages of AD and that help distinguish it from other dementing conditions.

Attention, Concentration, and Processing Speed

Multiple areas of attentional function are reduced in AD although to a lesser extent than memory (Rosenstein 1998). Impairments have been identified in attentional focus, attention shifting, and processing speed (Lezak et al. 2004), although simple attention span may be relatively normal (Butters et al. 1988; Wilson and Kaszniak 1986) in the initial stages of the disease.

Language and Verbal Abilities

Disruptions in semantic knowledge are thought to underlie disturbances in spontaneous speech and language that can be evident in the early course of AD (Salmon and Lange 2001). Spontaneous speech may be characterized by a vague quality and circumlocutions that reflect word-finding difficulties. Disruptions in verbal fluency and naming may be elicited by tests of controlled oral word association (e.g., category and letter fluency tests) and confrontation naming (e.g., Boston Naming Test). Studies have shown that patients with AD generally perform more poorly on tests on category fluency like Animal Naming as opposed to letter fluency measures such as the FAS test (Butters et al. 1987; Canning et al. 2004). Patients with AD also show impairments in confrontation naming as elicited by the Boston Naming Test, and the qualitative nature of their errors (inclination to produce a superordinate category (e.g., animal) as opposed to the target exemplar (e.g., rhinoceros) suggests a "bottom-up" deterioration of semantic knowledge (Salmon and Lange 2001). As AD progresses deficits are evident in other aspects of language including comprehension and writing (Bayles et al. 1989).

Visuoanayltic Functions

Visuospatial functions are thought to decline "fairly early" in AD (Rosenstein 1998), although some reviewers (Salmon and Lange 2001) suggest that deficits in visuoperceptual abilities, visuospatial abilities, and constructional praxis occur in AD but emerge "after the early stages" of the disease and may have little to contribute in differentiating early dementia from normal aging. AD patients demonstrate deficits across a broad range of visuoanalytic functions including visuoperception as assessed by the Judgement of Line Orientation (Ska, Poissant, and Joanette 1990), visuoconstruction as assessed by the Block Design Test (Larrabee, Largen, and Levin

1985), and complex figure drawings (Binetti et al. 1998). The Clock Drawing Test is a popular assessment tool and has proven useful in detecting dementia in patients with AD where qualitative features of their performance
reveal disruptions in semantic knowledge early in the course of the disease
(Rouleau et al. 1992).

Memory

Memory dysfunction is considered the hallmark characteristic of AD
(Rosenstein 1998), and deficits in memory may be present well before criteria are met for a diagnosis of dementia (Albert et al. 2001). Numerous
studies have demonstrated memory deficits in patients with AD (Carlesimo and Oscar-Berman 1992) and have shown that measures of the ability to learn and retain new information can differentiate between patients
with mild dementia associated with AD and normal older adults (Salmon
and Lange 2001). The nature of the explicit memory deficit in AD also has
been investigated and findings have suggested that the deficit is not so
much a problem of impaired retrieval of learned information, but more
so an impairment in the consolidation process itself—the transfer of information from short-term to long-term memory (Rosenstein 1998;
Salmon and Lange 2001). This phenomenon was demonstrated in a study
(Delis et al. 1991) in which various dimensions of verbal memory processing in patients with AD were investigated using the California Verbal
Learning Test, and deficits were revealed not only on measures of immediate and delayed recall (i.e., retrieval) but also on a measure of recognition discriminability. As Rosenstein (1998) stated in her review: "Impaired performance on explicit memory tasks in Alzheimer's patients, in
other words, is not secondary to impaired retrieval of learned information
from memory; rather, the information is not 'there' to be retrieved (freely
recalled)."

Executive Functioning and Conceptual Problem-Solving

Disruptions in executive functioning can be seen in the early stages of
AD, although performances may not be uniformly impaired on tasks aimed
at abilities collectively known as "executive functions" (e.g., concurrent manipulation of information or cognitive flexibility, concept formation, and
cue-directed behavior). Lafleche and Albert (1995) demonstrated that
mildly impaired AD patients had significant deficits on tasks that required
concurrent manipulation of information (e.g., set shifting, self-monitoring,
sequencing) such as Trails-B and the FAS test. In another study, Bondi et al.
(1993) demonstrated that an index derived from a measure of conceptual
problem solving and set shifting (i.e., categories achieved from the Wiscon-

sin Card Sorting Test) was able to differentiate patients with mild dementia associated with AD from normal elderly controls.

Psychological and Emotional Features

Patients with AD can exhibit disturbances in mood, and changes in behavior and personality. Depressive symptoms are common in AD and can be seen in approximately 40% of patients, although major depressive episodes and suicide have been noted to be rare (Cummings and Kaufer 1996). Patients may exhibit suspicious and paranoid thinking, and delusions (e.g., burglary, infidelity, misidentification-Capgras syndrome) are not uncommon, being seen in 40%–70% of patients at some time in the course of the illness (Cummings and Kaufer 1996). Agitation that can manifest in oppositional behavior can be a significant challenge for caregivers, and can occur in approximately 70% of people with AD (Cummings and Kaufer 1996). Personality changes also can accompany AD and include apathy, irritability, and mild disinhibition (Cummings and Kaufer 1996), with apathy being the most common change observed (Mega et al. 1996).

PARKINSON'S DISEASE

Epidemiology

PD is the most prevalent movement disorder in the elderly, and is thought to be more common in men than women (Cummings and Mega 2003). The typical age of onset is in the 50s (Lezak et al. 2004). The etiology of idiopathic PD is unknown, but parkinsonism as a clinical syndrome can have a number of causative factors including viral encephalitis and reactions to dopamine antagonistic drugs (Lezak et al. 2004).

Pathophysiology

PD is associated with loss of neurons in the brain stem nuclei, particularly the substantia nigra, resulting in the depletion of the neurotransmitter dopamine. There are additional pathophysiological features including cell loss in structures like the nucleus basalis of Meynert that provide major cholinergic input to the cortex. See Cummings and Mega (2003) and Lezak et al. (2004) for detailed discussions. Prior to the use of dopamine replacement therapies, the average duration of the illness was 8 to 10 years; now survival has increased to approximately 15 years following diagnosis (Cummings and Mega 2003), with a majority of patients living beyond age 75 (Lezak et al. 2004).

Clinical Features

The core clinical features of PD are resting tremor, rigidity, and bradykinesia (slow movement). Patients with PD may also demonstrate monotonic speech, micrographia (i.e., progressive diminution in size of writing), shuffling gait, absence of facial expression ("masked facies"), difficulty initiating walking, festination (tendency to accelerate when walking), and decreased arm swing while walking (Cummings and Mega 2003; Lezak et al. 2004).

Cognitive Features

Cognitive deficits are considered "ubiquitous" in PD and tend to be less pronounced in patients who have tremor at onset or tremor-predominant syndrome (Cummings and Mega 2003). The nature of the cognitive impairment seen in the early stages of PD has been characterized as a subcortical dementia with predominant executive or frontal system dysfunction that can include cognitive slowing, difficulties with set shifting and sequencing, problems generating strategies, and abnormalities with organization and planning (Cummings and Mega 2003; Lezak et al. 2004; Rosenstein 1998). It is estimated that 30%–40% of patients with PD meet DSM diagnostic criteria for dementia (Cummings and Mega 2003).

Attention, Concentration, and Processing Speed

Immediate auditory attention span is generally within normal limits in PD but deficits are identified when demands are placed on more complex attention abilities such as shifting or sustained attention, and mental tracking. Patients with PD also demonstrate slowed mental processing, an aspect of subcortical dementia, referred to as "bradyphrenia" (Lezak et al. 2004).

Language and Verbal Abilities

The language dysfunction associated with PD primarily involves problems with word finding which manifest in poor performances on verbal fluency tasks (Lezak et al. 2004; Rosenstein 1998). Speech has a monotone quality, and the writing of patients with PD may be characterized by micrographia (Cummings and Mega 2003).

Visuoanalytic Functions

Visuospatial functions decline in patients with PD with advancing disease, and deficits have been demonstrated on measures of visuoperception, for example, Judgment of Line Orientation, Hooper Visual Organizational Test; and visuoconstruction, for example, Block Design (Levin et al. 1991; Rosenstein 1998).

Memory

Rosenstein (1998) reviewed a number of studies investigating memory processing and PD which revealed that patients with the condition were impaired relative to controls on measures of free recall but not recognition (Breen 1993; Gabrieli et al. 1996). In commenting on the use of the California Verbal Learning Test in studies with PD (Delis et al. 2000) noted that patients with PD have difficulty utilizing the more efficient internally generated semantic clustering strategy as opposed to externally generated serial clustering. They reported no evidence for decrease in retention or for the supranormal increase in recognition that has been reported in people with Huntington's disease. Also patients with PD seemed susceptible to intrusion errors but only on cued recall as opposed to free recall tests. Delis and colleagues concluded that this pattern is consistent with the idea that PD is a subcortical dementia.

Executive Functioning and Conceptual Problem Solving

A characteristic feature associated with the cognitive profile of PD is disruption in frontal system functioning; and Lezak et al. (2004) have noted that patients with the condition consistently fail tests comprising both conceptual and executive functions. Patients with PD have demonstrated poor performances on tests requiring concept formation and set shifting like the Wisconsin Card Sorting Test (Bondi et al. 1993) and the Category Test (Matthews and Haaland 1979). They also have demonstrated deficits in planning on measures like the Tower of London Test (Owen et al. 1995).

Psychological and Emotional Features

Depression is the most common psychiatric disturbance in patients with PD and occurs in approximately 40%; anxiety is also a common symptom occurring in 20%–40% of patients and being more prevalent in patients with depression (Cummings and Mega 2003). Psychiatric symptoms in patients with PD may also be associated with dopaminergic therapy, with hallucinations and delusions respectively occurring in approximately 30% and 10% of patients treated with dopaminergic medications. See Cummings and Mega (2003) for a comprehensive review of neuropsychiatric aspects of PD.

DEMENTIA WITH LEWY BODIES

Epidemiology

DLB shares clinical and pathological characteristics with AD and PD (Luis et al. 1999) and therefore blurs the distinction between cortical and subcortical dementias. AD has long been identified as the predominant cause of dementia in the elderly, and it was thought that vascular dementia was responsible for remaining cases. However it is now known that DLB may be the second leading cause of dementia in the elderly with estimates ranging from 15%–20% (McKeith et al. 1996) to 20%–34% (Luis et al. 1999) of all dementia cases. Onset of DLB is generally after age 50 (McKeith 2002), and men are more susceptible and have a worse prognosis (McKeith et al. 1996).

Pathophysiology

The defining pathological feature of DLB is the presence of Lewy bodies in the brain. Lewy bodies are intracytoplasmic, spherical, eosinophilic neuronal inclusion bodies that occur in the brain stem, subcortical nuclei, limbic cortex, and neocortex; and disease course tends to be rapid with duration estimates from 1 to 5 years (McKeith et al. 1996).

Clinical Characteristics

Consensus guidelines for the clinical and pathological diagnosis of DLB were established in the report of the consortium on DLB international workshop (McKeith et al. 1996), and the following description of clinical characteristics is based on that review.

Central Feature

The central feature for the diagnosis of DLB is progressive cognitive decline of sufficient magnitude to interfere with normal social or occupational functioning. Evidence of prominent or persistent memory impairment is not always present early in the course of the disease. The consortium suggested that prominent deficits in executive functioning may be identified by tests such as the Wisconsin Card Sorting Test, the Trail Making Test, and measures of verbal fluency. Possible disproportionate disruption in visuospatial abilities may be evident on tests such as Block Design, clock drawing, and copying figures. In a review that considered the neuropsychological characteristics of DLB, Luis et al. (1999) commented that available neuropsychological research supported the cognitive deficit pattern suggested by the consortium.

Core Features

The consortium recommended that at least one of the following three core features be present for making the diagnosis of DLB.

Patients with DLB may demonstrate fluctuations in cognitive function that manifest in variations in attention and alertness. Deficits in cognitive functioning may alternate with periods of normal or near normal performance. The fluctuations may occur rapidly (minutes to hours) or in a more prolonged fashion (weekly or monthly).

Patients with DLB may demonstrate recurrent and detailed visual hallucinations that may include themes of people or animals intruding into the home. Hallucinations may also include inanimate objects or abstract perceptions (e.g., writing on the wall).

Patients may demonstrate motor features of parkinsonism with rigidity and bradykinesia being more prominent than resting tremor.

Supportive Features

The consortium also noted a number of supportive features for diagnosis of DLB including repeated falls, syncope, and transient loses of consciousness; neuroleptic sensitivity, and systematized delusions, and hallucinations in other modalities.

Psychiatric Features

Luis et al. (1999) reviewed several studies that suggested depression is a common symptom in DLB (present in 50%), and that patients with the condition may present initially in psychiatric settings with symptoms of agitation, severe anxiety, psychotic depression or personality changes reminiscent of Pick's disease.

FRONTOTEMPORAL DEMENTIA

Epidemiology

FTD affects cortical structures and, like AD, it is classified as a cortical dementia. It is considered one of the most common neurodegenerative syndromes after AD, but with an earlier age of onset (about 52 years), and it is more common in men than women (Harciarek and Jodzio 2005). In contrast to AD, the risk of FTD does not appear to increase with age (Grossman 2002). The incidence of FTD in dementia and memory disorder clinics ranges between 4% and 20% (Grossman 2002).

Pathophysiology

FTD is associated with focal atrophy in the frontal and anterior temporal lobes. Subcortical white matter also may be affected, and Pick bodies are found in the Pick's disease subtype of FTD (Cummings and Mega 2003). The clinical course of FTD is thought to progress through three stages, with the first being characterized by disruptions in personality and behavior; the second stage is characterized by increasing cognitive problems with language deficits being most prominent; in the last stage patients become aphasic and progress to complete muteness; and the usual survival after symptom onset is 10 years (Harciarek and Jodzio 2005).

Clinical Characteristics

FTD describes a spectrum of non-Alzheimer's degenerative conditions that are associated with focal atrophy of the frontal and/or temporal lobes and present with two principal variants: a frontal variant associated with early behavioral disorders and executive dysfunction and a temporal variant associated with language and semantic impairments (Harciarek and Jodzio 2005). Other typologies include three clinical subgroups: progressive nonfluent aphasia characterized by disordered expressive speech; semantic aphasia characterized by impairment in word meaning and object identity; and frontotemporal degeneration characterized by a deterioration in personality and social conduct (Grossman 2002).

From a neuropsychological perspective, patients with FTD demonstrate disruptions in personality and behavior that reflect frontal system involvement and can include: disinhibition, impulsivity, loss of insight, poor judgment, diminished sense of social propriety, lack of concern for the feelings of others, and declines in personal hygiene (Cummings and Mega 2003; Grossman 2002; Harciarek and Jodzio 2005).

At the early stages disruptions in cognition are characterized more by executive dysfunction than by memory impairment—a pattern opposite AD (Lezak et al. 2004). In contrast to AD, in the early stages of the disease patients with FTD tend to have better performances on word-list recall and delayed verbal recall, and recognition memory tends to be well-preserved (Harciarek and Jodzio 2005). Patients with FTD may perform even more poorly on verbal fluency tests than patients with AD (Lezak et al. 2004), but tend to perform relatively well on measures of visuospatial abilities, distinguishing them from patients with AD.

MILD COGNITIVE IMPAIRMENT

For many patients whose neuropsychological status has declined to the point of warranting a diagnosis of dementia, participation in psychotherapy often will include a caregiver and the focus of treatment will be supporting coping resources and maintaining quality of life. However, a psychotherapist is also likely to encounter elderly patients who either begin to demonstrate deficiencies in cognitive functioning during the course of therapy or who present for treatment with symptoms of anxiety or mood disturbance secondary to perceived declines in cognitive functioning. This group of patients may not meet the diagnostic criteria for one of the progressive dementias we have been discussing, however their perceived decline in memory or other cognitive abilities is sufficient to cause concern in some and alarm in others. For some patients disruption in cognitive status may be associated with systemic illness, medication effects, or depression; however for others their cognitive difficulties reflect what has come to be known as "mild cognitive impairment" or MCI.

"Clinically, MCI is defined as impairment in one or more cognitive domains (typically memory), or an overall mild decline across cognitive abilities that is greater than would be expected for an individual's age or education, but that is insufficient to interfere with social or occupational functioning, as is required for a dementing syndrome" (Luis et al. 2003). MCI has been considered an intermediate state between normal aging and dementia (Luis et al. 2003) or a transitional phase between normal aging and early AD (Rivas-Vazquez et al. 2004). There have been earlier terms used to describe cognitive dysfunction among elderly patients who did not have dementia, and these included benign senescent forgetfulness, age-associated memory impairment, late-life forgetfulness, and aging-related cognitive decline (Kral 1962; Ritchie and Touchon 2000; Tuokko and Frerichs 2000; Rivas-Vazquez et al. 2004). However, the concept of MCI is intended to meet the objective of providing a conceptual framework and clinical criteria that would assist in predicting the appearance of dementia at an earlier stage, thus permitting better patient management and allowing pharmacologic interventions targeted at secondary prevention to be offered with better specificity and earlier in the disease process (Bozoki et al. 2001). To this end the American Academy of Neurology (Petersen et al. 2001) established criteria for defining a pre-AD form of MCI. Rivas-Vazquez et al. (2004) have suggested the mnemonic "SOUND" as a helpful tool for remembering these criteria, which include: Subjective memory complaints, Objective memory deficit, Unaffected overall cognition, Normal capacity to perform ADLs, and Dementia criteria not met. What proportion of patients with MCI ultimately develops AD? It has been estimated that individuals with MCI convert to AD at a rate of approximately 12% per year as opposed to 1%–2% for the normal elderly population (Petersen et al. 2001; Rivas-Vazquez et al. 2004) and studies reviewed by Luis et al. (2003) show conversion rates from MCI to dementia ranging from 10%–30% annually, 20%–66% over 3 to 4 years, and 60.5%–100% in 5 to 10 years.

Studies have suggested there are monosymptomatic presentations (e.g., visuospatial impairment) of a pre-AD stage besides isolated memory impairment which is a defining feature of MCI (Mapstone, Steffenella, and Duffy 2003); and MCI subtypes representing a prodromal stage for dementing conditions other than AD (e.g., vascular, depressed, parkinsonian) also have been described (Luis et al. 2003). Improving the detection of pre-AD and ultimately other degenerative conditions affords the opportunity to consider treatments aimed at the prevention or delay of dementia. To this end, researchers are exploring how neuropsychological assessment methods might better identify MCI patients who are likely to develop or convert to AD. One approach has been to improve detection by considering impairment in cognitive domains besides memory. Bozoki et al. (2001) demonstrated that nondemented patients with mild cognitive impairments in several domains in addition to memory were more than twice as likely compared to those patients with memory impairment alone to develop AD over a period of 2 to 5 years. Other approaches have considered tests of neuropsychological functioning that may be particularly sensitive to the prodromal phase of AD, and measures of memory (e.g., total learning score of CVLT) and executive functioning (e.g., Trails-B) consistently have emerged as sensitive indices (Albert et al. 2001; Rivas-Vazquez et al. 2004).

SUMMARY POINTS FOR PSYCHOLOGICAL INTERVENTION

- Dementia is largely a condition of the elderly and refers to a chronic, progressive, and irreversible condition that is characterized by cognitive deficits that are in excess of the normal decline in cognitive functioning associated with aging.
- Dementia can be associated with many neurological conditions having primary involvement either in the cortical (e.g., AD) or subcortical (Parkinson's disease) regions.
- Neuropsychiatric features are common with the dementias and can include depression, anxiety, agitation, delusions, hallucinations, and disruption in personality.

- Elderly patients who do not meet criteria for dementia may nevertheless have cognitive disruption—known as MCI—that can have a negative impact on quality of life. MCI is considered an intermediate stage between normal aging and dementia.
- Involvement of caregivers or family members is an essential component in the assessment and treatment of patients with dementia.

A Closing Note

Within a series of articles on neurodegenerative diseases that appeared in the *British Medical Journal*, Findley and Baker (2002) challenged the notion that the quality of life of people with neurodegenerative disorders depends primarily on the severity of the disease and the effectiveness of pharmacological interventions. Clearly these factors are important, and research will continue in efforts to develop pharmacological agents to reduce symptom severity, retard disease progression, and perhaps even find cures for diseases now considered incurable. However as research builds upon the foundations of the past with an eye toward the future, there is the challenge of "now" for anxious patients with MCI whose faulty memory may be the harbinger of a more dreaded loss of "mind"; or for other patients and their caregivers for whom the process of dementia has already taken hold and forever changed their lives. Commenting on a study of patients with Parkinson's disease and their caretakers (Findley 2002), Findley and Baker (2002) noted that when face-to-face interviews were carried out with more than 1,000 patients and carers in six countries, only 17.3% of the variation in perceptions of health-related quality of life could be explained by severity of illness or effectiveness of drug treatment. In contrast, mood (depression) accounted for approximately 40% of the variation. Their concluding message that maintaining and improving health-related quality of life are objectives of any treatment program for neurodegenerative disorders is a challenging invitation for psychotherapy to take a place in the treatment of neurodegenerative disorders.

Our review has shown that the comorbidity of depression and anxiety in patients with progressive neurological conditions associated with dementia can sometimes approach 50%. Pharmacotherapy plays a role in addressing psychiatric symptoms associated with these conditions thereby reducing patient suffering and caregiver burden, but medication alone does not address the quality of life challenges that patients and families face. However, psychological intervention can make a valuable contribution in this area, not only in reducing psychological/emotional suffering but also in promoting an engagement in life that strengthens coping resources and builds resilience to deal with current and future stress.

A welcomed development in professional psychology is the increasing recognition that patients with dementia syndromes are not outside the scope of effective psychological services to address the cognitive and psychological/emotional consequences of their conditions, as well as the overall quality of their lives and that of their caregivers (Koltai and Branch 1998, 1999; Teri, McKenzie, and LaFazia 2005). A common theme in these approaches is the need for flexibility in adapting psychological intervention strategies to meet the specific needs of patients (e.g., impact of cognitive dysfunction), and the involvement of caregivers in the therapy process. For example, Attix (2004) emphasizes that the focus of therapeutic work for patients with progressive conditions and dementia is coping, adjustment, and the use of compensatory strategies and residual abilities. In a review of psychological treatment for depression in older adults with dementia, Teri, McKenzie and LaFazia (2005) identified a number of successful approaches including behavioral strategies (e.g., supervised exercise program) focused on increasing positive interactions (Teri et al. 2003), and social engagement therapies (e.g., therapeutic biking) aimed at improving socialization, and increasing sensory stimulation and positive events (Buettner and Fitzsimmons 2002). They also provided several "take-home messages" for clinicians to consider: depression in patients with dementia does not remit over time; psychosocial treatment is effective for depression associated with dementia; treatment approaches need to be flexible and multifaceted to address deteriorations in functioning and the range of problems challenging patients and their caregivers; and assessment and treatments should include and assist caregivers.

The message is clear. Psychotherapeutic approaches are effective in treating people with dementia and should be offered to patients and their caregivers. With its emphases on active involvement, openness and flexibility, and strengthening coping resources through cultivating positive emotions and mindful engagement in the "ordinary" moments of daily living—the attitude of mind perspective for psychotherapy can provide a helpful foundation in developing specific interventions for patients and caregivers. In chapter 12 we will consider in more depth the application of the attitude of mind perspective in developing a psychoeducational group program for caregivers.

REFERENCES AND READINGS

Albert, M. L., R. G. Feldman, and A. L. Willis. 1974. The "subcortical dementia" of progressive supranuclear palsy. *Journal of Neurology, Neurosurgery, and Psychiatry* 37 (2): 121–130.

Albert, Marilyn S., Mark B. Moss, Rudolph Tanzi, and Kenneth Jones. 2001. Preclinical prediction of AD using neuropsychological tests. *Journal of the International Neuropsychological Society* 7 (5): 631–639.

American Psychiatric Association and American Psychiatric Association Task Force on DSM-IV. 2000. *Diagnostic and statistical manual of mental disorders: DSM-IV-TR.* 4th ed. Washington, D.C.: American Psychiatric Association.

Arango-Lasprilla, Juan Carlos, Heather Rogers, Jean Lengenfelder, John DeLuca, Sonia Moreno, and Francisco Lopera. 2006. Cortical and subcortical diseases: Do true neuropsychological differences exist? *Archives of Clinical Neuropsychology* 21 (1): 29–40.

Attix, D. K. 2004. Maximizing coping and compensation in dementia: Geriatric neuropsychological intervention. *American Psychological Association: Division of Clinical Neuropsychology* 22: 3–4.

Bayles, K. A., D. R. Boone, C. K. Tomoeda, T. J. Slauson, and A. W. Kaszniak. 1989. Differentiating Alzheimer's patients from the normal elderly and stroke patients with aphasia. *Journal of Speech and Hearing Disorders* 54 (1): 74–87.

Binetti, G., S. F. Cappa, E. Magni, A. Padovani, A. Bianchetti, and M. Trabucchi, 1998. Visual and spatial perception in the early phase of Alzheimer's disease. *Neuropsychology* 12 (1): 29–33.

Bondi, Mark W., Alfred W. Kaszniak, Kathryn A. Bayles, and Katherine T. Vance. 1993. Contributions of frontal system dysfunction to memory and perceptual abilities in Parkinson's disease. *Neuropsychology* 7 (1): 89–102.

Bozoki, A., B. Giordani, J. L. Heidebrink, S. Berent, and N. L. Foster. 2001. Mild cognitive impairments predict dementia in nondemented elderly patients with memory loss. *Archives of Neurology* 58 (3): 411–416.

Breen, E. K. 1993. Recall and recognition memory in Parkinson's disease. *Cortex: A journal devoted to the study of the nervous system and behavior* 29 (1): 91–102.

Buettner, L. L., and S. Fitzsimmons. 2002. AD-venture program: therapeutic biking for the treatment of depression in long-term care residents with dementia. *American Journal of Alzheimer's Disease and Other Dementias* 17 (2): 121–127.

Butters, N., E. Granholm, D. Salmon, I. Grant, and J. Wolfe. 1987. Episodic and semantic memory: A comparison of amnesic and demented patients. *Journal of Clinical and Experimental Neuropsychology* 9:479–497.

Butters, N., D. P. Salmon, C. M. Cullum, P. Cairns, A. I. Trosten, D. Jacobs, M. Moss, and L. S. Cermack. 1988. Differentiation of amnesic and demented patients with the Wechsler Memory Scale–Revised. *Clinical Neuropsychologist* 2 (2): 133–148.

Canning, S. J., L. Leach, D. Stuss, L. Ngo, and S. E. Black. 2004. Diagnostic utility of abbreviated fluency measures in Alzheimer disease and vascular dementia. *Neurology* 62 (4): 556–562.

Carlesimo, Giovanni A., and Marlene Oscar-Berman. 1992. Memory deficits in Alzheimer's patients: A comprehensive review. *Neuropsychology Review* 3 (2): 119–169.

Cummings, J. L. 1986. Subcortical dementia: Neuropsychology, neuropsychiatry, and pathophysiology. *British Journal of Psychiatry* 149:682–697.

Cummings, J., D. F. Benson, and S. LoVerne, Jr. 1980. Reversible dementia. Illustrative cases, definition, and review. *Journal of the American Medical Association* 243 (23): 2434–2439.

Cummings, J. L., and D. Kaufer. 1996. Neuropsychiatric aspects of Alzheimer's disease: The cholinergic hypothesis revisited. *Neurology* 47 (4): 876–883.

Cummings, J. L., and Michael S. Mega. 2003. *Neuropsychiatry and behavioral neuroscience.* New York: Oxford University Press.

Delis, D., E. Kaplan, J. H. Kramer, and B. A. Ober. 2000. *California Verbal Learning Test–Second Edition (CVLT-II) Manual*. San Antonio, TX: Psychological Corporation.

Delis, Dean C., Paul J. Massman, Nelson Butters, David P. Salmon et al. 1991. Profiles of demented and amnesic patients on the California Verbal Learning Test: Implications for the assessment of memory disorders. *Psychological Assessment* 3 (1): 19–26.

Findley, Leslie J. 2002. Factors impacting on quality of life in Parkinson's disease: Results from an international survey. *Movement Disorders* 17:60–67.

Findley, L. J., and M. G. Baker. 2002. Treating neurodegenerative diseases. *British Medical Journal* 324: 1466–1467.

Gabrieli, John D. E., Jaswinder Singh, Glenn T. Stebbins, and Christopher G. Goetz. 1996. Reduced working memory span in Parkinson's disease: Evidence for the role of frontostriatal system in working and strategic memory. *Neuropsychology* 10 (3): 321–332.

Grossman, Murray. 2002. Frontotemporal dementia: A review. *Journal of the International Neuropsychological Society* 8 (4): 566–583.

Harciarek, M., and K. Jodzio. 2005. Neuropsychological differences between frontotemporal dementia and Alzheimer's disease: A review. *Neuropsychology Review* 15 (3): 131–145.

Knopman, D. S., S. T. DeKosky, J. L. Cummings, H. Chui, J. Corey-Bloom, N. Relkin, G. W. Small, B. Miller, and J. C. Stevens. 2001. Practice parameter: Diagnosis of dementia (an evidence-based review). Report of the Quality Standards Subcommittee of the American Academy of Neurology. *Neurology* 56 (9): 1143–1153.

Kokmen, E., C. M. Beard, P. C. O'Brien, K. P. Offord, and L. T. Kurland. 1993. Is the incidence of dementing illness changing? A 25-year time trend study in Rochester, Minnesota (1960–1984). *Neurology* 43 (10): 1887–1192.

Koltai, Deborah C, and Laurence G. Branch. 1998. Consideration of intervention alternatives to optimize independent functioning in the elderly. *Journal of Clinical Geropsychology* 4:333–349.

———. 1999. Cognitive and affective interventions to maximize abilities and adjustment in dementia. *Annals of Psychiatry: Basic and Clinical Neurosciences* 7:241–255.

Kral, V. A. 1962. Senescent forgetfulness: benign and malignant. *Canadian Medical Association Journal* 86: 257–260.

Lafleche, G., and M. S. Albert. 1995. Executive function deficits in mild Alzheimer's disease. *Neuropsychology* 9 (3): 313–320.

Larrabee, Glenn J., John W. Largen, and Harvey S. Levin. 1985. Sensitivity of age-decline resistant ("hold") WAIS subtests to Alzheimer's disease. *Journal of Clinical and Experimental Neuropsychology* 7 (5): 497–504.

Levin, B. E., M. M. Llabre, S. Reisman, W. J. Weiner, J. Sanchez-Ramos, C. Singer, and M. C. Brown. 1991. Visuospatial impairment in Parkinson's disease. *Neurology* 41 (3): 365–369.

Lezak, Muriel D., Diane B. Howieson, David W. Loring, H. Julia Hannay, and Jill S. Fischer. 2004. *Neuropsychological assessment*. 4th ed. New York: Oxford University Press.

Luis, C. A., D. A. Loewenstein, A. Acevedo, W. W. Barker, and R. Duara. 2003. Mild cognitive impairment: directions for future research. *Neurology* 61 (4): 438–444.

Luis, Cheryl A., Wiley Mittenberg, Carlton S. Gass, and Ranjan Duara. 1999. Diffuse Lewy body disease: Clinical, pathological, and neuropsychological review. *Neuropsychology Review* 9 (3): 137–150.

Mapstone, M., T. M. Steffenella, and C. J. Duffy. 2003. A visuospatial variant of mild cognitive impairment: Getting lost between aging and AD. *Neurology* 60 (5): 802–808.

Matthews, C. G., and K. Y. Haaland. 1979. The effect of symptom duration on cognitive and motor performance in parkinsonism. *Neurology* 29 (7): 951–956.

McKeith, I. G. 2002. Dementia with Lewy bodies. *The British Journal of Psychiatry: The Journal of Mental Science* 180: 144–147.

McKeith, I. G., D. Galasko, K. Kosaka, E. K. Perry, D. W. Dickson, L. A. Hansen, D. P. Salmon, J. Lowe, S. S. Mirra, E. J. Byrne, G. Lennox, N. P. Quinn, J. A. Edwardson, P. G. Ince, C. Bergeron, A. Burns, B. L. Miller, S. Lovestone, D. Collerton, E. N. Jansen, C. Ballard, R. A. de Vos, G. K. Wilcock, K. A. Jellinger, and R. H. Perry. 1996. Consensus guidelines for the clinical and pathologic diagnosis of dementia with Lewy bodies (DLB): report of the consortium on DLB international workshop. *Neurology* 47 (5): 1113–1124.

McKhann, G., D. Drachman, M. Folstein, R. Katzman, D. Price, and E. M. Stadlan. 1984. Clinical diagnosis of Alzheimer's disease: Report of the NINCDS-ADRDA Work Group under the auspices of Department of Health and Human Services Task Force on Alzheimer's Disease. *Neurology* 34 (7): 939–494.

Mega, M. S., J. L. Cummings, T. Fiorello, and J. Gornbein. 1996. The spectrum of behavioral changes in Alzheimer's disease. *Neurology* 46 (1): 130–135.

Mesulam, M. M. 2000. Aging, Alzheimer's disease, and dementia. In *Principles of behavioral and cognitive neurology*, edited by M. M. Mesulam. New York: Oxford University Press.

Owen, A. M., B. J. Sahakian, J. R. Hodges, B. A. Summers, C. E. Polkey, and T. W. Robbins. 1995. Dopamine-dependent frontostriatal planning deficits in early Parkinson's disease. *Neuropsychology* 9 (1): 126–140.

Petersen, R. C., J. C. Stevens, M. Ganguli, E. G. Tangalos, J. L. Cummings, and S. T. DeKosky. 2001. Practice parameter: Early detection of dementia: mild cognitive impairment (an evidence-based review). Report of the Quality Standards Subcommittee of the American Academy of Neurology. *Neurology* 56 (9): 1133–1142.

Ritchie, K., and J. Touchon. 2000. Mild cognitive impairment: conceptual basis and current nosological status. *Lancet* 355 (9199): 225–228.

Rivas-Vazquez, Rafael A., Cecilia Mendez, Gustavo J. Rey, and Enrique J. Carrazana. 2004. Mild cognitive impairment: New neuropsychological and pharmacological target. *Archives of Clinical Neuropsychology* 19 (1): 11–27.

Rosenstein, Leslie D. 1998. Differential diagnosis of the major progressive dementias and depression in middle and late adulthood: A summary of the literature of the early 1990s. *Neuropsychology Review* 8 (3): 109–167.

Rouleau, I., D. P. Salmon, N. Butters, C. Kennedy, and K. McGuire. 1992. Quantitative and qualitative analyses of clock drawings in Alzheimer's and Huntington's disease. *Brain and Cognition* 18 (1): 70–87.

Salmon, David P., and Kelly L. Lange. 2001. Alzheimer's disease and dementia: Cognitive screening and neuropsychological assessment in early Alzheimer's disease. *Clinics in Geriatric Medicine* 17 (2): 229–254.

Ska, Bernadette, Arlette Poissant, and Yves Joanette. 1990. Line orientation judgment in normal elderly and subjects with dementia of Alzheimer's type. *Journal of Clinical and Experimental Neuropsychology* 12 (5): 695–702.

Teri, L., L. E. Gibbons, S. M. McCurry, R. G. Logsdon, D. M. Buchner, W. E. Barlow, W. A. Kukull, A. Z. LaCroix, W. McCormick, and E. B. Larson. 2003. Exercise plus behavioral management in patients with Alzheimer disease: A randomized controlled trial. *Journal of the American Medical Association* 290 (15): 2015–2022.

Teri, Linda, Glenise McKenzie, and David LaFazia. 2005. Psychosocial treatment of depression in older adults with dementia. *Clinical Psychology: Science and Practice* 12 (3): 303–316.

Tuokko, Holly, and Robert J. Frerichs. 2000. Cognitive impairment with no dementia (CIND): Longitudinal studies, the findings and the issues. *Clinical Neuropsychologist* 14 (4): 504–525.

Wilson, R. S., and A. W. Kaszniak. 1986. Longitudinal changes: Progressive idiopathic dementia. In *Handbook for clinical memory assessment of older adults*, edited by L. W. Poon. Washington, D.C.: American Psychological Association.

8

Cerebrovascular Disorders

The brain requires a continuous supply of blood to provide glucose and oxygen while dispersing heat and the metabolic products of cerebral activity (Brown, Baird, and Shatz 1986; Toole and Patel 1974). Disruption in this essential process either through hemorrhage or ischemia (i.e., restricted blood flow) is the basis of cerebrovascular disease, which includes the categories of transient ischemic attack (TIA), an acute loss of neurological function lasting less than 24 hours; stroke, which is defined by rapidly developing symptoms or signs of cerebral dysfunction with symptoms lasting more than 24 hours and having no cause other than cerebrovascular disease; and vascular dementia, which is characterized by an impairment in memory and disturbance in at least one other cognitive domain produced by cerebrovascular disease (Cummings and Mega 2003).

EPIDEMIOLOGY

Cerebrovascular disease is the third leading cause of death in the United States ranking behind heart disease and cancer (Cummings and Mega 2003), and stroke is the leading cause of disability in people over 60 (Lezak et al. 2004). Approximately 2 per 1,000 individuals have a stroke between the ages of 55 and 64, and the incidence of stroke doubles every 10 years after age 55 (Cummings and Mega 2003). It is estimated that approximately half a million people per year in the United States are expected to have a stroke (Weinstein and Swenson 1998). Men are more susceptible to stroke than women, and risk factors include hypertension, elevated cholesterol, diabetes, and cigarette smoking, all of which contribute to atherosclerosis—pathologically thickened arterial walls—which is a significant factor in the pathophysiology of stroke (Lezak et al. 2004; Norris and Hachinski 2001).

PATHOPHYSIOLOGY

TIAs are caused by temporary disruption in blood supply (i.e., reversible ischemia) frequently resulting from thrombotic microemboli; and within the first months after a TIA, a stroke can manifest in approximately 30% of patients (Bogousslavsky, Hommel, and Bassetti 1998; Lezak et al. 2004). Although the symptoms associated with TIAs technically can last up to 24 hours, many attacks may last from only several hours to less than an hour (Lezak et al. 2004). Cummings and Mega (2003, 385) have noted that "The distinction between TIA and stroke is arbitrary and they represent a continuum of increasingly severe and irreversible brain infarction."

Cerebral infarctions (areas of damaged or dead tissue) are the cause of approximately 80% of cerebrovascular events (Cummings and Mega 2003), with thrombotic obstructions being responsible for up to 75% of obstructive strokes (Bogousslavsky, Hommel, and Bassetti 1998; Lezak et al. 2004) and emboli causing from 20%–30% of obstructive strokes (Castillo and Bogousslavsky 1997; Lezak et al. 2004). A thrombotic obstruction (i.e., thrombosis) is the result of the accumulation of fatty deposits (i.e., atherosclerotic plaques) within the artery wall. Emboli are circulating bodies (e.g., thrombus fragment from the heart) that lodge in a smaller vessel and cause ischemia. Hemorrhage is the cause of 10%–20% of strokes (Bogousslavsky, Hommel, and Bassetti 1998), and hypertension is the primary risk factor for hemorrhagic strokes (Lezak et al. 2004).

Although the concept of vascular dementia (VaD) has been the focus of an evolving debate as to the criteria that define the syndrome (Bowler 2000), the neuropathologic basis of vascular dementia is viewed as being composed of a variable combination of multiple infarcts, single strategic infarcts, noninfarct ischemic lesions affecting the white matter and basal ganglia, hypoperfusion, and hemorrhage (Româan et al. 1993; Sachdev, Brodaty, Valenzuela, Lorentz, Looi, Wen, and Zagami 2004).

NEUROPSYCHOLOGICAL CONSEQUENCES

Patients who have had an obstructive stroke tend to have a lateralized pattern of neuropsychological dysfunction, with left hemisphere lesions generally producing aphasic syndromes that have been well described by

Goodglass and Kaplan (1983), and right hemisphere lesions producing perceptual and visual-spatial dysfunction (Benton, Sivan, and Hamsher 1994). Although the symptoms associated with TIAs by definition are considered "transient," patients who have had a TIA indeed may demonstrate residual neuropsychological deficits (Brown, Baird, and Shatz 1986). When considering the neuropsychological consequences of vascular dementia, which is thought to be the second most common cause of dementia behind Alzheimer's disease (Bowler 2000), we encounter a construct still in search of consistent defining criteria. In a multicenter study of the comparability and interrater reliability of clinical criteria for the diagnosis of VaD, Chui et al. (2000) conclude, "the choice of diagnostic criteria for VaD remains a critical but elusive methodological issue for clinical and epidemiological studies." In addressing this problem of inconsistency in the diagnosis of VaD, Bowler (2000) stresses the need for diagnostic criteria to reflect evidence about cerebrovascular disease rather than models of dementia based on Alzheimer's disease, which emphasize memory loss as a cardinal symptom. Furthermore, he notes the importance for early treatment of patients identified with cognitive impairment associated with vascular causes prior to development of dementia (i.e., cognitive impairment affecting activities of daily living), and recommends a "moving away from the concept of dementia" to a perspective of cognitive impairment due to cerebrovascular disease—"vascular cognitive impairment."

Vascular Cognitive Impairment

Vascular cognitive impairment (VCI) is considered a superordinate construct that includes all levels of cognitive impairment of vascular origin (Sachdev, Brodaty, Valenzuela, Lorentz, and Koschera 2004). Wentzel et al. (2001) identify three subtypes of VCI that include VaD, mixed dementia (Alzheimer's disease with a vascular component), and impairment that does not meet dementia criteria (vascular cognitive impairment—no dementia, or vascular CIND). Like mild cognitive impairment (MCI) associated with a prodromal stage of Alzheimer's disease, which we reviewed in chapter 7, vascular CIND also includes a group of patients who will progress to dementia (46% within 5 years) with 54% remaining cognitively stable (Wentzel et al. 2001). VCI also has been conceptualized as a continuum that includes three primary stages: brain-at-risk, R-CVD; cognitive impairment—no dementia, CIND; and VaD (Garrett et al. 2004). Stage one (R-CVD) includes patients who have cardiovascular or other diseases that place them at risk for developing cerebrovascular disease. Stage two (VaCIND) includes patients who demonstrate vascular cognitive impairment but do not meet criteria for dementia. Stage three (VaD) includes patients who have progressed to a vascular dementia. The neurocognitive profile associated with VaCIND includes poor cognitive flexibility and impaired verbal retrieval in the presence of intact recognition memory (Garrett et al. 2004). Other studies have suggested that the nature of neuropsychological impairment is similar for VaD and VCI with psychomotor slowing and frontal-executive dysfunction being prominent for both but more severe with VaD (Sachdev et al. 2004).

Psychological and Emotional Consequences

Post-stroke depression (PSD) is considered the most common emotional outcome of stroke, and it has been reported as occurring in 20%–50% of patients in the acute stages or the first year following a stroke, and in 30% of patients in the more chronic stages (Hosking, Marsh, and Friedman 1996). Variations in prevalence estimates for PSD may reflect different classification criteria (e.g., DSM criteria for major and minor depression, or various rating scales), but the presence of depression following stroke is a significant treatment challenge because it can affect not only the natural recovery process but also the process and benefits of rehabilitation (Agrell and Dehlin 1989; Hosking, Marsh, and Friedman 1996).

Studies have examined the relationship between PSD and lesion location, and the ultimate outcome may be more complex than simply ascribing depression to being more likely associated with either left or right hemisphere lesions. Some researchers (Astrèom, Adolfsson, and Asplund 1993) have reported a higher incidence of PSD with lesions in the left anterior hemisphere, while others suggest that lesions in either hemisphere are associated with depression but the nature of depression may differ as a function of hemispheric localization (Gainotti 1992; Hosking, Marsh, and Friedman 1996). Cummings and Mega (2003) reviewed studies (Morris et al. 1996; Shimoda and Robinson 1999) that suggested a relationship between depression and lesion location with time since stroke. A higher frequency of depression was associated with left hemisphere lesions in the immediate post-stroke period (7–10 days); no hemispheric asymmetry was evident after 3–6 months; and after 1 year patients with right hemisphere lesions were more likely to be depressed than patients with left hemisphere involvement.

Patients who have had a stroke also may struggle with generalized anxiety. Castillo, Schultz, and Robinson (1995) found a frequency of 27% for early onset (i.e., while patient was hospitalized for stroke) and 23% for late onset (i.e., 3 months or more after stroke) post-stroke generalized anxiety, and three-quarters of the patients diagnosed with anxiety also had comorbid depression.

SUMMARY POINTS FOR PSYCHOLOGICAL INTERVENTION

- VCI refers to all levels of cognitive impairment of vascular origin.
- The neuropsychological consequences of obstructive strokes tend to have a lateralized pattern with left hemisphere lesions generally being associated with aphasic symptoms, and right hemisphere lesions causing perceptual and visual-spatial dysfunctions.
- Post-stroke depression is the most common emotional outcome of stroke and often coexists with generalized anxiety.
- The neuropsychological profile of vascular cognitive impairment without dementia can include frontal-executive dysfunction, poor cognitive flexibility, verbal retrieval deficits, and psychomotor slowing.
- VCI can progress to dementia (46% in five years) with increasing severity seen in those neurocognitive areas disrupted in the earlier stage.

A Closing Note

On his way to completing a book on aging, and imagining one evening what it would be like to be "very old," Ram Dass—spiritual teacher and social activist—had a stroke. He suffered a cerebral hemorrhage that left him partially paralyzed and wheelchair-bound, with residual symptoms of aphasia and memory problems. His lifestyle changed dramatically, yet he still went on to complete *Still Here: Embracing Aging, Changing, and Dying* (2000), his wonderful book about aging and so much more. I can think of no better guide not only for dealing with challenges of loss and change, but for embracing life with the aftereffects of a stroke, than the firsthand lessons of this wise and compassionate teacher. And among the many teaching gems Ram Dass offers is his distinction between curing and healing. For many of the neurological conditions we have been considering, "cures" remain elusive because we are not yet able to restore life to the way it had been. But Ram Dass offers a guide for "healing" heart and mind that may not undo the after-effects of a stroke, but instead opens a space to experience a sense of wholeness when so much has been taken away—a recognition of that spirit that cannot be diminished by illness.

Psychotherapy may not offer a cure for the after-effects of a stroke or other neurological conditions, but it can accept the challenge to guide a process of healing which in turn may have a positive effect on the condition itself. We have the firsthand experiences of superb writers like Ram Dass and Reynolds Price to inform the psychotherapy approaches we offer patients to reduce suffering and promote an embracing of life as it is now and as it continues to change.

REFERENCES AND READINGS

Agrell, B., and O. Dehlin. 1989. Comparison of six depression rating scales in geriatric stroke patients. *Stroke: A Journal of Cerebral Circulation* 20 (9): 1190–1194.

Astrèom, M., R. Adolfsson, and K. Asplund. 1993. Major depression in stroke patients. A 3-year longitudinal study. *Stroke: A Journal of Cerebral Circulation.* 24 (7): 976–982.

Benton, A. L., A. B. Sivan, and K. Hamsher. 1994. *Contributions to neuropsychological assessment. A clinical manual.* 2nd ed. New York: Oxford University Press.

Bogousslavsky, J., M. Hommel, and C. Bassetti. 1998. Stroke. In *Outcomes in neurological and neurosurgical disorders,* edited by M. Swash. Cambridge: Cambridge University Press.

Bowler, J. V. 2000. Criteria for vascular dementia: replacing dogma with data. *Archives of Neurology* 57 (2): 170–171.

Brown, G. G., A. D. Baird, and M. W. Shatz. 1986. The effects of cerebrovascular disease and its treatment on higher cortical functioning. In *Neuropsychological assessment of neuropsychiatric disorders,* edited by I. Grant and K. Adams. New York: Oxford University Press.

Castillo, C. S., S. K. Schultz, and R. G. Robinson. 1995. Clinical correlates of early-onset and late-onset poststroke generalized anxiety. *American Journal of Psychiatry* 152 (8): 1174–1179.

Castillo, V., and J. Bogousslavsky. 1997. Brain embolism. In *Primer on cerebrovascular diseases,* edited by K. A. Welch, et al. San Diego, CA: Academic Press.

Chui, H. C., W. Mack, J. E. Jackson, D. Mungas, B. R. Reed, J. Tinklenberg, F. L. Chang, K. Skinner, C. Tasaki, and W. J. Jagust. 2000. Clinical criteria for the diagnosis of vascular dementia: A multicenter study of comparability and interrater reliability. *Archives of Neurology* 57 (2): 191–196.

Cummings, Jeffrey L., and Michael S. Mega. 2003. *Neuropsychiatry and behavioral neuroscience.* New York: Oxford University Press.

Dass, Ram. 2000. *Still here: Embracing aging, changing, and dying.* New York: Riverhead Books.

Gainotti, G. 1992. Post-stroke depression: Psychological and biochemical interpretations. In *Neuropsychological rehabilitation,* edited by N. V. Steinbuchel, D. Y. V. Cramon, and E. Poppel. New York: Springer-Verlag.

Garrett, K. D., J. N. Browndyke, W. Whelihan, R. H. Paul, M. DiCarlo, D. J. Moser, R. A. Cohen, and B. R. Ott. 2004. The neuropsychological profile of vascular cognitive impairment—no dementia: Comparisons to patients at risk for cerebrovascular disease and vascular dementia. *Archives of Clinical Neuropsychology* 19 (6): 745–757.

Goodglass, H., and E. Kaplan. 1983. *Assessment of aphasia and related disorders.* 2nd ed. Philadelphia: Lea and Febiger.

Hosking, Shirley G., Nigel V. Marsh, and Paul J. Friedman. 1996. Poststroke depression: Prevalence, course, and associated factors. *Neuropsychology Review* 6 (3): 107–133.

Lezak, M. D., D. B. Howieson, D. W. Loring, H. J. Hannay, and J. S. Fischer. 2004. *Neuropsychological assessment.* 4th ed. New York: Oxford University Press.

Morris, P. L., R. G. Robinson, B. Raphael, and M. J. Hopwood. 1996. Lesion location and poststroke depression. *Journal of Neuropsychiatry and Clinical Neurosciences* 8 (4): 399–403.

Norris, J. W., and V. C. Hachinski, eds. 2001. *Stroke prevention*. New York: Oxford University Press.

Român, G. C., T. K. Tatemichi, T. Erkinjuntti, J. L. Cummings, et al. 1993. Vascular dementia: Diagnostic criteria for research studies. Report of the NINDS-AIREN International Workshop. *Neurology* 43 (2): 250–260.

Sachdev, P. S., H. Brodaty, M J. Valenzuela, L. Lorentz, J. C. Looi, W. Wen, and A. S. Zagami. 2004. The neuropsychological profile of vascular cognitive impairment in stroke and TIA patients. *Neurology* 62 (6): 912–919.

Sachdev, P. S., H. Brodaty, M. J. Valenzuela, L. M. Lorentz, and A. Koschera. 2004. Progression of cognitive impairment in stroke patients. *Neurology* 63 (9): 1618–1623.

Shimoda, K., and R. G. Robinson. 1999. The relationship between poststroke depression and lesion location in long-term follow-up. *Biological Psychiatry* 45 (2): 187–192.

Toole, J. F., and A. N. Patel. 1974. *Cerebrovascular disorders*. 2nd ed. New York: McGraw-Hill Book Company.

Weinstein, A., and R. A. Swenson. 1998. Cerebrovascular disease. In *Clinical neuropsychology: A pocket handbook for assessment*, edited by P. Snyder and P. Nussbaum. Washington, D.C.: American Psychological Association.

Wentzel, C., K. Rockwood, C. MacKnight, V. Hachinski, D. B. Hogan, H. Feldman, T. Ostbye, C. Wolfson, S. Gauthier, R. Verreault, and I. McDowell. 2001. Progression of impairment in patients with vascular cognitive impairment without dementia. *Neurology* 57 (4): 714–716.

9

Elusive Diagnoses

There are more things in heaven and earth . . .
Than are dreamt of in your philosophy.

—Shakespeare

In his book *Freud's Requiem,* von Unwerth (2005) notes Freud's fondness for quoting Hamlet's admonition to Horatio when tackling especially difficult problems that challenged conventional ways of thinking. Such an open-minded attitude also may serve us well when working with patients whose symptoms and experiences do not conform neatly to our current "philosophies" of diagnostic classification and treatment strategy. This open-minded sensitivity to the validity of our patients' experiences and their protean manifestations is no more important than in psychotherapy, with people whose conditions inhabit the borderlands of neurology and psychology where they can elude either-or conceptual classifications and formulaic treatment approaches. Conditions that present with neurological symptoms in the absence of confirmatory signs of neurological disease or in excess of any disability attributed to an existing neurological condition—"hysteria" in the era of Charcot and Freud, or "conversion disorder" (hysterical conversion disorders) in today's nomenclature—continue to challenge our clinical approaches but in doing so also provide gateways for a better understanding of mind-body interactions and ultimately our patients' experience.

Once considered the "most enigmatic of all nervous diseases" (Freud 1893), hysteria evolved from a "symptom-complex definition" to a "personality-configuration definition" (Krohn 1978), and now its features have been conceptualized under two separate conditions: conversion, a symptom-complex formulation; and histrionic personality, a personality-configuration formulation. Krohn (1978) aptly characterized hysteria "The Elusive Neurosis," and the "transformation from psychic into organic phenomenon" (Deutsch 1959), whether defined as hysteria, conversion, psychogenic disorder, unexplained neurological symptom, or yet to be articulated formulation, is a dramatic example of mind-body interactions that have yet to be fully explained. Even as we approach a better understanding of the neuropsychological processes that underlie conversion phenomena, the challenges of providing helpful therapies remain, with leading neuroscientists concluding that "the most defensible clinical approach is to regard conversion phenomena as important harbingers of an underlying condition that must be identified and treated" (Cummings and Mega 2003, 341).

To begin our discussion I will use the commonly accepted term "conversion" (American Psychiatric Association and American Psychiatric Association Task Force on DSM-IV 2000) to refer to neurological symptoms that are not fully explained by diagnosable neurological illness employing currently available diagnostic procedures. Conversion phenomena manifest in symptoms affecting voluntary sensory and motor functions, and the symptoms are not intentionally produced or feigned. Symptoms may include motor dysfunction (problems with coordination and balance, paralysis and weakness, difficulty swallowing, and urinary retention), sensory deficits (loss of touch or pain sensation, double vision, blindness, deafness, and hallucinations), and seizures (psychogenic nonepileptic seizures). Psychological factors contribute to symptom expression—thus "conversion"—and thereby psychological approaches can offer useful methods for symptom reduction and maintaining quality of life even as symptoms may persist. Despite psychological influences on a patient's functional status, it must be acknowledged that a number of neurological conditions may be misdiagnosed as conversion disorders—among them are multiple sclerosis, myasthenia gravis, and idiopathic or substance-induced dystonias (APA and APA Task Force on DSM-IV 2000). Conversion symptoms also may co-exist with a diagnosable neurological condition; and given the limitations of our current understanding and methods of diagnosis, medical etiologies ultimately may be found for the symptoms expressed by people presently diagnosed with conversion disorder (Slater 1965; Mace and Trimble 1996), although for some patients a clear neurological diagnosis may not emerge (Crimlisk et al. 1998).

PSYCHODYNAMIC AND
NEUROPHYSIOLOGICAL PERSPECTIVES

Concepts of hysteria and conversion have deep roots in the psychoanalytic tradition; and despite advancements elucidating the neural mechanisms that underlie conversion phenomena, a psychodynamic perspective still may be helpful in understanding the person with the symptoms, and the psychological processes that are being expressed in symptoms via physiological brain activity. In his argument for the continuing importance of a psychodynamic perspective for the understanding, evaluation, and treatment of patients with psychosomatic illnesses, Nemiah (2000) offers a definition of hysterical conversion that may serve as a springboard for thinking about the integration of psychodynamic perspectives with emerging neurophysiological views on conversion: "The hysterical conversion symptom is an attempt to relieve an emotional tension in a symbolic way; it is a symbolic expression of a definite emotional content. The mechanism is restricted to the voluntary neuromuscular or sensory perceptive systems whose function is to express and relieve emotions." The relief of emotional tension, albeit in a dissociated form, via somatic symptoms is a product of conflictual psychological processes that preclude the integration of affect, thought, and behavior. The expressive function of somatic symptoms is not only a manifestation of emotional content that cannot be experienced in a fully integrated way, but also a communication of the patient's fragmented experience that may at least be recognized, and perhaps better understood from a psychodynamic perspective. This functional duality of tension relief and expression/communication will manifest in relationship dynamics between patients and treatment providers where frustrating interactions may represent an "isomorphic replay" (Levenson 1972) of the conditions that originally gave rise to the conversion process and continue to sustain the expression of conflicted emotional experience in somatic symptoms.

Rather than view recent advances in mapping the underlying neurophysiology of conversion symptoms as an alternative to psychodynamic understanding, a complementary perspective may offer a broader appreciation of the complexities of mind-body interactions that elude either-or formulations, and thus may better inform our treatment approaches. Let's review some recent studies using functional brain imaging procedures and consider the relationships between postulated neurophysiological mechanisms underlying conversion symptoms and psychodynamic processes.

Using PET technology (regional cerebral blood flow, rCBF), Marshall et al. (1997) studied a female patient with left sided paralysis who met diagnostic criteria for conversion disorder. The patient showed no significant asymmetries in rCBF activation of the motor cortices at rest. The activation patterns when she prepared to move her paralyzed left leg and good right leg were similar, providing evidence against the idea that she might be feigning the deficit. However, in contrast to activation patterns evident when she moved her good right leg, her attempt to move her paralyzed left leg did not activate the right motor cortex, but did activate the right anterior cingulate and the right orbitofrontal cortex. The anterior cingulate cortex is considered a powerful cortical suppressor area and also is involved in the integration of mental processes with bodily systems (Luu and Posner 2003). Marshall et al. (1997) hypothesized that the brain activation pattern evidenced by their patient represented a "functional disconnection" with the orbito-frontal cortex operating as a distal source of "unconscious inhibiting," while the anterior cingulate operated as the proximal source that "disconnects" premotor/prefrontal areas (intention) from the primary motor cortex (action).

Recognizing that "psychological processes responsible for hysterical paralysis occur via physiological brain activity," Halligan et al. (2000) using PET functional imaging demonstrated that hypnotically induced left leg paralysis in an otherwise healthy young man shared common neurophysiological mechanisms with conversion hysteria. The researchers suggested that the activations of the right orbito-frontal cortex and anterior cingulate, when the participant attempted to move his left leg, could represent "the management of mental dissonance" that occurs when the suggestion of paralysis conflicts with the instruction to move the "paralyzed" limb. They further suggested this process might apply to patients with conversion symptoms, "hysterical people," in their attempts to manage "a similarly generated internal conflict."

Other functional neuroimaging studies suggest the operation of "unconscious" processes in the production of conversion symptoms. Spence et al. (2000) demonstrated activation differences between patients with conversion motor symptoms and individuals instructed to consciously feign similar motor dysfunction. Vuilleumier et al. (2001) demonstrated activation asymmetries in patients with conversion symptoms involving the thalamus and basal ganglia that resolved after recovery from symptoms and suggested that hysterical paralysis may reflect the inhibition of action through the modulation of basal ganglia and thalamocortical systems that may be "triggered outside conscious will by various emotional stressors, through limbic inputs from amygdala and orbito-frontal cortex."

It would seem fair to conclude that the purpose of these studies was to explore neurophysiological processes that underlie conversion symptoms and associated phenomena (hypnotic paralysis), and not necessarily to provide biological support for Freudian theory or psychodynamic concepts. After all, Halligan, Bass, and Wade (2000), citing the work of Crimlisk et al. (1998), noted that "conversion hysteria retains the doubtful distinction among psychiatric diagnoses of still invoking Freudian mechanisms as an explanation." And in considering the evolution of theory on hysterical conversion, Vuilleumier et al. (2001) expressed the opinion: "Purely psychodynamic accounts are now recognized as insufficient, but a modern theoretical framework is still lacking." Psychodynamic theory, however, also has evolved since the time of Freud (Mitchell and Black 1995), and fundamental concepts such as unconscious motivation, psychological defense, and the management of conflict are still relevant for understanding the processes expressed via neurophysiological activity that may underlie conversion symptoms. If we consider some of the concepts and hypotheses offered to explain neurophysiological mechanisms and hysterical symptom production, themes of "disconnection," "inhibition," and "dissonance" emerge (Marshall et al. 1997; Halligan et al. 2000). It would seem then that the therapeutic challenge would be to address these factors as they manifest psychologically in our patients' attempts to manage conflictual experiences by providing the conditions within a psychotherapy relationship that facilitate an increasing awareness of psychological experience and integration of thought, feeling, and behavior. Psychotherapy informed by a psychodynamic perspective may be particularly well suited for this task. And perhaps our theorizing also may be better served by considering neurophysiological and psychodynamic perspectives not as alternatives to each other but as components to be integrated into an evolving "modern neuropsychological theory" of unexplained neurological symptoms.

CLINICAL FORMULATION AND
THE ATTITUDE OF MIND PERSPECTIVE

Within neurological circles, clinical presentations that in psychiatry are considered manifestations of "conversion disorder" more commonly may be referred to as "psychogenic disorders"—as in psychogenic movement disorders (Miyasaki et al. 2003) and psychogenic seizures (Lesser 1996). Sometimes the perspectives are combined, and psychogenic movement disorders and pseudoepileptic seizures (psychogenic seizures) are discussed as manifestations of conversion disorders (Cummings and Mega 2003). Despite such differences, however, there is consensus between neurology and psychiatry in acknowledging that conversion or psychogenic disorders can coexist with a diagnosable neurological condition (Lesser 1996; APA and APA Task Force on DSM-IV 2000; Miyasaki et al. 2003). Therefore depending on referral sources and their particular diagnostic philosophy, patients presenting for psychotherapy may be accompanied by a variety of diagnoses possibly including past and/or current neurological illness, and different labels for neurological symptoms that are not fully explained by medical or organic factors. The privilege of seeing such patients has provided me the opportunity to note some common themes in their struggles, encounters with health care providers, and experiences in psychotherapy.

Diagnostic Dilemmas

Despite recommendations for tact, empathy, and a nonjudgmental attitude when presenting psychogenic diagnoses to patients (Lesser 1996; Miyasaki et al. 2003), the diagnosis of conversion still may be considered "pejorative" (Halligan, Bass, and Wade 2000) regardless of the labels that may be used to describe the condition. For one patient who had been through multiple work-ups for seizures and motor dysfunction, among her stated goals for psychotherapy was "to deal with feelings of being judged by the medical establishment." Like psychotherapists, medical providers bring their own attitudes and biases into the consulting room and the potential for such predispositions to affect the doctor-patient interaction is a fact in any encounter. The best attempts to exercise tact and empathy may belie judgmental or pejorative attitudes of which the doctor is not fully aware. However even if the doctor is free of judgmental bias, some patients may be exquisitely sensitive to the slightest hint of such attitudes because their vulnerable position is reminiscent of past encounters with other significant figures where their experiences had been minimized, shamed, or ignored. These disruptive developmental experiences continue to be reinforced by the repetition of conflicted interpersonal dynamics in present-day encounters, and as a result the dissociations in emotional life that underlie the expression of conflict in somatic symptoms are sustained.

On a manifest level the patient with unexplained neurological symptoms seeks the assistance of medical providers to clarify their complex symptom presentation, diagnose a condition, and provide appropriate treatment. On a latent level, however, the patient wants their experience validated and understood. As one patient said after another disappointing experience with a neurological consultation that failed to find an organic basis for her symptoms, "I wish they would try to get to know me and not just my past medical records." And therein lies the dilemma: the validation of experience is different than the diagnosis of a medical condition. Failure to find a reason—an organic etiology—for compromising symptoms can leave the patient with the feeling of yet another invalidation of her experience in an interaction in which she has made herself vulnerable to a replay of a painful emotional past. The scene is all too familiar because she is left with the alternative that her condition is psychologically based, which translates into being a product of her own imagination, something of her own doing, an experience without validation.

Patients do not necessarily resist the idea that psychological factors may affect their status, but in their experience, this formulation remains incomplete, simply because it is. A patient's reaction revealed a quiet disappointment as we reviewed the results of a recent neuropsychological evaluation that seemed to be an accurate reflection of her cognitive status. She could agree that weaknesses identified by the examination paralleled problems she was having in daily functioning, but she added: "It just seems incomplete, there's more to me than that," and of course there was, but it wouldn't be found even in the most comprehensive of neuropsychological evaluations.

Sometimes patients, especially those with medically unexplained symptoms, seek from an authority of a physician or other health care provider something that was lacking in their developmental encounters, something that continues to be missing in their current relationships, and something they yet are unable to provide for themselves—the honoring of the totality of their experience and its expression. Fears of abandonment, anticipation of shame, and anxiety about overwhelming others with their affect all may work to keep our patients' emotional experiences strangulated, fueling the possibility that this psychological state of affairs will find expression in perhaps a more oblique but no less dramatic fashion. While this honoring of experience would seem essential for successful therapy, it may be difficult to find within neurological and psychological diagnoses, because it really is the other way around—psychological and neurological factors are both part of a larger life experience that is manifesting now in a particular way. To demonstrate an acceptance of a patient's experience as valid—even as manifested in "conversion" or "psychogenic" symptomatology—and not get caught in either-or diagnostic dilemmas, initiates the therapeutic conditions that are essential if the patient is to risk coming to know and honor the full range of his or her own experience. The therapist begins the process with a "benevolent curiosity" about the patient's experience. This nonjudgmental attitude considers symptoms, the context in which they occur, their impact on the patient's life and relationships, the patient's thoughts and feelings about them, and so forth and so on—coming to know the patient with the symptoms instead of the symptoms but not the patient. Through the process psychotherapy, the patient eventually adopts this attitude of benevolent curiosity in coming to know his or her own experience. It is from this foundation that the integration of thought, feeling, and behavior can grow.

Developmental Origins and the Process of Integration

Returning from a consultation at a tertiary care medical center, a patient commented how her symptoms of neurological dysfunction "didn't fit neatly into a diagnostic box." As a youngster, her playful spirit fueled by ADHD didn't find ready acceptance in a family that placed a premium on proper decorum. Her physical exuberance and emotional expressiveness were routinely met with shaming reprimands to contain herself and stay in line. Her childhood memories were characterized by incessant demands, performance expectations, and boundary violations all of which would make her feel "physically ill." Yet illness itself was a conflictual experience, "something to be gotten over quickly so you could be productive again." She spoke of being a sad, lonely, disappointed, and angry child who would become increasingly "disconnected and disengaged" from her body.

During the course of her psychotherapy the patient cultivated a parallel interest in mindfulness and meditation which proved to be an invaluable support in her process of coming to know and honor the totality of her experience without trying "to contain it or box it up in some neat package." Mindful awareness provided her with a foundation to experience painful memories and the associated feelings, and to catch and interrupt reactive tendencies that otherwise would lead to the repetition of painful self-criticism and unfulfilling relationships. She would come to recognize the persistent power of internalized childhood experiences as she noticed how she became angry with herself during a recent illness and "making promises to be productive" after the illness subsided. As a youngster it would seem that the duration of her illness was measured by clock time as opposed to the more natural pace of a recovery aided by rest and the attention of a caring adult.

As therapy progressed the patient could allow herself to actually feel anxious and fearful about the possibility of a debilitating condition rendering her totally dependent on others, and it appeared that at times she countered these fears by overextending herself, which would exacerbate her symptoms. However the spirit of her youth hadn't been completely dampened and she worked gamely to find a balance between activity and rest, between engagement and solitude that made sense for her life as it was now.

Her lifestyle had become pared down, perhaps more simple, but no less true. She spoke of beginning "to reconnect" with herself through the feeling she experienced working with wet clay on a potter's wheel. With an expressiveness that spoke of her integration of physicality and emotion, she would describe immersing herself in the textures of wet clay and motion of the potter's wheel. Her studio became her "safe and sacred place" that allowed her the freedom to "physically express" her emotions. She spoke of noticing the difference in her experience when she allowed the process of throwing a pot to unfold moment by moment rather than trying too hard to achieve some predetermined idea of what it was supposed to be. She would see parallels between this process and her own self-exploration and growing self-acceptance; she would say "sometimes there is no need to change or fix anything, but just that awareness and acceptance is a change for the better."

SUMMARY POINTS FOR PSYCHOLOGICAL INTERVENTION

- Conversion or psychogenic disorders—once known as hysteria—are conditions that present with neurological symptoms in the absence of confirmatory signs of neurological disease or in excess of any disability attributed to an existing neurological condition.

- A number of neurological conditions may be misdiagnosed as conversion—among them are multiple sclerosis, myasthenia gravis, and idiopathic or substance-induced dystonias.
- Conversion symptoms may co-exist with a diagnosable neurological condition, and medical etiologies ultimately may be found for symptoms diagnosed as conversion.
- Psychological processes play a role in conversion symptom formation via physiological brain activity.
- From a psychological perspective, conversion symptoms represent an attempt to relieve emotional tension in a symbolic way. The expressive function of the somatic conversion symptom is a manifestation of emotional content that cannot be experienced in a fully integrated way, and also a communication of a patient's fragmented experience. Attention to the manifest and latent aspects of the patient's communication may not always occur in medical settings but it is an essential component in psychotherapy.

A Closing Note

A history of abuse has been associated with psychogenic disorders such as psychogenic nonepileptic seizures (Cragar et al. 2002), and a common theme for many patients presenting with unexplained neurological symptoms is having experienced a violation of boundaries and personal integrity with the subsequent minimization or denial of the traumatic experience by those on whom the patient may have depended. This experience, at least in part, may fuel the need to have subjective experience—as expressed through symptoms—validated by some external authority. For other patients, who may have been the victims of abuse, the diagnosis of a neurological illness can reawaken fears associated with vulnerability, dependency, and trust that will manifest in relationships with caretakers and health care providers, but this reawakening also provides the opportunity for the patient in psychotherapy to finally address the wounds of trauma and neglect.

Past trauma and neglect can set the stage for a host of later psychological difficulties including perhaps a susceptibility to conversion or psychogenic disorders; and a current stressor, which may be symbolic of the past trauma, may "trigger" the emergence of symptoms. However, for other patients with medically unexplained neurological symptoms, a specific psychological precipitant may not be discerned suggesting that for some the emergence of symptoms may represent the release of the accumulated press of strangulated emotions.

The success of psychotherapy efforts with patients whose conditions represent the Elusive Diagnoses is often supported by the patient's interaction with others outside the therapy session. These "supportive personnel" have primary relationships with the patient in their own right as spouses, family members, primary care physicians, psychiatrists, or neurologists. They have been an integral part of my patients' therapy process, and their positive contributions echo a common theme. A psychotherapy challenge for many patients, which is especially prominent with elusive diagnoses, is the integration of thought, feeling, and behavior as they relate to their inner experience and the external world. This integration requires the capacity to hold conflictual thoughts and feeling in awareness, which is the process of coming to know and honor our experience with a benevolent curiosity. More often than not this process is challenged when our experiences differ with, or perhaps more forcefully come into conflict with the experiences of another. There is ample opportunity for such dissonance to occur in a relationship with a physician. In expressing a medical opinion that may not be congruent with a patient's thoughts or wishes, while still acknowledging the patient's perspective on his or her own experience, a physician provides an experiential context for working with conflicting thoughts or feelings as represented by different perspectives in an interaction. Essentially intrapsychic dynamics manifest in an interpersonal sphere. Within a supportive but noncollusive physician-patient relationship, individual autonomy and opinion are respected, and a patient's developing intrapsychic integration is practiced in an interpersonal context. As one patient commented on her relationship with her primary care physician, "We don't always agree, but he has his experience and I have mine and there's room enough in our relationship for both."

REFERENCES AND READINGS

American Psychiatric Association and American Psychiatric Association Task Force on DSM-IV. 2000. *Diagnostic and statistical manual of mental disorders: DSM-IV-TR.* 4th ed. Washington, D.C.: American Psychiatric Association.

Cragar, Dona E., David T. R. Berry, Toufic A. Fakhoury, Jean E. Cibula, and Frederick A. Schmitt. 2002. A review of diagnostic techniques in the differential diagnosis of epileptic and nonepileptic seizures. *Neuropsychology Review* 12 (1): 31–64.

Crimlisk, H. L., K. Bhatia, H. Cope, A. David, C. D. Marsden, and M. A. Ron. 1998. Slater revisited: 6 year follow-up study of patients with medically unexplained motor symptoms. *BMJ (Clinical research ed.)* 316 (7131): 582–586.

Cross, Wilbur L., and Tucker Brooke, eds. 1993. *The Yale Shakespeare.* New York: Barnes & Noble Books.

Cummings, Jeffrey L., and Michael S. Mega. 2003. *Neuropsychiatry and behavioral neuroscience.* New York: Oxford University Press.

Deutsch, F. 1959. On the formation of the conversion symptom. In *The mysterious leap from the mind to the body,* edited by F. Deutsch. New York: International Universities Press.

Freud, Sigmund. 1893. Charcot. In *Sigmund Freud collected papers,* edited by J. Riviere. New York: Basic Books.

Halligan, P. W., B. S. Athwal, D. A. Oakley, and R. S. Frackowiak. 2000. Imaging hypnotic paralysis: Implications for conversion hysteria. *Lancet* 355 (9208): 986–987.

Halligan, P. W., C. Bass, and D. T. Wade. 2000. New approaches to conversion hysteria. *BMJ (Clinical research ed.)* 320 (7248): 1488–1489.

Krohn, Alan. 1978. *Hysteria: The elusive neurosis.* New York: International Universities Press.

Lesser, R. P. 1996. Psychogenic seizures. *Neurology* 46 (6): 1499–1507.

Levenson, Edgar A. 1972. *The fallacy of understanding; an inquiry into the changing structure of psychoanalysis.* New York: Basic Books.

Luu, P., and M. I. Posner. 2003. Anterior cingulate cortex regulation of sympathetic activity. *Brain: A Journal of Neurology* 126: 2119–2120.

Mace, C. J., and M. R. Trimble. 1996. Ten-year prognosis of conversion disorder. *British Journal of Psychiatry: Journal of Mental Science* 169 (3): 282–288.

Marshall, J. C., P. W. Halligan, G. R. Fink, D. T. Wade, and R. S. Frackowiak. 1997. The functional anatomy of a hysterical paralysis. *Cognition* 64 (1): B1–B8.

Mitchell, Stephen A., and Margaret Black. 1995. *Freud and beyond: A history of modern psychoanalytic thought.* New York: Basic Books.

Miyasaki, J. M., D. S. Sa, N. Galvez-Jimenez, and A. E. Lang. 2003. Psychogenic movement disorders. *Canadian Journal of Neurological Sciences. Le journal canadien des sciences neurologiques* 30 (Supp. 1): S94–S100.

Nemiah, J. C. 2000. A psychodynamic view of psychosomatic medicine. *Psychosomatic Medicine* 62 (3): 299–303.

Slater, E. 1965. Diagnosis of "Hysteria." *British Medical Journal* 5447:1395–1399.

Spence, S. A., H. L. Crimlisk, H. Cope, M. A. Ron, and P. M. Grasby. 2000. Discrete neurophysiological correlates in prefrontal cortex during hysterical and feigned disorder of movement. *Lancet* 355 (9211): 1243–1244.

von Unwerth, Matthew. 2005. *Freud's requiem: Mourning, memory, and the invisible history of a summer walk.* New York: Riverhead Books.

Vuilleumier, P., C. Chicherio, F. Assal, S. Schwartz, D. Slosman, and T. Landis. 2001. Functional neuroanatomical correlates of hysterical sensorimotor loss. *Brain: Journal of Neurology* 124: 1077–1090.

Part III

PSYCHOLOGICAL INTERVENTION

10

Foundations for Therapy

May you have a strong foundation
When the winds of changes shift

—Bob Dylan, "Forever Young" (2004)

A neurological condition disrupts the course of a life, and the resulting disequilibrium of uncertainty can narrow our patients' view to grasping for what was and fearing what's to come. Our approach is to transcend dichotomous reactivity that narrows options to either fighting the truth of what is, or falling victim to it. Through the "elements of a way" and "mindfulness," we endeavor to help our patients change their relationship to their conditions by placing the reality of their losses and limitations within the context of a larger life perspective that continues to unfold. Our aim is to engage our patients in a reciprocal therapeutic process that reduces suffering and promotes an engagement in life. These factors build upon each other, providing a foundation for active and meaningful participation in other treatment modalities, and fueling the resilience needed to cope with present and future stress. A patient's story may help illustrate how the "attitude of mind" approach becomes a foundation for treatment and reengagement with life.

A PATIENT'S STORY

Jack was in his early 30s when he was diagnosed with MS, although some problems with tripping and falling over the years hinted that symptoms of the condition were present well before the diagnosis was made. He was an avid outdoor sportsman who felt equally at home tracking game through autumn fields, or fishing the cold lakes and streams of northern Michigan. After graduating high school and completing a tour in the Navy, he began working in the building trades. He enjoyed his job, especially since much of his time was spent outdoors, and he had risen through the ranks to become a crew foreman with a large construction company.

Jack was a proud man, not in a haughty sense, but someone who placed great value in "carrying my own weight and not whining." He initially minimized his symptoms, or as he said, "fought them back." Numbness and weakness in his left arm and leg were the first challenges to his job that placed a premium on strength and agility. His attempts to "work through" the symptoms exacerbated an increasingly obvious susceptibility to fatigue that brought him home after a workday feeling exhausted, impatient, and irritable. Whatever energy had once been left to play ball with his kids or garden with his wife now had been spent hours before at the construction site.

Eventually Jack had to consider the offer of being reassigned to an "indoor desk job" in the company office. He tried to counterbalance his feelings of loss with the optimistic perspective that the accommodations of his new position would allow him to continue to work, and perhaps even have something left to share with his family. Working at a desk in an air-conditioned office seemed like a reasonable alternative to his losing battle in the field.

Jack's difficulties in managing his new position initially were attributed to the challenges of transition. After all, a change of role often calls into question our sense of who we are—and for Jack, sitting behind a desk was a far cry from being behind the wheel of a company pick-up. Having known the operations of his company quite well, he didn't anticipate the problems he would have juggling phone calls, data entry, and crew assignments, while at the same time remembering to begin a new project his supervisor had given him a week ago. With self-doubt mounting on a daily basis, Jack began to question his own motives—wondering if he "wasn't trying hard enough." A job reassignment that was thought to be less demanding was becoming a nightmare. Again Jack simply wasn't getting the job done, but this time the reasons for his difficulties seemed more elusive. Jack would later recall: "At least in the field I knew my problems with balance and walking were because of my MS, but it was hard to blame MS sitting behind a desk in an air-conditioned office."

A Referral for a Neuropsychological Evaluation

Recognizing Jack's problems with his desk job may be related to cognitive weaknesses and not necessarily lack of effort, his neurologist referred him for a neuropsychological evaluation. The psychologist began the evaluation by taking a history of Jack's illness. As his story unfolded, a picture emerged of a man whose struggles at work had taken a toll on his sense of who he was. Jack couldn't find an explanation for his failures in his job reassignment, because he wasn't yet aware that cognitive difficulties could be associated with MS. And so—like many of us—he filled in the gaps of awareness with his own mental constructions. Simply stated, Jack's approach to life was to work through adversity by trying harder; therefore if he wasn't meeting the challenge of his current circumstances, he must not have been trying hard enough.

Jack was caught in a negative spiral of failure, frustration, and fatigue; and his painful situation was no more obvious than when he described an incident that overwhelmed his coping resources. He had been trying to teach his twelve-year-old daughter how to tie a particular fishing knot, but he was having problems manipulating the thin monofilament line. As he continued to press himself, the line became a tangled mess. Having felt helpless and humiliated, he was stuck in self-blame: "I couldn't even hold it together long enough to teach Josie how to tie a clinch knot."

Evaluation Results

Jack underwent several hours of neuropsychological testing, and the results confirmed his neurologist's suspicions. It wasn't lack of effort that was compromising Jack's performance at work; in fact his attempts to deal with failure by increasing his effort—"trying harder"—actually may have been making his situation worse.

The psychologist's report described reductions in processing speed, weaknesses in memory retrieval, and deficiencies in executive abilities that included problems with organization and planning, and mental flexibility. Jack's personality test profile also showed that he was experiencing a high level of psychological distress that was probably magnifying his cognitive processing difficulties.

The results of Jack's neuropsychological evaluation were helpful in providing objective evidence of the cognitive weaknesses that were making his transition to a new job more difficult than he had ever anticipated. His attempts to "beat MS" through sheer will of effort only served to compound his problems, and with his options dwindling, he was increasingly feeling helpless and hopeless. Jack's test profile also would be useful in guiding a rehabilitation approach that would include developing cognitive compensatory strategies and eventually considering alternative job options, but something else would come first—an attitude of mind that would provide a foundation for treatment and living with the uncertainties of MS.

THE ATTITUDE OF MIND: THEMES IN PSYCHOTHERAPY

Jack was invited to consider changing his relationship to MS and its neuropsychological challenges. Accomplishing this reorientation would call for an *open mind* to consider ways of living with MS other than fighting it. Jack would come to know that giving up his fighting posture did not mean falling victim to MS. He would step out of this either-or dilemma, and transform the energy of the battle into the determination that would fuel his *active involvement* in treatment, and equally if not more important, his reengagement with life.

Expanding Our Vision of Who We Are

Sometimes when change threatens our self-image, we tend to react by clinging to the illusory security offered by beliefs about ourselves that are at best only part-truths. For Jack, the more his world changed, the more steadfastly he tried to live his self-concept as the man of action—the fighter who would not give up. Most of us may not be very different from Jack. Frequently our response to threat is to hold on to the aspect of ourselves that feels most threatened, and in doing so we narrow our focus and lose sight of all that we truly are. "Hold on; brace yourself"—even our language during times of challenge can evoke images of a clinging and rigid posture that won't withstand the next gale. Jack was never really far from the substance of his foundation, and the therapeutic task was to help him see and experience that which always was and continued to be, but had been obscured by his battle with MS.

Beginning Foundations for Psychotherapy:
Talking, Language, and Experience

Sometimes the language of psychotherapy also can obscure what it is trying to describe, if a preoccupation with explanation replaces a nonjudgmental appreciation of the experience for what it is. Perhaps this point may be illustrated by a story about a great pianist being asked about the meaning of a piece of music he had just played—to which he responded by playing the piece again. We can't ascribe a specific intention to the maestro's repeating the piece, but perhaps it had something to do with not wanting the essence of his music lost in explanation. Examples of "being in the experience" and "talking about the experience" also occur in our daily lives. Just consider the difference between taking a bite of a juicy peach and describing the taste of a peach.

In our approach to living with neuropsychological challenges and thinking about the role of psychotherapy, we don't want to get caught in either-

or thinking; because having an experience and talking about an experience both can be valuable if we maintain a perspective of balance. And sometimes the duality of language and experience may even dissolve in the immediacy of a moment, when words not only convey meaning but also are the experience itself. Such moments are available in haiku poetry.

> Sweet springtime showers,
> and no words can express
> how sad it all is
>
> —Buson, 1715–1783 (Hamill and Seaton, 2004)

Psychotherapy is a dynamic process of experiencing and talking that occurs within the unfolding context of a relationship where a patient's story resonates with the available skills of a therapist to open "avenues of understanding" (Mueller 1973) and opportunities for transformation. Initially a bit skeptical about psychological treatment, Jack's questions about "how is talking going to help" reflected both his fear of being vulnerable and his willingness to try.

Shifting from Fighting to Living: Touching the Positive

Changing Jack's relationship to MS started by placing his illness within the context of something larger—his life. The challenge would call for an ongoing acceptance—not a once and for all notion of acceptance—that MS was a part of, but not all of life. We don't deny the pain and suffering of the losses that can be associated with a neurological condition. We acknowledge the truth of our experience as it is in the moment, and then as best we can, we allow that experience of pain simply *to be* within the context of the larger unfolding process of our life.

"Touching the positive" is how Thich Nhat Hanh—a Zen master, poet, and peace activist—describes the process of shining awareness on those parts of life for which we are grateful—be it the midnight sound of the surf crashing on a distant shore, or perhaps having a cup of coffee with a friend. Whatever the special moments may be for a particular person, they provide balance and an essential foundation for being with the suffering that also is an inevitable part of life.

There are people in our lives who touch us with their simple presence—people whose being in the world is a benefit for others. In Buddhist circles, they are called bodhisattvas. Thich Nhat Hanh and the Dalai Lama are well-recognized examples of the bodhisattva ideal, but these special people also live among us in our communities and maybe even in our families. You will know them not by fanfare, but by the feeling you have after an encounter with them—maybe something like returning home after a long journey.

City Streets

A vibrant personality, and before the onset of MS, a star player of the Sassy-9 softball team, Linn's acceptance of MS began with the diagnosis and continued with the challenges that became part of her daily life. There came a time when her doctor suggested she consider a brace to provide needed support for walking. For a former athlete who had run the bases with abandon, being fitted for a brace brought a hollow feeling that she could only describe as "homesick." The feeling began the night before her appointment for the fitting and continued through most of the next day. She didn't fight the rush of emotions that were mixed with memories of running the bases as a young woman, or dodging New York City traffic to make a meeting with a book publisher. She told her husband she simply was having a sad day, and she let it be as she sat watching a cardinal at the birdfeeder on a dreary December afternoon. But in time the "homesick" feeling took its place within the larger context of her life that included gratitude for the joys that remained—outside her window, a red splash of color against a background of gray. Later that evening, she spoke of plans of visiting her daughter in Chicago and taking the brace with her. This time she would be walking the boulevards of the Windy City, perhaps at a slower and more mindful pace than she had negotiated the streets of New York, but arm in arm with her daughter and with no particular place to go.

A Connection with Nature

From a mother who was a former softball star to a Zen poet who was a peace activist, there are many teachers along the way whose lessons are available to us, if for a moment we can quiet the chatter of our minds and empty ourselves of our notions of how we think life ought to be. Jack also knew a great teacher, but his fight with MS had for a time obscured her wisdom. But Nature hadn't abandoned her student; she remained of and around Jack like "the day-blind stars waiting with their light" (Berry 1998).

The foundations of psychological treatment are best served when patients discover their personal way through coming to know their own experience and not necessarily the preconceived notions of their therapists. Jack had been an avid outdoorsman, and his love of nature would provide a central theme around which his therapist could help him reconnect with the meaningful elements of his life and find his way. This psychotherapy process would be the foundation for an attitude of mind that then could consider, in an active and engaged way, specific techniques and strategies for working with neurocognitive challenges.

Wendell Berry is a poet and farmer who knows the refuge that nature once again could provide Jack, or any of us caught up in the sound-bite world of glitz and anxiety.

> When despair for the world grows in me
> and I wake in the night at the least sound
> in fear of what my life and my children's lives may be
> I go and lie down where the wood drake
> rests in his beauty on the water, and the great heron feeds.
> I come into the peace of wild things
> who do not tax their lives with forethought
> of grief. I come into the presence of still water.
> And I feel above me the day-blind stars
> waiting with their light. For a time
> I rest in the grace of the world, and am free.
>
> —Wendell Berry, "The Peace of Wild Things" (1998)

A Glimpse of the Therapy Process

To develop an attitude of mind that could serve as a foundation for treatment and for living with the uncertainty of MS, an initial step in psychotherapy would be helping Jack recognize that elements of a way did not have to be newly learned because they already existed in those moments in his life when he experienced peace and contentment. Once Jack could reconnect with his personal experience and see its relationship to the different parts of a way, he would be in a better position to translate these elements into an active engagement with the challenges that faced him.

Sometimes when life with a neurological condition calls upon a person to deal with pain and loss, it is best to include some time to touch the positive. And so Jack was invited to help his therapist come to know aspects of his life that had brought him joy, and in doing so, discover the wisdom of his own experience. Their conversation went something like this:

Therapist: *I was thinking about the day we first met when you told me how bad you felt when you had a hard time showing Josie how to tie a fishing knot.*

Jack: *Yeah. My hands just weren't working right, and having her see that made it worse.*

Therapist: *You were focusing so hard on trying to teach her about a part of life that meant a lot to you.*

Jack: *Yeah, I felt like MS was robbing me again just like it did at work, and the harder I tried, the worse it got.*

Therapist: *Right. But you're not the kind of guy who gives up. If you felt you were being robbed, you were going to fight back, but forcing it just wasn't going to help.*

Jack: *I know, but I just didn't see any other options.*

Therapist: *Sometimes we push extra hard when there is something important at stake.*

Jack: *What do you mean?*

Therapist: *Well, like your job. And with Josie, being her dad and doing something together. Maybe teaching her to tie the fishing knot was part of something bigger.*

Jack: *How so?*

Therapist: *I remember your telling me that you release most of the fish you catch. What's the sense of catching them if you're going to let them go?*

Jack: *You're missing the point.*

Therapist: *What's the point?*

Jack: *Going fishing is about more than catching fish. Sure it's great to hook into a big one, and it's even better to watch Josie reel one in, but that's only part of it. It's a whole lot of things like getting up before dawn, sipping hot cocoa as we drive to the lake, setting up our tackle, launching the boat—best of all, having time with Josie.*

Therapist: *Sounds like you wouldn't want to miss any part of it.*

Jack: *That's right because it's all part of it* . . . (a smile brightened Jack's face and he began to laugh). *I'm onto you doc.; I think I know where you're going.*

Therapist: *Where's that?*

Jack: *Tying the clinch knot was never the main thing, it was having time with Josie and teaching her how to do it—like we've been talking, just one part of something bigger. Like MS being part of life, but not all of life. Like the other pieces we've been talking about the past few weeks—being there in the moment so that I'm not so stuck in the past or worried about the future. That's the thing with fishing—my mind is not at the job, and most of the time, it's not even with MS*

Therapist: *It looks like a lot of the pieces we have been talking about have been a part of your experience for some time, but maybe your battle with MS kept you from seeing that they were still there and available to guide your way.*

Jack: *I guess they never really went away.*

Therapist: *Just needed to be reawakened. Nature can do that sometime.*

Jack: *I know what you mean.*

Continuing Treatment and Living Life: Finding a Way Back Home

Jack continued in psychotherapy for some time. His treatment expanded to incorporate mindfulness approaches for working with difficult emotions, developing strategies for dealing with cognitive limitations that had been compromising his work performance, and eventually considering job options that would be better suited for him. Jack ultimately left his job with the construction company and began working at Ed's Rod and Gun—a local sporting goods store where he had been a customer for years. This opportunity had the makings of a right match, but for a while Jack remained a bit cautious, remembering the failure of his last job change. Even though this new situation tapped into his strengths and minimized demands on his cognitive weaknesses, success wasn't guaranteed. Jack would remain actively involved in making this new job work—this time not by forcing the solution, but by maintaining his balance. With time, the cognitive tools of making lists to prompt memory and using a day planner to organize his activities became part of his daily routine. Like most of us, he wasn't immune to slipping into habitual patterns of thought that disconnect us from our present experience and engagement with life; but Jack had discovered *A Way* to guide himself back. Calling upon his wilderness experiences and working with one customer at a time, Jack now introduced newcomers to outdoor adventures. He was no longer behind the wheel of a pick-up, supervising construction projects; but he was back home.

WORKING WITH PAINFUL EMOTIONS

For Jack and many other patients living with neurological conditions, a shift in attitude of mind guided by the elements of a way and mindfulness can provide an essential foundation for dealing with the losses and uncertainties that come with the winds of change. The approach also offers "tools," as Jack called the methods, for working with painful emotions.

The emotional disturbances seen with neurological conditions can reflect a complex interplay of primary effects associated with the pathophysiology of an illness and secondary effects that are psychological reactions to symptoms, limitations, loss, and uncertainty. Such complexity calls for openness to a range of treatment options that are best suited to a patient's unique set of needs and circumstances, and flexibility to adapt to changes in a patient's condition over time. Pharmacological options are frequently used to address emotional disturbances that are primary effects of a condition, such as symptoms of depression and anxiety that can accompany stroke, Parkinson's disease, and multiple sclerosis; or the disinhibition, impulsivity, and irritability that are seen with frontal lobe involvement in traumatic brain injury. Secondary emotional effects are no less common and represent reactions to illness—that interaction between long-standing personality and new adaptive challenges. The co-occurrence of primary emotional effects with secondary psychological reactions can magnify disturbances in mood and behavior as can be seen with multiple sclerosis. In other situations, there may be a delayed onset of reactive mood disturbance such as late-onset depression that is common with traumatic brain injury (Jorge et al. 1993).

Our aims in psychotherapy with neuropsychological challenges are to reduce suffering by addressing symptoms and maladaptive behavior patterns, and to promote a reengagement with life as it is now and as it continues to unfold. We approach our aims through expanding our patients' adaptive possibilities. By increasing their repertoire of psychological resources we hope to counter reactive psychological patterns that fuel secondary painful emotions and exacerbate primary psychological effects. Countering reactive psychological patterns—what Pema Chödrön calls "interrupting the momentum to fixation" (Chödrön 2004)—is a key element in working with painful emotions, and the elements of a way and mindfulness approaches are the adaptive possibilities we invite our patients to consider.

Depression

Symptoms of depression are common to many neurological conditions. Multiple sclerosis has a lifetime prevalence of major depression between 25%–50% (Minden and Schiffer 1990). Depression is seen in 25% of patients in acute post-traumatic brain injury (Cummings and Mega 2003), and delayed onset depression is common. Between one-third and two-thirds of patients with stroke struggle with depression and difficulty in social adjustment (Eslinger, Parkinson, and Shamay 2002). Depression is common in subcortical conditions where 50% of patients with Parkinson's disease will manifest depressive symptoms of varying severity (Cummings and Mega 2003). Patients with cortical dementias such as Alzheimer's disease may show less severe depression than those with subcortical conditions, but the prevalence of depressive symptoms is still high and seen in approximately 40% of patients (Cummings and Mega 2003).

Depression is a multidimensional syndrome and disturbance in mood is a hallmark characteristic. Depressive reactions to loss, compromised functioning, future uncertainty can include sadness, guilt, feelings of worthlessness, and loss of interest in what were once pleasurable activities—essentially a loss of interest in life. Depression can exacerbate cognitive problems associated with neurological conditions and compromise active participation in treatment and rehabilitation.

Cognitive models of emotional disorders assert how we think has a major effect on our mood and behavior (Beck 1976). In their seminal work in developing a mindfulness-based cognitive therapy for depression, Segal, Williams, and Teasdale (2002) discuss the other direction of the equation: how depressed mood can affect thinking in terms of promoting negative biased thought, and how people who are or who have been depressed are particularly vulnerable to react to small changes in mood with large changes in negative thinking, which renders them susceptible to deepening depression or relapse. This formulation is an interesting counterpoint to Fredrickson's (2001) broaden-and-build theory of positive emotions that asserts positive emotions also have an effect on thinking but in a different direction. Specifically, positive emotions expand attention in ways that are flexible and open to new information; furthermore, they fuel psychological resilience, thus increasing capacities to deal with current and future stress. Our approach in working with neuropsychological challenges incorporates both perspectives: countering reactive negative thoughts and cultivating positive emotions.

Let's recap the attitude of mind perspective and consider some applications for depression associated with neuropsychological challenges.

- Our psychotherapy aims of reducing suffering and promoting an active engagement with life are reciprocal processes/goals that build upon each other.
- These goals are effected by changing our relationship to adversity. This change promotes an active and ongoing process of acceptance of life as it is.
- The practice of mindfulness meditation develops a foundation of awareness to counter reactive psychological patterns that manifest in how we feel, think, and relate to others.
- The practice of mindfulness meditation also cultivates capacities to live in the present moment, which promotes an engagement with life as it is now.
- The five elements of a way are reminders that guide efforts in changing our relationship to adversity and in reengaging in life.
- The attitude of mind perspective develops coping resources that cultivate positive emotions which in turn may undo the after-effects of negative emotions and build resilience to deal with current and future stress.

Depressive reactions associated with neuropsychological challenges frequently include painful attachments to what has been lost; sadness and hopelessness; feelings of worthlessness, self-recrimination and guilt; and a lack of interest and involvement in life. We want to expand our patients' adaptive resources for dealing with the adversities that fuel depression, and with the elements of a way and mindfulness meditation we offer possibilities for transformation.

Depression is often accompanied by narrowed cognitive perspective and judgmental attitude, especially regarding the self. We ask our patients as best they can to suspend judgment and maintain an *open mind* as we consider factors that contribute to their suffering. In the initial stages of therapy, patients may be supported by the therapist's hopeful perspective as they begin to learn about the nature of depression and the possibilities for transformation. Patients are encouraged to adopt an *active orientation* in whatever way best suits their circumstances, and in doing so they begin to counter the passive resignation and hopelessness that can accompany depression. We cultivate a *present-moment awareness* infused with gratitude for what is positive in life to counter painful attachments to the past and fearful anticipation of the future. We place psychotherapy within a *process perspective* where a "goal" is developing an attitude of mind that views acceptance and change as an ongoing process of living rather than an achieved end. We practice a *balanced view* to counter depression's reactive patterns of focusing on the negative to the exclusion of the positive, having unrealistic expectations, getting caught in rigid either-or propositions, and predicting the future by imagining the worse.

With mindfulness meditation, we help our patients maintain an awareness of reactive thought patterns that fuel depression. Mindfulness increases their capacity to "interrupt the momentum to fixation" that can rigidify into unrealistic expectations, negative self-judgments, and painful attachments to the past. We try to help our patients understand how the suffering of painful emotions is compounded by getting carried away with a storyline (i.e., negative thoughts prompted by depressed mood), or by trying to push away painful feelings. By becoming aware of their reactive tendencies, our patients interrupt negative momentum and take a first important step in changing their relationship to depression. We practice pausing to notice, suspending criticism, and returning to the present moment with our breath as an anchor to the here and now. Painful emotions may not be eradicated; but with continuing practice, reactivity is replaced by stability and our patients are better able to tolerate affective storms and find stillness in the waves. In the process of bringing mindful attention to the activities of daily living, our patients place painful emotion within a larger context of a life being lived; and cultivate the adaptive coping resources of positive reappraisal, problem-focused coping, and infusing ordinary events with positive meaning. Such efforts need not be complicated or elaborate, because the accomplishment is in bringing care and attention to the activity of the present moment, and the outcome is the cultivation of positive emotions that counter painful affect and fuel resilience. Sometimes the simple act of caring for another life—a pet, a potted plant—can help counter negative self-preoccupations with loss, vulnerability, and dependency on others; and invite our patients to once again take their place in a larger life context of giving and receiving.

Anxiety

Anxiety often accompanies neurological conditions and frequently co-occurs with depression. Anxiety is among the symptoms of postconcussion syndrome that complicate depression in patients with traumatic brain injury (Lezak et al. 2004). Nearly half of patients with multiple sclerosis can experience a painful emotional complex—so-called subsyndromal distress—that includes symptoms of anxiety and depression that may not meet criteria for major depression or anxiety disorder, but nevertheless can cause considerable psychological distress (Feinstein and Feinstein 2001). Post-stroke anxiety co-occurs with depression, and symptoms of generalized anxiety disorder are seen in patients hospitalized for stroke (Castillo, Schultz, and Robinson 1995). Anxiety commonly is seen with depression in subcortical conditions like Parkinson's disease (Cummings and Mega 2003), and anxiety can be part of a complex of emotional disruption that accompanies cortical dementia of Alzheimer's disease.

Symptoms of anxiety are pervasive in our fast-paced society that can feel as though it is spinning dizzyingly out of control. We know the symptom profile well through our work with patients in psychotherapy, and perhaps even through our own experience—feeling restless, keyed up, or on edge; being easily fatigued, having difficulties concentrating, being irritable, experiencing muscle tension, and having problems with sleep. And then there is "worry," the defining feature of generalized anxiety disorder and the frequent companion of many people living with neurological disorders, their loved ones, and caretakers. Illusions of certainty, if not shattered, are mightily challenged by neurological conditions that magnify the reality that everything changes and uncertainty is a fact of life. Acceptance of this fact is more frequently an ongoing process than a once and for all phenomenon, and it involves coming to terms with worry.

The attempt of our patients and their families to steady themselves in the disequilibrium of uncertainty often involves trying to bring some degree of certainty back into their lives. This can be a tricky proposition. Efforts at problem-focused coping such as learning about a neurological condition can reduce uncertainty (i.e., by expanding awareness and knowledge) and provide a foundation for active involvement in treatment. On the other hand, efforts to reduce uncertainty by predicting the future, albeit a negative one, with worry (i.e., by creating an illusion of certainty) are counterproductive and ultimately lead to more anxiety and fear. In helping our patients change their relationship to uncertainty, we expand their options for dealing with anxiety and fear. Our observation of the ability of neurological patients to profit from an approach that incorporates an acceptance of uncertainty perspective and mindfulness techniques has parallels with recent developments in the treatment of generalized anxiety disorder that integrate mindfulness/ acceptance-based approaches with existing cognitive-behavioral models (Roemer and Orsillo 2002).

Similar to our efforts with depression, working with anxiety involves dealing with reactive patterns and "interrupting the momentum to fixation," which in this situation is the reactive pattern of worry. Let's consider some steps that may be helpful to our patients.

- We start by inviting our patients to maintain an *open mind* as they learn—to the best of their abilities and without self-judgment—about the nature of anxiety and their capacities to interrupt reactive patterns of worry.
- We encourage an *active orientation* in which our patients learn first to recognize reactive worry tendencies, and then take action by refocusing their attention with a breathing relaxation exercise, followed by reengaging in the present moment with mindfulness.
- Coming back to the *present moment* is the antidote to being carried away in a storyline about the future—worry. We can come back to the present moment by any one of the several avenues: returning to our breath, or perhaps by bringing awareness to sense perception such as the sense of our body—alive, sitting in a chair with feet touching the floor and hands resting calmly in the lap.
- In interrupting reactive patterns that otherwise would perpetuate distressing feelings, we work with our patients in developing a *process perspective* by first noting a distressing thought or feeling—neither pushing it away nor being carried away by it—and then letting it pass.
- We emphasize a *balanced view* in which our patients come to *accept* uncertainty but *change* their relationship to adversity.
- With the practice of *mindfulness,* our patients become less susceptible to the reactive tendencies that would lead to more suffering and painful emotion, and they also reengage with living through infusing ordinary events with positive meaning.

AN ADJUNCT TO OTHER TREATMENT MODALITIES

The attitude of mind perspective also can provide a helpful foundation for our patients' involvements in other treatment modalities. The cognitive and physical challenges associated with neurological conditions often call for our patients to participate in neurorehabilitative programs that may include cognitive/speech therapy, occupational therapy, and physical therapy. These efforts are aimed at improving adaptive abilities, but the therapies themselves bring attention to functions that have been compromised. An open mind and suspension of self-judgment are essential if our patients are to be active participants in expanding their adaptive options while simultaneously confronting their limitations and painful emotions that accompany them.

Through their practice with the five elements and mindfulness meditation, patients are developing the resilience to deal with frustrations, and the capacities for focusing their attention with present-moment awareness on therapeutic activities that capitalize on reorganizational plasticity of the brain. One such approach is Constraint-Induced Movement Therapy, or CI therapy, which has been shown to be effective in improving adaptive functioning in patients with motor deficits associated with mild to moderately severe stroke (Taub 2004). Essentially CI therapy involves training by a shaping procedure of the more affected arm, and using additional behavioral techniques (e.g., behavioral contracts, daily home diary, home practice exercises, problem solving, and less affected limb restraint) to effect transfer of treatment gains from the therapeutic setting to the home. Although use of less affected arm restraints (e.g., protective safety mitt) has been part of the approach, Edward Taub—who developed CI therapy—has noted the common factor for success appears to be repeatedly practicing use of the paretic arm and not necessarily the use of an affected arm restraint (Taub 2004).

CI therapy has been extended to successfully treat a number of other conditions (Taub 2004), including arm use deficits in persons with traumatic brain injury (Taub, Uswatte, and Pidikiti 1999). The potential for enhancing beneficial effects of cortical adaptive plasticity also provides a neurobiological rationale for rehabilitation therapies aimed at other neurological conditions like multiple sclerosis (Reddy et al. 2002). In commenting on the range of treatments that incorporate principles from CI therapy, Taub (2004) described "an emerging picture of a very plastic adult human brain that appears to keep reorganizing itself to adjust to the environmental demands placed on it." This is a compelling proposition for psychotherapy because it points to the inherent reciprocity between brain functioning and behavior. Our thoughts, emotions, and actions—our behavioral repertoire—are manifestations of brain activity, and reciprocally they also influence brain organization and function. Psychotherapy has been shown to have demonstrable positive effects on behavior, and there now is an increasing body of evidence that shows the impact psychological interventions have on brain functioning (Gabbard 1998), and specifically the effects mindfulness meditation approaches have on brain organization and symptoms of neurological illness. Davidson et al. (2003) have demonstrated that mindfulness meditation has an effect on brain electrical activity by producing increases in relative left-sided anterior activation that are associated with reductions in anxiety and negative affect and increases in positive affect. Mills and Allen (2000) have shown mindfulness of movement training can maximize physical and psychological functioning, and be a helpful method of symptom management for people with multiple sclerosis.

Let's consider an example of the attitude of mind approach providing a supportive foundation for interventions based on the principles of CI therapy and adaptive plasticity of the brain. These guidelines were incorporated into weekly psychotherapy with a patient whose left-sided motor functioning had been compromised. She had begun psychotherapy before interventions based on CI therapy were initiated, and she therefore had the advantage of a beginning foundation in mindfulness meditation practice that would support her involvement in this new therapeutic effort.

- Practice with an *open and nonjudgmental mind*. Our language can shape our experience, so rather than refer to your left arm and hand as "the bad one," let's just try a shift in attitude and bring some loving attention and care to the arm that needs help in getting stronger.
- Your *active involvement* is needed to transfer the gains you are making in therapy to your everyday life. Your right arm will have a tendency to take over as it had been doing, but with ongoing practice you will become more aware of that tendency. You will be able to notice it, and shift your attention to put energy into the effort of your left arm doing the task. You will be working with your brain's capacity for reorganization.
- Bring your mindful attention to the *present moment* as you work with you left arm and hand, perhaps in lifting a shoe or holding a fork. If frustrations arise, just note them as you have been doing in your meditation practice, let them pass, and bring your attention back to your breath. Then with mindfulness, begin again working with your left hand.
- Remind yourself that this practice is an *unfolding process*. Capitalizing on the brain's capacity for reorganization takes time, but your mindful effort can make a difference, and every moment of practice helps. Like drops from a faucet filling a bucket—it may not seem like anything is happening, but the bucket does fill with water.
- Let your practice be guided by a *balanced view*. We are working to bring your left hand into a balanced relationship with your right. This will not be the familiar balance of the past but a new and evolving balance in which your left side continues to participate as best it can in concert with your right—not pushing to exhaustion and frustration, but also not passively allowing the right side to upset the balance. With practice you will notice when the balance is shifting to the right. When that happens, there is no need to criticize yourself; just note that the balance has shifted, bring your attention back to your center—your breath, and with mindfulness bring your left side back into the activity.

THE ESSENTIAL FOUNDATION:
THE PSYCHOTHERAPY RELATIONSHIP

The core feature of psychotherapy is the relationship between the patient and therapist, and this relational context is the essential foundation for therapeutic intervention and personal transformation. We have been discussing ways in which the attitude of mind perspective may serve as a foundation for specific psychological interventions aimed at addressing distressing emotions and placing the challenges of illness within the larger context of a living. This perspective reflects both a therapeutic sensibility, as well as a set of guiding points for patients that are intended to expand their adaptive possibilities. The therapist's sensibility—attitude of mind—provides a bridge of hope for patients as they grieve the losses of what was and consider possibilities of now, and the carrier of this transformative process is the psychotherapy relationship. Given its primacy as a foundational element for treatment, we will conclude our discussion with a focus on relational aspects of psychotherapy in working with patients living with neuropsychological challenges.

Characteristics of the Relationship

Patients who are struggling with the losses and adaptive challenges of neurological conditions more often than not feel overwhelmed, bewildered, and disoriented. Their psychological coping resources are strained and their adaptive reserves may be limited further by neuropsychological compromises. These conditions call for a flexible psychotherapeutic attitude and more active involvement by the therapist than may be the case in traditional psychotherapy approaches. In many ways, the nature of the psychotherapy relationship with a neurological patient shares elements in common with supportive psychodynamic psychotherapy (Ursano, Sonnenberg, and Lazar 2004), where the goal is less change-oriented and more directed toward maximizing functioning. Within this framework, an atmosphere of trust and safety is created by the therapist's regular availability and mindful attention to the patient's experience. The therapist's sensibility represents hope not as an attachment to the past, but as openness to the possibilities in the present. Naturally the therapist's supportive activity is a matter of degree depending on the needs and circumstances of a particular patient, but in general the relationship to the patient is "more one of a guide and mentor" who creates a "holding environment" within which help is provided in organizing experiences and exploring alternatives (Ursano, Sonnenberg, and Lazar 2004).

Transference

Simply stated, transference is experiencing another person (i.e., thinking or feeling, or behaving toward another) as a figure from one's past.

Although the intensity of transference may vary considerably, I would suggest that transference is ubiquitous regardless of one's theoretical orientation because our current experiences and interactions are affected by past conditioning and learning; or if one prefers, by internalized object representations of which we are not completely aware. As maladaptive interpersonal interaction patterns manifest in the present, transference can be both an impediment in developing and sustaining relationships, as well as an opportunity for transformation within a therapy relationship. The transformative potential is fueled by our patients' attempts to master or resolve conflictual states by repeating and drawing others into a dynamic reenactment of earlier traumatic or developmentally arresting experiences. A classic example is the female hysterical personality creating a triadic relationship with a married man. If her motivations are simply ascribed to supplanting the wife and winning the affections of the husband, then her complexity and desire for mastery are minimized, for her deeper motivation may be to awaken the wife (mother surrogate) from her passive resignation, and to elicit from the husband (father surrogate) a responsible attitude that was missing in her developmental years (Mueller and Aniskiewicz 1986).

Neuropsychological challenges do not preclude the emergence of transference phenomena in psychotherapy; however a patient's neuropsychological status can complicate the nature of the transference. Lewis (1999) has offered the observation that patients with frontal lobe injury, especially orbitofrontal involvement, tend to have more "chaotically shifting transferences" in contrast to patients with more posterior neurological involvement. Disruptions in executive functions associated with frontal lobe involvement can result in problems with affect and behavioral regulation that contribute to intensity and instability of the transference.

To illustrate the interaction between psychological dynamics and neurological compromises as demonstrated in different transference experiences, let's consider the cases of Bob and Randy who were in high school when they sustained brain injuries.

Bob's head trauma resulted in frontal lobe involvement that manifested in impulsive behavior, lowered frustration tolerance, affective lability, and poor behavioral control. His parents were often embroiled in conflict before his injury, and now his behaviors brought more disruption to an already strained family system. His normal developmental challenges of separation and autonomy were complicated by regulatory dysfunction associated with a frontal brain injury, and Bob's intensely conflicted emotional experiences and chaotic family dynamics would now find their way into his relationship with his psychotherapist. Bob's reckless bids for autonomy involving risky money-making schemes, alcohol use, and noncompliance with medical recommendations were often followed by dependent and regressive behaviors—all of which confused and exasperated his parents, and ultimately his therapist. He frequently would show up late or not at all for a scheduled therapy session only to appear in crisis at an unscheduled time several days later, or call the answering service with after-hour emergencies. Slowly developing steps toward progress in maintaining an organizational planner or completing class assignments were more quickly undone by what seemed like giving up and self-sabotage. Bob's attitude toward his brain injury and its consequences also suggested a diminished awareness that reflected both a psychological defense against severe narcissistic injury, and compromised insight secondary to frontal lobe dysfunction. For example, he would speak of plans of attending an elite university but saw little need to make a transition back to academics by perhaps taking a limited course load at a community college. Bob's therapist indeed came to know the frustration his parents were experiencing, but by reflecting on this "complimentary countertransference" (Racker 1974) and not reacting to it, the therapist also gained a deeper appreciation of Bob's narcissistic injury, conflicted dependency needs, and frontal-executive dysfunction, and how these factors played out in his interactions at home and subsequently in therapy. Bob's family situation mirrored his chaotic inner experience and neither he nor his parents saw a way out. Helping Bob negotiate the developmental challenges of autonomy and individuation within a dysfunctional family system, and with the added burden of a head injury, would first require bringing some organization to the chaos of his life—lending frontal executive functioning, if you will—in the form of supportive family therapy. The aim would be to provide a structured and safe holding environment for him and his parents as they attempted to appreciate and understand each other's experiences, identify maladaptive interaction patterns as they would emerge within sessions, and consider alternative ways of responding. Insight into these therapeutic possibilities emerged with Bob's therapist recognizing the factors contributing to his patient's transference, its parallel dynamics within his family situation, and its elicitation of countertransference reactions that echoed the frustrations experienced by his parents.

Randy too was in high school when he suffered his brain injury, but the neurological involvement was in the posterior aspects of his brain, leaving him with motor coordination problems that affected his speech and walking, and with residual cognitive weaknesses in processing speed, attention, and complex memory. In contrast to Bob, however, Randy was fully cooperative and engaged in his rehabilitation treatments. He also had the advantage of supportive parents who took an active part in his rehabilitation planning. Randy's dogged determination and optimistic attitude brought him the admiration of many, and at least for a time the special attention of his classmates. Like Bob, Randy also had aspirations of attending college and pursuing a professional career; but unlike Bob, he appeared aware of his limitations which seemed to push him all the more to overcome them. However, after a while, his parents and members of his rehabilitation team began to wonder if he too might have been "in denial" because he did not demonstrate the anger or sadness that might have been expected given his losses. If indeed denial or diminished awareness were operative in the early stages of Randy's recovery, it was less an issue of neurologically driven lack of insight and perhaps more a reflection of his maintaining "hope" or maybe a positive illusion that with effort he would somehow keep pace with his classmates and attain the academic and social goals they once shared. With time, however, Randy's classmates drifted away as their developmental paths took them to college, new relationships, and exciting challenges. Randy simply couldn't keep pace and was being left behind. Mounting frustrations began to take the place of the determination that once had fueled his efforts and garnered the admiration of others. He became increasingly sullen and seemed to be pushing away his family and a diminishing circle of friends, who in turn were feeling more and more helpless in the face of his depression, anger, and withdrawal. What his psychotherapist had once considered a positive working relationship now took on an angry and disappointed tone that reflected Randy's painful inner turmoil, and the therapist was now challenged to maintain "hope" amidst Randy's expressions of hopelessness and suicidality. The therapist's coming to know—on an experiential level— Randy's hopelessness and frustration (concordant countertransference, Racker 1974) without reacting to it, but instead holding the distressing experience as if in a supportive vessel, was a critical point in psychotherapy. Unproductive reactions to such concordant countertransference might have included the therapist defending against his own feelings of helplessness by reprojecting his frustration back to Randy and encouraging him to try harder and reengage with his past positive outlook. Instead, by providing a space for the patient to have the emotional experience (i.e., fear, rage, sadness, despair) or stated otherwise—to be with the patient as the patient is with his or her experience of the moment, the therapist creates the necessary conditions for developing a new kind of hope (i.e., an identification with the therapist's hope) in the possibilities of life as it is now and not as we wish it might have been. Perhaps Randy's earlier version of hope provided the necessary support to absorb the trauma of his functional losses at so early an age, but the process of letting go—that was necessary for his continuing growth—can touch upon despair before a new face of hope can be seen. The therapy relationship "contains" this despair and provides the bridge to new hope. Even in the midst of a stormy transference, the patient may continue to rely on the therapist as a carrier of hope, something akin to the "containing-transcendent" transference described by Young-Eisendrath (2003) that "is filled with the hope of transforming one's suffering and one's life."

Countertransference

Definitions of countertransference and its varied manifestations in psychotherapy have undergone revisions and modifications since the term was introduced by Freud (Racker 1974). For the purposes of our discussion, we will adopt a more recent conceptualization that considers countertransference as describing "nearly all emotional reactions of the therapist to the patient in the therapeutic setting" (Ursano, Sonnenberg, and Lazar 2004). Like the transference of a patient, a therapist's countertransference can be both an impediment to progress as well as a powerful means of understanding a patient's experience and its impact on others. In working with patients whose lives often have been dramatically altered by a neurological condition, the potential for intense countertransference reactions looms large. The key to working with such reactions is first to recognize that they will inevitably occur, and they are not necessarily indications of lack of skill or personal inadequacy. Awareness of the factors within one's own history or current circumstances that may affect reactions to patients also is an ongoing necessity, and this attention is sharpened by an openness to one's experience as it may be cultivated by personal psychotherapy, consultations with colleagues, or other awareness practices like meditation. Finally, transference-countertransference interactions are as varied as the personalities and life circumstances of patients and their therapists; yet some common features do emerge, and being attuned to these possibilities can provide a framework that informs our understanding of our patients' experiences and guides our interventions.

We already have alluded to Racker's (1974) distinction between concordant and complimentary countertransference in the preceding clinical vignettes. Let's underscore these dimensions because their operations offer opportunities for appreciating patients' experiences in ways that words may not communicate, as well as offering an experiential perspective on our patients' internalized self-object relationships and interaction dynamics with current caregivers. In concordant countertransference, the therapist experiences or identifies with the emotional experiences of the patient. These feelings may not have arisen fully into consciousness in a way that the patient can verbally articulate, and so this countertransference dimension involves a critical communicative function for patients whose inner experiences have not been acknowledged either by themselves or by significant others in their lives.

Such is often the case with feelings of anger, hopelessness, and despair that can accompany the losses and challenges of neurological conditions. The process of grieving such losses has no specific timetable, and it is prudent to exercise caution in "attempting to facilitate an unnatural, forced progression through generic stages of grief when working with brain-injured individuals" (Coetzer 2004). In fact, patients may persist in trying to communicate their painful inner experiences to others until such experiences are acknowledged, and this persistence may take the form of creating in the other an experiential counterpart of that which has not been "heard" or validated. If the therapist reacts defensively to this concordant experience and suggests for example that the patient is caught in a prolonged attachment to grief, then the therapist has identified with a significant person in the patient's life (complimentary countertransference) whom the patient may feel is blaming or not understanding. Through the operations of transference-countertransference dynamics there exists the potential for a patient to elicit from a therapist either a reaction that is yet another repetition of a failed encounter (a transference-countertransference interlock), or an emphatic understanding that maintains the momentum of therapy. However the "concordant" experience or empathic link with someone who has lost a version of themselves that cannot be recaptured can be more than unsettling because it touches upon a primal vulnerability about the integrity of the self—as Freud wondered, "What is one to do on the day when thoughts cease to flow and the proper words won't come" (Bloom 1994). Our patients' experiences with loss, disability, and mental impairment can awaken our worse fears; and magnify the reality of impermanence and uncertainty in our lives. Reacting to such feelings defensively solidifies an entrapment in fear that serves neither therapist nor patient; but bringing attention to the emergence of these feelings—holding them in awareness—can forge an empathic link with a patient and reawaken for the therapist an appreciation of the immediacy of life (remember Jane Kenyon's poem "Otherwise" in the first chapter).

Sometimes our work with patients also can stimulate voices from our past, or perhaps bring to the surface present-day conflicts. A psychiatry resident was treating symptoms of depression in an elderly female patient who had Parkinson's disease. Antidepressant medication seemed to have provided some relief, but the patient frequently left the resident with a feeling of being vaguely dissatisfied with the progress of their work together ("I guess there really aren't many other options and I'm just going to have to live with this"). The resident left her sessions with the patient often feeling defeated, inadequate to the task, and thinking she was a disappointment to the patient whom she thought would have fared far better with a more experienced psychotherapist.

In discussing the case in supervision, the resident recognized that her patient was about the same age as her own mother for whom she could never do enough to elicit approval for "being okay as I am." This resident had superlative academic credentials and achievements yet these accomplishments just weren't sufficient—at least not yet—to sustain her budding professional confidence and self-acceptance, especially in the face of a daunting challenge like Parkinson's disease for which the patient's medical team was doing all that could be done. In exploring the case further, the resident and her supervisor considered the possibility that the patient may have felt defeated and disappointed in herself, feeling as though she were no longer good enough given the compromises in functioning with which she was now living. Perhaps what sounded like a pessimistic statement of resignation ("I guess there really aren't many other options and I'm just going to have to live with this") belied the untouched grief that if experienced might open the way for other options and a different way of living. The resident was able to consider that the patient may have communicated her own experience of inadequacy and not feeling whole through stimulating similar feelings in her (concordant countertransference). She also recognized that by defending against her feelings of inadequacy by redoubling her efforts to try harder—a familiar pattern for her—perhaps by more aggressively treating the patient's depression with a medication adjustment or by transferring her to a more seasoned therapist, she would have missed the opportunity to provide the therapeutic context within which the patient could experience her grief and reclaim her wholeness.

Reflecting on her countertransference reactions in a nonjudgmental way allowed the resident to appreciate the painful defeat her patient was experiencing while also understanding how feelings about her own life circumstances may have precluded "hearing" her patient's message. With her expanded awareness the resident could now use her reactions to form an empathic link to her patient, and provide the context for the patient to expand her own awareness and allow for the expression of feelings that likely were fueling her depression yet had remained untouched.

A Closing Note

The attitude of mind perspective can inform psychotherapies with patients whose challenges are not necessarily neurologically based, however the perspective largely evolved from my work with neurological patients and I think it is particularly well-suited to the needs for openness and flexibility in therapy that neuropsychological challenges often require. I consider the perspective a foundational element in psychotherapy for neuropsychological challenges because it can inform a therapeutic attitude, as well as provide a framework and methods that patients and families may use as they attempt to reorient lives that have been disrupted by a neurological condition. However like any other psychotherapy approach, the therapist's sensibility and the interventions offered to patients are brought to life when therapist and patient encounter each other in the psychotherapy relationship, which for neurological patients is a bridge of hope and remains the essential foundation for their treatment.

> In the difficult are the friendly forces, the hands that work on us.
> Right in the difficult we must have our joys, our happiness, our dreams:
> there, against the depth of this background they stand out,
> there for the first time we see how beautiful they are.

—Rainer Maria Rilke (1947, 77–78)

REFERENCES AND READINGS

Beck, A. T. 1976. *Cognitive therapy and the emotional disorders.* New York: International Universities Press.

Berry, Wendell. 1998. *The selected poems of Wendell Berry.* Washington, D.C.: Counterpoint.

Bloom, Harold. 1994. Freud: A Shakespearean Reading. In *The Western Canon.* New York: Riverhead Books.

Castillo, C. S., S. K. Schultz, and R. G. Robinson. 1995. Clinical correlates of early-onset and late-onset poststroke generalized anxiety. *American Journal of Psychiatry* 152 (8): 1174–1179.

Chödrön, Pema. 2004. A Bodhichitta Practice. *Shambhala Sun,* May 2004, 32.

Coetzer, B. R. 2004. Grief, self-awareness, and psychotherapy following brain injury. *Illness, Crisis and Loss* 12 (2): 171–186.

Cummings, Jeffrey L., and Michael S. Mega. 2003. *Neuropsychiatry and behavioral neuroscience.* New York: Oxford University Press.

Davidson, R. J., J. Kabat-Zinn, J. Schumacher, M. Rosenkranz, D. Muller, S. F. Santorelli, F. Urbanowski, A. Harrington, K. Bonus, and J. F. Sheridan. 2003. Alterations in brain and immune function produced by mindfulness meditation. *Psychosomatic Medicine* 65 (4): 564–570.

Dylan, Bob. 2004. *Bob Dylan Lyrics 1962–2001.* New York: Simon & Schuster.

Eslinger, P. J., K. Parkinson, and S. G. Shamay. 2002. Empathy and social-emotional factors in recovery from stroke. *Current Opinion in Neurology* 15 (1): 91–97.

Feinstein, A., and K. Feinstein. 2001. Depression associated with multiple sclerosis. Looking beyond diagnosis to symptom expression. *Journal of Affective Disorders* 66 (2–3): 193–198.

Fredrickson, Barbara. 2001. The role of positive emotions in positive psychology: The broaden-and-build theory of positive emotions. *American Psychologist* 56 (3): 218–226.

Gabbard, Glen. 1998. The impact of psychotherapy on the brain. *Psychiatric Times,* September.

Hamill, Sam, and Jerome P. Seaton. 2004. *The poetry of Zen, Shambhala library.* Boston: Shambhala.

Hanh, Thich Nhat. 2001. *Thich Nhat Hanh.* Edited by R. Ellsbery, Modern Spiritual Masters Series. Maryknoll, NY: Orbis Books.

Jorge, R. E., R. G. Robinson, S. V. Arndt, A. W. Forrester, F. Geisler, and S. E. Starkstein. 1993. Comparison between acute- and delayed-onset depression following traumatic brain injury. *Journal of Neuropsychiatry and Clinical Neurosciences* 5 (1): 43–49.

Lewis, Lisa. 1999. Transference and countertransference in psychotherapy with adults having traumatic brain injury. In *Psychotherapeutic Intervention for Adults with Brain Injury or Stroke: A Clinician's Treatment Resource*, edited by K. G. Langer, L. Laatsch, and L. Lewis. Madison, CT: Psychosocial Press.

Lezak, Muriel D., Diane B. Howieson, David W. Loring, H. Julia Hannay, and Jill S. Fischer. 2004. *Neuropsychological assessment*. 4th ed. New York: Oxford University Press.

Mills, N., and J. Allen. 2000. Mindfulness of movement as a coping strategy in multiple sclerosis. A pilot study. *General Hospital Psychiatry* 22 (6): 425–431.

Minden, S. L., and R. B. Schiffer. 1990. Affective disorders in multiple sclerosis. Review and recommendations for clinical research. *Archives of Neurology* 47 (1): 98–104.

Mueller, W. J. 1973. *Avenues to understanding: The dynamics of therapuetic interactions*. Englewood Cliffs, NJ: Prentice-Hall.

Mueller, William J., and Albert S. Aniskiewicz. 1986. *Psychotherapeutic intervention in hysterical disorders*. Northvale, NJ: Aronson.

Racker, Heinrich. 1974. *Transference and countertransference*. London: Hogarth Press.

Reddy, H., S. Narayanan, M. Woolrich, T. Mitsumori, Y. Lapierre, D. L. Arnold, and P. M. Matthews. 2002. Functional brain reorganization for hand movement in patients with multiple sclerosis: Defining distinct effects of injury and disability. *Brain: A Journal of Neurology* 125: 2646–2657.

Rilke, Rainer Maria. 1947. *Selected letters of Rainer Maria Rilke*. Translated by R. F. C. Hull. London: Macmillan & Co. Ltd.

Roemer, Lizabeth, and Susan M. Orsillo. 2002. Expanding our conceptualization of and treatment for generalized anxiety disorder: Integrating mindfulness/acceptance-based approaches with existing cognitive-behavioral models. *Clinical Psychology: Science and Practice* 9 (1): 54–68.

Segal, Zindel V., J. Mark G. Williams, and John D. Teasdale. 2002. *Mindfulness-based cognitive therapy for depression: A new approach for preventing relapse*. New York: Guilford Press.

Taub, E., G. Uswatte, and R. Pidikiti. 1999. Constraint Induced Movement therapy: A new family of techniques with broad application to physical rehabilitation—A clinical review. *Journal of Rehabilitation Research and Development* 36: 237–251.

Taub, Edward. 2004. Harnessing brain plasticity through behavioral techniques to produce new treatments in neurorehabilitation. *American Psychologist* 59 (8): 692–704.

Ursano, Robert J., Stephen M. Sonnenberg, and Susan G. Lazar. 2004. *Concise guide to psychodynamic psychotherapy*. Arlington, VA: American Psychiatric Publishing, Inc.

Young-Eisendrath, Polly. 2003. Transference and transformation in Buddhism and psychoanalysis. In *Psychoanalysis and Buddhism: An unfolding dialogue*, edited by J. D. Safran. Somerville, MA: Wisdom Publications.

11

Individual Psychotherapy

It is better to know the patient who has the disease
than the disease the patient has.

—attributed to Hippocrates

People living with neuropsychological challenges may share common clinical characteristics and neurological diagnoses, but their experiences with the conditions are unique and represent a complex interplay of medical and neuropsychological factors, preexisting personality, current circumstances including family and social support, accessibility to treatment, and future perspective—hope. There is no "one size fits all" psychological treatment approach for the challenges associated with stroke, traumatic brain injury, or for that matter any of the neurological disorders we have been considering in our review. But psychotherapy with these conditions can be informed by an overarching sensibility to the experiences of people living with neuropsychological challenges, and the "attitude of mind" orientation may serve as a guiding perspective in this effort. We suggest to our patients that they change their relationship to their conditions, neither fighting the truth of what is, nor passively being a victim of their circumstances. In a similar fashion, this perspective guides our psychotherapeutic efforts by not forcing methods that are unsuited to our patients' circumstances, nor retreating in the face of neuropsychological challenges by considering psychological interventions inadequate to assist our patients. With this perspective as a foundation, specific therapeutic approaches are adapted to fit the particular needs and circumstances of the patient, and are modified as the therapeutic relationship evolves and the psychotherapist develops an increasing understanding of the patient's unique experience.

CONSTRAINTS AND CHALLENGES

As simple as it may sound, patients bring themselves to psychotherapy, neu-ropsychological challenges and all. The compromises with which they are living have placed constraints on how they go about their daily activities, and for many patients seeking treatment is fueled by the motivation to ac-cept the reality of these constraints and learn how to best live with them. For others, however, the process of adaptation is more arduous because their beginning treatment may be motivated initially by a desire to return to what was. Indeed, some people who have had CVAs and others with mul-tiple sclerosis still maintain employment with appropriate accommoda-tions, and individuals who have sustained mild traumatic brain injuries may return to previous jobs; but ultimately their lives have changed and liv-ing with the truth of this reality is essential to support the very adaptive strategies that often permit a return to work.

Our patients' neuropsychological challenges also are viewed as placing constraints on how we traditionally go about psychotherapy; and of course they do, but what better place to deal with the truth of our patients' experi-ence than as it manifests in the psychotherapy process. Sweeping conclu-sions miss the point if neuropsychological limitations are thought to pre-clude patients' benefiting from psychotherapy, or if traditional perspectives are considered too constrained to offer anything meaningful. Our patients' experiences with neurological illness or trauma reflect the direct conse-quences of the condition as well as their individual reaction to the condi-tions' disruptive effects on living. These neuropsychological challenges be-come our challenges to be open minded and creative in our psychotherapy methods, and above all, to be aware of expectations and how congruent they are with our patients' needs, circumstances, and abilities.

Patients' motivation to participate in psychotherapy must be matched by our ability to meet their challenges with hope and flexibility because a wide range of neuropsychological factors may influence their engaging in and benefiting from the process. Loss of an abstract attitude (Miller 1993), dis-orders in awareness (Prigatano 1999), and deficiencies in executive abilities (Pollack 2005) all challenge psychotherapy methods that rely on self-aware-ness and reflection, capacities to tolerate frustration and disturbing affect, ability to generalize from one situation to another, and transfer gains from therapy to daily living. Limitations with information processing capacity and speed may call for adaptations within a session, and deficiencies in memory can affect continuity between sessions. For some patients, disrup-tions in neuropsychological functioning may be relatively mild and they will be able to engage in psychotherapy with only minor modifications in method, perhaps to accommodate a susceptibility to information overload or processing speed deficiencies—the very weaknesses that may be compromising their work performances or management of household tasks. For other patients, however, the primary goal may be more limited but no less worthy, as in supporting coping resources and maintaining quality of life in the face of a degenerative neurological condition.

The neurological evaluation begins the diagnostic process for most of our patients by identifying the conditions that underlie their symptoms. The neuropsychological evaluation takes the diagnostic process to the next level by clarifying a patient's neuropsychological status and its impact on daily living, including participation in psychotherapy. In describing the unique manifestation of a patient's neuropsychological challenges, this procedure also is an important component in initial treatment planning. Psychotherapy then advances the unfolding "diagnostic" process as our understanding evolves from knowing the patient's condition to knowing the patient who has the condition. This evolving diagnostic process, or put another way, this coming to know the patient's experience, becomes an essential element of psychotherapeutic treatment.

PERSONALITY AND ATTITUDE OF MIND THEMES IN PSYCHOTHERAPY

We have discussed the psychotherapy relationship being the essential foundation for treatment and how the attitude of mind perspective can inform a therapeutic sensibility as well as provide a foundation for patients and families as they meet the challenge of reengaging in life with neuropsychological challenges. In reviewing the relational dynamics of psychotherapy we also touched upon the interactions of patient and therapist personalities in transference and countertransference experiences. Building upon this foundation, let's now consider how attitude of mind themes inform the beginning stages of individual psychotherapy, and then, illustrated by clinical vignettes, see how the themes may serve as a backdrop as we consider the personality dynamics of the patient and their impact on adaptation, relationships with treatment providers, and interactions with the therapist.

Open Mind

With an open mind we can see possibilities, and with possibilities there is hope. At the beginning stages of therapy it is often the therapist's hopeful attitude that provides a stabilizing foundation for patients as they develop their own hope in accepting the reality of their condition and changing their relationship to it. Drawing upon research in positive psychology (Fredrickson 2001), an open mind reflects a positive but realistic attitude that expands our awareness and allows us to see a broader array of possibilities for our patients. From this foundation we offer assistance in developing coping resources that support a reengagement with life and fuel resilience to deal with current and future stress.

Active Orientation

The therapist maintains an active orientation in psychotherapy, which is especially important during the initial stages of treatment. We start by inviting our patients to participate in a process of creating meaning from the confusion and disorientation that can be the aftermath of a neurological diagnosis; and this process begins with a clear explanation for patients and perhaps family members of "what happened." Discussing the results of a neuropsychological evaluation is often the starting point. The therapist can explain how test results reflect the patient's neurological condition and the relevance of the findings for the patient's rehabilitative treatments and daily functioning. Patients and family members are invited to consider how the findings match or sometimes do not totally represent their experience. In taking this first step of sharing their perspective of what has happened, patients begin an active engagement with the therapist that can serve as a foundation for an active reengagement with life as it is now and as it will continue to unfold.

Recognizing that goals for psychotherapy often are simply starting points and not fixed destinations, patients are invited to talk about what would be helpful to them. Their expressions of need, vulnerability, and anxiety, tinged with perhaps only a slight glimmer of hope during those initial moments, guide the therapist's responses. If the therapist's awareness has fostered a sensitivity to the patient's experience as expressed in those moments, then a helpful comment may be offered and the therapy interaction gains momentum. On the other hand, if a therapist's awareness is narrowed by a personal agenda of what constitutes effective psychological intervention for the patient's condition, then patients' communications about their experience with the condition are missed, the interactional momentum is stalled, and the therapist is left to come up with another intervention to encourage the patient to become engaged in the process. If the therapist persists on this tack, he runs the risk of treating a "concept" of the patient that reflects his own constructions (e.g., the patient is passive and reluctant to engage in the treatment), and patients indeed do become passive bystanders because their participation in the process has yet to be acknowledged. We are then contributing the very scenario we are describing, thus reinforcing our concepts but losing the patient. Patients' experiences of themselves and their world have been altered by brain dysfunction and they already feel lost, bewildered, and alone. If their challenge is to accept the reality of their conditions and learn how to best live with them, the process begins with an acceptance of their experience as it is. The therapist's ability to respond to patients' productions in a way that demonstrates an appreciation of their experiences sets the tone for acceptance, which is the prerequisite for change.

Present-Moment Awareness

An appreciation of the historical antecedents that shape our patients' personalities is essential for understanding their current experience, but psychotherapy occurs now in the present moment and this perspective is especially important with neuropsychological challenges because a patient's attachment to "what was" can forestall an engagement with "what is." And "what is" is not restricted to the neurological condition that has interrupted a life course, but reflects the larger context of the life that remains and now includes neuropsychological challenges. In psychotherapy we appreciate that a patient's attitude, feelings, and interaction at any moment can reflect the interlocking of the past experiences, current realities, and dynamics in the patient-therapist relationship. The patient's neuropsychological challenges may influence the expression of this triply charged process, but the dynamic operation is not necessarily different from that which occurs in psychotherapy with other patients.

A Clinical Vignette

A patient's neurological disability reawakened emotions related to past neglect that would manifest in conflictual feelings about vulnerability and dependency in her marriage, and would eventually find expression in her psychotherapy. During her childhood the patient had been repeatedly disappointed by the minimization of her needs and lack of support which crystalized in the memory of a time when her complaints about painful symptoms, which eventually led to serious medical complications, were met with punishment for crying and not wanting to go to school. She had grown to become an independent and self-sufficient woman whose keen sensitivity to the experiences of others belied the insensitivities she had experienced as a child. It was little surprise to those who knew her that she accepted her neurological challenges with the strength and resilience to which her family and friends had grown accustomed. At the suggestion of her neurologist, she began psychotherapy "to strengthen (her) coping resources." During an early session, she appeared more obviously dejected than was typical of her mood as she described her husband becoming frustrated with her "being distant" especially when the burden of her illness weighed heavily upon her. He complained that she seemed to "pull away" when she appeared "most vulnerable" and in need of help. She already had acknowledged not wanting to be a "burden" to her family, but she didn't think she was being distant or rejecting help either from her husband or her health care providers. If anything, she viewed herself as compliant and fully cooperative with her treatments, which indeed she was.

If the therapist focuses narrowly on the content of the patient's comments and construes the situation as reflecting her husband's need to help and her difficulty in accepting help, he may direct his efforts toward a problem occurring outside the session (i.e., a conflict in the marriage), but miss the point of what is occurring now in the present-moment therapy interaction. However, if an expanded awareness can allow for the possibility that the themes embedded in the patient's comments reflect the triply charged dynamic of past experience, current circumstances, and present-moment interaction, then the therapist can recognize that the point of this content emerging at this time in the therapy interaction is to repeat the very dynamics reflected within the content and to elicit a response from the therapist (Mueller and Aniskiewicz 1986).

In maintaining an awareness of the communicative salience of the present-moment interaction, the therapist is able to consider the message within the content; and equally important, to consider why the content is emerging now. For example, the content of the patient's productions may have been a response to what had happened just moments before in the therapy interaction (Kell and Mueller 1966). Perhaps she was feeling the press of frustrated needs for attention and support that were countered by equally strong fears of rejection. Indeed she may have been experiencing the "burden" of conflicted emotions as reflected in the themes within her comments: that is, being a burden, being vulnerable, being distant, and pulling away. If the patient is to allow herself to experience her vulnerability and have her needs responded to in a sensitive and helpful way, the therapy conditions have to be present to allow such risks to be taken.

These conditions are realized within the interaction with the therapist, and are not a given simply because the patient is engaged in psychotherapy. Moreover, the therapist's beliefs about himself as a caring and sensitive clinician are not sufficient to engender the trust necessary for the patient to risk vulnerability. Endeavoring to provide what he thinks the patient's husband has been unable to do reflects the therapist's narrow view of the meaning of the patient's production, as well as his own countertransference and ego-inflating needs. On the other hand, if the therapist is able to respond to the conflicted emotional undercurrents in the patient's productions as they manifest in the present-moment interaction, he fosters the conditions that enable the patient to risk having and expressing her experience, and therein lies the potential for transformation.

Process Perspective

Psychotherapy is an evolving process where what has occurred just moments before influences what is occurring now in the present moment, which in turn affects what's to come. The clinical vignette we just reviewed illustrates the moment to moment unfolding of the process within a therapy session that fosters the conditions necessary for a patient to risk vulnerability and reduce suffering. Another dimension of the process perspective is that we are not necessarily focused on getting somewhere with the hope that, once there, our patients are somehow better prepared to accept the consequences of a neurological condition and engage in life. Instead our goal is less a destination and more an attitude of mind that acknowledges the reality of neuropsychological challenges but places them within the larger context of a life that is available to be lived now. Engaging in the psychotherapy then is not simply preparatory for a more effective living once treatment is completed, but a moment to moment involvement in an evolving process that is both reflected in and informed by the unfolding process of a patient's living with a neurological condition. Ultimately the product of this parallel process is better preparedness, as seen in increased resilience and greater adaptive capacity, which enables patients to engage more fully in living and handle current and future stress.

A recurring theme in our work is that patients bring themselves to psychotherapy, and addressing neuropsychological challenges does not exclude the person living with them. Being diagnosed with a neurological condition can reawaken emotions related to past traumas and painful experiences; and the influences of the past as manifested in the present can affect self-care, relationships with health care providers, dynamics within a family, dealing with loss and uncertainty, and hope—that necessary element that undergirds an investment in living. Because the persisting effects of past wounds will manifest in present adaptive challenges, psychotherapy provides a twofold opportunity. In addressing current realities we also can begin a process of transforming the residuals of a painful past.

Patients may be conflicted about their experience and its expression (e.g., needs for support vs. anxiety about vulnerability), and there are multiple ways for their experience to manifest in the course of psychotherapy. We already discussed how themes embedded in the content of a patient's comments about a situation outside of therapy reflect the ongoing process of the patient-therapist interaction. Themes embedded in dream material or perhaps a poem will also reveal a patient's experience and inform the therapist of the conditions that are necessary to maintain the momentum of the therapy process.

A Clinical Vignette

A patient whose background included demanding expectations and violations of personal boundaries had ambivalent feelings about participating in the health care system where her experiences with providers during the course of her illness sometimes felt more demeaning than helpful. Her personal needs and feelings of discomfort had been discounted during her development, and she adopted a "tough girl" persona to get through the difficult times. Her past experiences with caretakers whose own agendas had taken precedence over her needs had also left her keenly sensitive to the reoccurrence of these dynamics with those with whom she was being asked to entrust with her medical care. Anticipating that when in need she would more likely experience hurt than help, her defensive posture with medical specialists could be well appreciated. However a past involvement with psychotherapy had included a trusting relationship with a psychologist who was sensitive to her experience, and this background provided an important foundation for her continuing work in therapy as she confronted the uncertainties of a future with a neurological condition.

Feelings of vulnerability and anxieties about dependency are not unusual when a neurological condition threatens independence and control. These challenges also can awaken feelings about past traumas as they did with our patient. Such reawakenings can complicate relationships with health care providers, but also provide an opportunity to address painful conflicts that have long affected self-acceptance and relationships with others. When such dynamics enter the therapy relationship, they challenge the therapist to maintain a sensitivity to the conditions that will enable the patient to experience the affect associated with past trauma and transform the experience within the context of a healing relationship. Patients will often alert the therapist about attitudes that will give rise to defense as well as the conditions that will be helpful in maintaining the momentum of the therapy process. If our responses suggest to patients that the conditions are not right for them to take additional risks, the therapy process may stall and the patient's experiences may be expressed in other ways until the message is heard.

Within the context of discussing a disappointing encounter with a doctor who seemed more preoccupied with the accuracy of his diagnosis than with her feelings about the diagnosis, the patient introduced a poem by Billy Collins.

> All you have to do is listen to the way a man
> sometimes talks to his wife at a table of people
> and notice how intent he is on making a point
> even though her lower lip is beginning to quiver,
>
> and you will know why the women in science
> fiction movies who inhabit a planet of their own
> are not pictured making a salad or reading a magazine
> when the men from earth arrive in their rocket,
>
> why they are always standing in a semicircle
> with their arms folded, their bare legs set apart,
> their breasts protected by hard metal disks.
>
> —Billy Collins, "Man in Space" (1995)

The poem was a beautiful expression of the themes the patient had been discussing, but if the therapist settles there in a comfortable position of thinking he is unlike the man in the poem or the diagnostician, he misses an important communication from the patient about her experience and readiness to take the next steps in the therapy process. The poem was introduced at a particular point in the therapy interaction, and if the therapist is able to "notice" the themes in the poem and the timing of it being shared with him, he has a deeper understanding of the patient's experience and its dynamic expression in the therapy process.

The evolving process of modifying defenses, which once may have eased pain but now truncate experiences in living, can be reflected in the patient's developing a benevolent curiosity about her own process of coming to know herself. Dream material provided an opportunity for the patient to reflect on the expression of her own experience in a way that allowed for self-pacing and self-control, which are key elements in maintaining the momentum of the therapy process especially for someone whose boundaries had been violated. The themes reflected in dreams helped reveal the patient to herself and also alerted the therapist to respect the pacing of her process of discovery rather than intrude by "making his point" with an interpretation.

The patient shared a sequence of dreams that included one in which she was in a yoga class that was being taught by a sensitive and helpful instructor. The patient was to sing folk songs from the 1960s, but she wasn't ready to do it yet, she didn't feel prepared. Her yoga group was disappointed but the teacher understood, and the patient knew she would be ready to play and sing at some point. Another dream that suggested the developmental origins for her feeling unprepared was followed by one in which she was getting some family photos developed. Her mother wanted all of them done now so she could have them for herself, but the patient told her she was paying for the processing and each photo took a lot out of her, so she wanted to develop them one at a time.

As patients come to honor and accept the validity of their own experience within the evolving process of a psychotherapy relationship, the experiential gains can translate into an acceptance and engagement in the unfolding process of living a life that includes but is not defined by a neurological illness.

Balanced View

A balanced view is fundamental to changing one's relationship to a neurological condition, neither fighting the truth of its reality nor falling victim to its challenges, and it is an essential component in our psychotherapy. Balance is not a matter of achieving a once and for all fixed point, but an ongoing process of awareness and responsiveness to changing circumstances that calls for an open mind and flexibility, and a balanced view is no more important than when considering expectations for change in psychotherapy with patients living with neuropsychological challenges. Our patients' conditions require the flexibility to adjust as advances or setbacks occur; and progress isn't measured by what did or did not occur in a particular session, but in a process of adaptation that evolves over time. A quiet or seemingly uneventful session may be a necessary prelude for advances to be made in future sessions, something akin to a period of rest that is necessary to consolidate gains and restore oneself before moving on to the next challenge. Neither forcing solutions not retreating from adversity, a balanced view strengthens our patients' foundations in adapting to change and uncertainty.

Sometimes our patients' neuropsychological challenges are compounded by aspects of personality that once supported achievement but now are less adaptive after a neurological insult. Finding the balance needed to be actively engaged in treatment and resume activities without overdoing it can be especially difficult for someone whose sense of self was measured by performance and whose response to challenge was "double the effort and plow ahead." In these situations the therapist's balanced view is essential in maintaining realistic expectations and appropriate pacing as patients develop new strategies that initially may feel somewhat alien to the person they've been, but eventually may be incorporated into an expanded view of self that is less dependent on performance and more open to being.

A Clinical Vignette

The patient had been a master at multitasking until a mild traumatic brain injury sustained in a car accident disrupted her fast-paced and high-performance lifestyle. A neuropsychological evaluation revealed mild deficiencies in processing speed and some inefficiencies in executive functioning that may not have constituted "significant deficits" when viewed within the context of performance expectations for someone of her age and educational level. However, for our patient, this so-called mild disruption in neuropsychological functioning would not support the speedy resumption of the full schedule of activities she had intended. Her psychotherapist suggested that she limit some of her involvements to permit the time and energy to participate in neurorehabilitative treatments, but taking time and slowing down was counterintuitive for someone whose success had been founded on a hard-driving and achievement-oriented personality style. Nevertheless the patient agreed and focused her energies on cognitive and physical therapies where her efforts were met with success. However, some lingering aftershocks of the accident persisted, and were difficult for family and colleagues to understand and even more challenging for her to accept. Prior to her accident she had maintained a busy social calendar but now found engagements that were once stimulating and enjoyable had become overwhelming. The conversational repartee she had welcomed with grace and wit now left her feeling depleted and exhausted. The frequent travel she once considered a perk of her job now felt like a demanding burden. Becoming increasingly anxious with the recovery process from a "mild injury" that was not matching her timetable, she called upon coping strategies that had served her well countless times before, but now would fail her—she tried to "double the effort and plow ahead." Her efforts only compounded her fatigue, which revealed cognitive processing weaknesses she thought had recovered—leaving her frustrated, even more depleted, and now scared. She thought her career was in jeopardy; she didn't feel her family and friends understood what had happened to her; her concept of herself was shaken by a trauma that was supposed to have been "mild."

Developing a sense of balance would become a recurring theme in the patient's psychotherapy. The challenge of shifting her perspective from forcing solutions to a balanced view that would support her recovery also provided an opportunity she hadn't expected—catching up with her own experience and finding a balance for living. The process would begin with her therapist explaining the negative interactive cycle that left her feeling lost and depleted. Situations that had been a regular part of her routine had always included potentials for sensory and information overload. But while her social circumstances and job expectations hadn't really changed, her capacities to deal with them had. Feeling overwhelmed, her perspective for coping was narrowed to what she had known—to try harder. Her reactive tendency to redouble her effort drained already depleted reserves, worsened her fatigue, and fueled the negative spiral of cognitive inefficiency, frustration, and anxiety. The patient had little difficulty appreciating the negative spiral explanation, at least from an intellectual perspective; the greater challenge would be doing something about it. The process began by first becoming aware of those situations that held the potential for overload and then slowing down enough to pause and notice reactive tendencies that could fuel the negative spiral. This approach did not mean giving up a career or avoiding social engagement, but changing a relationship to the demands inherent in those situations. To effect this change, the overarching theme for the psychotherapy process would be cultivating balance, and the beginning stages would take place on the cognitive level of pausing and noticing reactive tendencies that disrupted balance. The second and more challenging stage would be dealing with the affective dimension—the feelings that emerge when reactive tendencies are interrupted. When productivity is a defining feature of who we have been, the emptiness of not doing can arouse discomfiting anxiety that propels reactive tendencies, and in our patient's case led to the unrealistic expectations and overexertion that were compromising her recovery. This stage of the therapy was supported by the patient's growing practice of mindfulness meditation, which had been introduced earlier in the process to help her notice reactive tendencies, and now would serve as a foundation for working with difficult emotions. In time and with her determination redirected into pausing, noticing, and slowing down—the empty space that had once been so intimidating provided room for an expanded sense of self less dependent on doing and more open to being. She continued in psychotherapy, taking the process to a deeper level of coming to know the person who had been obscured by all the doing and achievement. She would make a successful transition back to work and resume some of her social activities, but her pace changed and she would allow for more space in her life. No longer just a therapy concept, a balanced view would become a way of living.

NOT THE ONLY WAY

Maintaining realistic expectations and not forcing solutions that either overwhelm or are beyond the capacities of our patients are critical for effecting the therapeutic balance that offers the best chances for success. However there will be times when "accepting the truth of what is" means recognizing that individual psychotherapy may not be the treatment modality best suited for a patient. Loosening an attachment to a particular method—in this case one on one psychotherapy—allows for the consideration of other possibilities that may reduce symptoms and promote an engagement in life.

Although the nature and extent of neuropsychological dysfunction is among the more obvious variables affecting participation in psychotherapy and engaging in living, it is by no means the sole determining factor. Cognitive reserve, premorbid personality, social support all interact with the primary effects of a neurological insult to influence the individualized expression of experience, recovery, and participation in psychotherapy. In a recent *New Yorker* article, "Recalled to Life," Oliver Sacks (2005) describes Patricia H., "a brilliant and energetic woman" who suffered a massive left hemisphere cerebral hemorrhage that left her severely aphasic. Aphasic syndromes can seriously compromise a patient's ability to participate in the "talking cure" of psychotherapy, however expressive and receptive language problems did not preclude Patricia H. from being "recalled to life" through the determination of her daughters, speech therapy, and social engagement. From Sacks's description, I would suspect Patricia's spirited personality also played no small part in her being recalled to live her life with engagement and vitality.

On the other hand we can consider Bob, the patient we introduced in chapter 10, who sustained a moderate traumatic brain injury in a car accident. Unlike Patricia, his language capacities and motor functioning were not compromised but his head trauma did result in frontal system effects that manifested in impulsive behavior, lowered frustration tolerance, affective lability, and poor behavioral regulation. He was referred for psychotherapy to help with temper control, but it seemed that any small gains were quickly undone by his reactivity to a chaotic family situation where he frequently was embroiled in arguments with his parents who were in conflict with each other. The strained family dynamics, which were present before Bob's accident, were now magnified by "the problems he was causing." Added to these strains were the normal developmental challenges of separation and autonomy—expected for a teenager about to graduate high school—which now were complicated by a traumatic brain injury. Bids for independence were exaggerated in reckless behaviors that vacillated with dependent yearnings for attention and support expressed in his seeming inability in his parents' words to "grow up and be responsible."

A basic formulation of Bob's irresponsible behaviors would consider several levels of interaction: 1) Frontal system brain dysfunction as manifested in initiation problems, poor planning, impulsivity, affective lability, and poor behavioral control; 2) Developmental challenges as manifested in conflicts between autonomy and dependency; 3) An expression of anger and frustration conjoined with an attempt to mobilize his parents to be responsible and responsive to his needs.

The developmental challenges of Level 2 and the elicitation behaviors of Level 3 are common themes in individual psychotherapy with patients making the transition from late adolescence to early adulthood, and the resolution of conflicts permitting the negotiation of this developmental hurdle calls upon the patient's abilities for self-reflection, tolerance of ambiguity and frustration, and self-control. However if these frontal system regulatory functions have been compromised by brain damage, the patient lacks essential aspects of the neural foundation needed to support the working through of this conflictual developmental process in individual psychotherapy. Moreover any gains made in terms of a budding understanding of maladaptive interaction patterns that fuel the family conflicts and leave the patient frustrated and misunderstood would be quickly eroded as he becomes reactively engaged in the repetition of the family dynamic that will leave him affectively and cognitively overwhelmed. His resulting tension is discharged by further "acting-out" behaviors that confirm the idea that he is the problem, and so the vicious negative cycle is reinforced. The best efforts of Bob and his therapist would not effect much of a change in this negative cycle until he and his parents worked together in family therapy. The neuropsychologically informed psychodynamic formulation of Bob's challenges provided a framework for understanding, and the Attitude of Mind perspective would eventually provide useful tools for working with difficult

emotions, but the conditions would have to be created to support psychotherapy; and at least in the earlier stages of Bob's treatment, those conditions would be better developed in family therapy with individual therapy being reserved for a later stage of treatment process.

ENDINGS

Perhaps more frequently than not our patients' crashes with fate precede
our own, and so we take our respective roles as patient and provider—at
least for now. But roles change as everything does and sooner or later it will
be "Otherwise," as Jane Kenyon's poignant poem (in chapter 1) reminds
us. Moment to moment our unfolding lives are a process of endings in the
flow of time: a daughter leaving for college, a colleague retiring, a patient
dying—all moments for awakening to the only life we have, the one that is
available now. Yet for some of us contentment remains elusive, and
thoughts of impermanence are more fearful than freeing. Challenged by the
passage of time, we cling tightly to what we have if only to preserve the illusion of stability and control for just a little while longer. Caught in "If
only I had . . . I would be . . . ," we bounce from regretting the past to fan-
tasizing a better future that will never come because we really wouldn't be
there to enjoy it. Letting go into the moment as it is, knowing when enough
is enough, is to know the wealth of contentment. Patients have shown me
that such possibilities exist even in the most difficult of times.

Lyle began psychotherapy when he was going through a painful divorce
and he made great strides in coming to terms with letting go of what he
once had, understanding the ways he may have contributed to his marital
problems, and moving on to less conflictual and more satisfying relationships. About three years after our last session, Lyle called to schedule an appointment. He had continued to maintain a close relationship with his two
daughters and spoke proudly of their achievements in school and music.
Growing up in Michigan he had fond memories of Detroit's automotive
heyday, and he was restoring the '66 GTO he couldn't afford as a college student. He even picked up his clarinet again and was playing in a community
band, where he met a woman who had become a "special friend." He was
creating a new life. He also had been diagnosed with a glioblastoma, an ag-
gressive brain tumor with a poor prognosis.

By the time Lyle returned to resume our sessions he already was involved
in a treatment protocol that he hoped would arrest the tumor. Despite his
weakened appearance, it seemed like his determination "to beat this" revealed reserves of strength he never thought he had, but something else
also was happening. He spoke of a heightened sensitivity and joked that it
may have been a positive symptom of his tumor. He would say, "There's
something about knowing there may not be a next year that makes every

day so special." He spoke of a "strange sensation of being scared one moment and just so peaceful the next." We did guided imagery and sometimes just sat quietly in meditation. Sometimes we laughed, more often we tried not to cry and then laughed again as our tears betrayed us. We would have a coffee together and I would steal a glance at Lyle as he lifted his cup and took a sip, just watching him extract the most of every moment was a lesson in living. As Lyle grew weaker there was a growing dignity about him. He seemed to be letting go but not giving up. He often spoke of his daughters and his gratitude for being their father. His oldest daughter would have his grandchild in the spring, and his younger daughter was playing his clarinet in her high school's marching band. Thinking about Lyle and his daughters now, I am reminded that Erikson's work (1980) remains instructive when we reach the end of a life cycle. Lyle had come to live the stage of *generativity*. And although he knew fear, he would not descend to despair. I remember Lyle being picked up by his two daughters after what was to be our last session at my office. The biting wind of a Michigan winter didn't hurry him to the warmth of the waiting car. He still had something to do; he introduced his daughters. Looking at Lyle for the last time that night, he showed me Erikson's *integrity* and the proud smile of a contented father.

> It was like this:
> you were happy, then you were sad,
> then happy again, then not.
>
> It went on.
> You were innocent or you were guilty.
> Actions were taken, or not.
>
> At times you spoke, at other times you were silent.
> Mostly, it seems you were silent—what could you say?
>
> Now it is almost over.
>
> Like a lover, your life bends down and kisses your life.
>
> It does this not in forgiveness—
> between you, there is nothing to forgive—
> but with the simple nod of a baker at the moment
> he sees the bread is finished with transformation.
>
> Eating, too, is now a thing for others.
>
> It doesn't matter what they will make of you
> or your days: they will be wrong,
> they will miss the wrong woman, miss the wrong man,
> all the stories they tell will be tales of their own invention.

Your story was this: you were happy, then you were sad,
you slept, you awakened.
Sometimes you ate roasted chestnuts, sometimes persimmons.

—Jane Hirshfield, "It Was Like This: You Were Happy" (2006)

REFERENCES AND READINGS

Collins, Billy. 1995. *The art of drowning: Pitt poetry series.* Pittsburgh, PA: University of Pittsburgh Press.

Erikson, Erik Homburger. 1980. *Identity and the life cycle.* New York: W. W. Norton & Co., Inc.

Fredrickson, Barbara. 2001. The role of positive emotions in positive psychology: The broaden-and-build theory of positive emotions. *American Psychologist* 56 (3): 218–226.

Hirshfield, Jane. 2006. *After.* New York: HarperCollins.

Kell, William L., and William J. Mueller. 1966. *Impact and change: A study of counseling relationships.* Englewood Cliffs, NJ: Prentice-Hall.

Miller, Laurence. 1993. Freud's brain: Toward a unified neuropsychodynamic model of personality and psychotherapy. *Journal of the American Academy of Psychoanalysis and Dynamic Psychiatry* 21 (2): 183–212.

Mueller, William J., and Albert S. Aniskiewicz. 1986. *Psychotherapeutic intervention in hysterical disorders.* Northvale, NJ: Aronson.

Pollack, I. W. 2005. Psychotherapy. In *Textbook of traumatic brain injury,* edited by J. M. Silver, T. W. McAllister, and S. C. Yudofsky. Arlington, VA: American Psychiatric Publishing, Inc.

Prigatano, George P. 1999. *Principles of neuropsychological rehabilitation.* New York: Oxford University Press.

Sacks, Oliver. 2005. Recalled to life: A neurologist's notebook. *New Yorker,* October 31.

12

Caregiving Challenges and a Group Approach

When a neurological illness or trauma interrupts a life, its shock waves reverberate beyond the person with the condition to affect the lives of family members, companions, and perhaps most directly those persons who have thrust upon them or have willingly accepted the responsibility of providing care. As an expression of their professional role, members of a patient's health care team have chosen to be in the position of providing specialized, although often delimited, care for people afflicted with neurological conditions. Delimited care by no means suggests less than adequate treatments or interactions devoid of compassion, but more so a circumscribed relationship in terms of time, personal involvement, and potential impact on well-being. Providing professional care to patients with neurological conditions is a privilege that offers the opportunity of receiving through giving, but the risks of depletion and "burnout" for health care providers also are a reality that must not be minimized. However, the circumstances for family members and companions (hereafter referred to as "caregivers") pose different challenges for a number of reasons. More often than not these caregivers have not had the advantages of prior preparation and training to deal with the challenges of a neurological condition and the uncertainty of what's to come. Resources available to support care can vary considerably in terms of financial stability, social and family assistance, and personal reserves. The responsibilities of primary caregivers—whatever their familial relationship may be (e.g., spouse, companion, adult child, parent)—are usually ongoing, sometimes with increasing pressures, and frequently with diminishing time to do what needs to be done. Caregivers face parallel challenges of adapting to change and uncertainty that share similarities with those experienced by the persons in their care, but the demands on each are also different. Caregivers may struggle with the "burden of responsibility" while those in their care struggle with the "burden of dependency," and these respective experiences can create a negative interlock that affects the balance in giving-receiving relationship dynamics, and ultimately the quality of life.

CAREGIVER CHALLENGES AND QUALITY OF LIFE

Quality of Life (QoL) is a multidimensional concept that has been the focus of numerous studies investigating the experiences of people with neurological illnesses (Murrell 1999) and their caregivers (Glozman 2004), and there are equally numerous ways that QoL has been conceptualized and measured. The "attitude of mind" approach is most compatible with a person-centered view of QoL in which patients' or caregivers' perception of the impact of conditions on their personal experience (e.g., physical, psychological/emotional, social, spiritual) is the focus of inquiry.

The challenges facing caregivers can be both daunting and unrelenting, and it is not surprising that these experiences can have a negative impact on QoL and pose an increased risk for psychological and physical morbidity. Many studies have shown high rates of psychological stress and depression, as well as increased susceptibility to physical illness, associated with caregivers of people living with neurological conditions. Glozman (2004) provides a comprehensive review of this body of work.

Glozman (2004) also investigated QoL for caregivers of patients with a particular neurological condition, Parkinson's disease, and suggested the results may be instructive for caregiving challenges associated with other neurological conditions as well. Using the Scale of Quality of Life of Caregivers (SQLC), QoL was assessed in three main levels of activity: professional activity (e.g., ability of caretaker to maintain employment), social and leisure activities (e.g., impact on caretaker's household responsibilities and leisure time), and responsibilities to help the patient in everyday living (e.g., need to assist patient with activities of daily living like bathing). Let's consider some of the findings:

1. 100% of the caregivers manifested some degree of disordered adaptation as graded on three levels: mild, moderate, and severe.
2. The main features of decreased QoL reflected difficulties in several areas, including: impact on employment, reduced holiday time and increased demands for household management, the experience of a permanent lack of time, and disruption in relationship balance with caregivers having increased decision-making responsibilities.
3. The main determinant of decreased QoL for caregivers was functional dependence on the caregiver to assist with the activities of daily living.

4. QoL of caregivers was not related to a summarized score of cognitive disorder for carereceivers but was related to specific areas of neuropsychological disruption. For example, memory disorders did not determine the degree of decreased QoL, but disruptions in emotional stability were related to diminished caregiver QoL.

5. Severe depression was not found in caregivers with mildly disordered adaptation, but was evident in 29% of the moderate group and 56% of the group classified with severe disadaptation.

PERSPECTIVES FROM PSYCHOTHERAPY

Studies investigating the QoL of caregivers are useful in expanding the awareness of the health care community to the challenges and potential negative consequences these family members and companions may face. Experiences from psychotherapy can provide yet another perspective on how these challenges are expressed between carereceivers and caregivers, and suggest interventions that may reduce the experience of "burden" and its negative impact on QoL. During the course of providing psychological services to patients with neurological conditions, there frequently comes a time when consultations will involve family members and more specifically, a caregiver. Sometimes this is one of the first opportunities for caregivers to provide their perspective on a patient's condition, and for some caregivers perhaps a time to offer the beginning hints of their own experience. Eventually some caregivers may participate with the carereceiver in couples or family psychotherapy, and for others individual psychotherapy can provide a much-needed context to share thoughts and feelings that, left unexpressed, would eventually manifest in increased stress, depression, and compromised health.

Caregivers experience a process of challenge and adaptation that often parallels that of the carereceiver. Both are faced with the losses of what was and of the dreams of what might have been. Both are confronted with the challenge of acceptance and reengagement in a life that is far different from what had been planned. The unfolding process of each life has taken a different course, but the nature of that unfolding, the timing of acceptance and adaptation, the personal meanings attributed to being a provider or recipient of care, can be as varied as the personalities whose lives have been disrupted by a neurological condition. And therein lies a significant relationship challenge—the reorientation of at least two, and sometimes several lives from parallel yet different experiences of loss and disequilibrium to an acceptance and engagement with life as it is now and as it continues to unfold.

Acceptance of the losses and adaptive challenges associated with a neurological condition is an individualized process and there can be no proscribed timetables that determine how it is to unfold for a particular patient or caregiver. That the timing of the process can be quite different was illustrated by Jennifer, the young mother we met in chapter 2 who had been recently diagnosed with multiple sclerosis but was reluctant to attend a support group despite her family's urgings. Her process of acceptance began with attending to her experience as it manifested in the moments of a psychotherapy session when she was talking about her perceived expectations of her family and her fears of uncertainty. Let's now consider the perspective of her family, and in particular her husband Ted's experience with loss and uncertainty. On the surface, his urging Jennifer to avail herself of the opportunities for treatment and support that existed in their community made sense and appeared to reflect his "acceptance" of his wife's condition in contrast to her apparent "denial." Indeed Jennifer's husband was a sensitive and caring man, but he also had experienced losses that would have their own timetable of challenge and acceptance. A successful man with a wonderful family, his illusions of control and stability had been shattered when his wife was diagnosed with a progressive neurological condition. He now faced an uncertain future that left him feeling anxious and out of control, but he wasn't about to let Jennifer know his experience, let alone himself. Jennifer's fear of the potential progression of her condition and what might become of her found its parallel in her husband's experience, but his reaction to his own anxiety was to try to reestablish control through managing his wife. If she did everything possible to ward off the anticipated threats of her condition, then perhaps their future might again be a bit more certain. Participation in medical and psychological treatment is certainly to be encouraged but our motivations are complex and sometimes our best intentions belie aspects of our experience of which we are unaware. Ted became very well informed and increasingly vigilant about Jennifer's status. He was managing his anxiety through managing her. Jennifer's sense of herself had already been threatened by a neurological condition, and now her shaken autonomy was challenged by an anxious husband, who appeared as though he had "accepted" her condition, but in the process was losing her. Ted was contributing to his own worse fear. The more he attempted to micromanage his wife's life, the more distant she became and not necessarily through her own doing. His relationship with Jennifer was being replaced by a relationship with a condition. Reestablishing a partnership of mutuality that can accommodate new roles of caregiver and carereceiver would first require an acceptance of his own and his wife's individual experiences as they were expressed now in the present and not in some imagined future. For Jennifer this process began during her first session of psychotherapy. Ted would later join her in sessions and was invited to attend to his own experience of uncertainty and anxiety, and the ways his feelings manifested in seemingly caring but controlling behaviors. In attending to his own experience, he could once again attend to Jennifer as the person she was now and not as a projected future condition. With a growing acceptance of life as it is now comes a growing feeling of equanimity that can temper our reactive tendencies to control a future that cannot be known with the certainty we wish.

Unfortunately for some patients and their caregivers, preexisting personality features or strained marital relationships compound the challenges of acceptance and adaptation to a neurological condition. For example, the personalities of some patients may have been shaped, at least in part, by frustrated needs for affection, attention, and support that have their roots in developmental experiences and now manifest in conflicted relationship patterns. These conflicted dynamics can become organized around a neurological condition in a way that confers a sense of legitimacy for the expression of exaggerated dependency needs. The long-standing frustrated needs that a patient may have had difficulty expressing in a direct and adaptive manner now find expression through an illness and its associated challenges. This solution, however, includes the seeds of its own failure because what are indeed legitimate needs are obscured by an exaggerated dependency that depletes and eventually may alienate a caregiver. The maladaptive pattern thus perpetuates itself; legitimate needs continue to be frustrated, participation in treatment may be conflicted, the patient may be viewed as not trying, and caregiver and carereceiver risk becoming increasingly estranged.

For some caregiver-carereceiver dyads, available caregiving resources may be limited as a function of physical and health status of the caregiver. The need to assist a carereceiver with the functional activities of daily living (e.g., transferring, bathing) was identified by Glozman (2004) as a major factor affecting quality of life for caregivers, and this challenge is compounded for caregivers whose physical stamina is less than optimal for the task. This situation can be fraught with anxiety and frustration for both and often requires the assistance of others (e.g., family members, professional aides) who can help address an immediate need (e.g., bathing) although lingering feelings of "burden" may remain for both carereceiver (burden of dependency) and caregiver (burden of responsibility).

Besides the physical and neuropsychological challenges with which our patients live, many struggle with the experience that they are a "burden" to their loved ones and especially to a companion who has the primary role of caregiver. Among the concerns most frequently voiced by patients in psychotherapy are worries about the impact of their condition on the lives of their families. And despite the best intentions of a caregiver to attend to self-care and maintain a balanced life, it is painfully obvious to the carereceiver that life has changed in so many ways for their companion or family member. This is no more evident than in the experience of time; it simply takes longer to get things done in this age when speed is the coin of the realm. So many patients feel they are not contributing their fair share to family responsibilities; they may also feel that their mere presence compromises the experiences of their loved ones—they get in the way and slow things down. Even in the best of times, the burden of dependency can rear its head. Consider the experience of a patient, who now relied on a cane to stabilize a slow and unsteady gait resulting from a neurological condition, on an evening out to dinner and a concert with her daughter and husband. The allowance of time for the evening's activities had already been expanded to accommodate the need to find parking that would minimize walking distances. Dinner had taken longer than expected and a visit to a restroom before a "short" walk to the concert hall would require yet another face-off with time as she glimpsed her husband's furtive yet anxious look at his watch. Moments later, on the street, concertgoers with the same destination hurried past them and she wished her husband and daughter could move along with the "normal" pace of the crowd, but they declined and what appeared as their dawdling steps only emphasized the "burden" of her slowness. Arriving at their seats only moments before the first performer took the stage, her husband turned to her with a look of relief and said, "We made it." As he and their daughter settled back into their chairs, she smiled and hoped the music would ease the lingering feelings of guilt that had become her familiar companion.

Sometimes in an attempt to assuage a patient's feelings of burden, a caregiver may minimize or deny his or her own experiences which then get lost in what comes to feel like a burden of responsibility. Other caretakers may feel that their experiences of loss and increased responsibility simply don't carry the weight of the challenges faced by their companion with a neurological condition. To consider their experience as different but equally legitimate smacks of selfishness and self-absorption. As one caretaker described the situation, "My wife's stroke always trumps my experience." Such minimization is ultimately more harmful than helpful. After initial diagnosis or trauma it is not unusual for family members and companions to focus their energies on the needs of the person with the neurological condition. But the passage of time may bring increasing responsibilities that occupy not only time but energy, and this press can narrow the focus of the caretaker to the tasks at hand while his or her own personal experience with loss and responsibility recede further into the background.

This territory is fertile ground for feeling overwhelmed, frustrated, angry, and resentful. Kept from awareness or minimized, these experiences can manifest in pervasive feelings of guilt that fuel the negative cycle and leave the caregiver depleted but determined to try harder if only to assuage his or her own guilty feelings. For many of us, the struggle with guilt is ultimately an exceedingly painful but self-absorbed exercise. Our focus is narrowly directed inward to actions, feelings, and thoughts we should or should not have done. In this preoccupation our awareness really does not include the other person, who may be the "reason" for our guilty feelings, in a way that would be most helpful. Guilt may provide the motivation to redouble our efforts, and indeed these efforts may be directed toward another, but the conflicted dynamics of the exchange can leave the giver and receiver both feeling unsatisfied when they "should" be feeling something else—and thus the cycle of guilt continues. Yet there can be another way, and it begins by providing a context where caregivers can come to know and honor their own experiences with an openness and benevolent curiosity that replaces minimization and self-judgment. From this perspective we at least have the possibilities for cultivating a caregiver-carereceiver relationship balance where parallel yet different experiences are acknowledged for what they are and the weight of "burden" is lifted by an attitude of mind that offers broader options and opportunities.

CHANGING PERSPECTIVES: FROM BURDEN TO OPPORTUNITY

In a comprehensive review on the quality of life of caregivers that considers the relationship between stressors associated with caregiving and the subjective experience of overload, Glozman (2004) offers the opinion that "caregiver burden is affected less by actual symptoms than by the caregiver's perception of the carereceiver's symptoms, attitude toward or emotional response to caregiving; perception of own adequacy for coping with stressors and the extent to which caregiving has an adverse impact on one's own life." These observations on caregiving challenges and adaptations are consistent with the perspectives that have informed the attitude of mind orientation, with a key element being that we may change our relationship to adversity—our attitude of mind—in such a way that reduces stress and strengthens coping reserves. Glozman (2004) also suggests that the results of their study with Parkinson's disease and caregiving might be generalizable to other neurological conditions, and further notes "caregiving for a family member with a severely debilitating chronic condition should be considered as a generic phenomenon." The lessons of psychotherapy also teach that each patient's and each caregiver's experience with a neurological condition is unique, yet there is a shared quality—perhaps generic—of loss, challenge of acceptance, potential to reengage with life.

It was from this shared perspective that the idea of offering a psychoeducational group experience for caregivers began to take form. In a broad sense, the goals for a group program for caregivers were not very different from those guidelines that informed the attitude of mind approach for patients living with neurological conditions. Their parallel challenges are accepting the reality of the condition and learning how to live with the truth of what is. The acceptance of loss challenges both patient and caregiver, but within the experience of loss their paths also diverge. For the patient and caregiver alike loss will involve letting go of what might have been. But in the present reality, loss for the patient will mean living with decreased functioning, and for the caregiver, living with increased responsibility. Both are dealing with adversity, and for both hope is offered by the possibility of changing one's relationship to the challenges—neither fighting their reality nor falling victim to them.

In considering the themes that could inform a group program for caregivers, the "five elements of a way" and "mindfulness meditation" provided the guideposts for dealing with challenge, and a practice to cultivate resilience needed for caregiving and the balance for remaining engaged in life. Perspectives from research on positive psychology—particularly the work on coping and cultivating positive emotions (Folkman and Moskowitz 2000; Fredrickson 2001)—provided a complementary theoretical orientation and the supporting evidence of empirical studies with caregivers to inform the themes and coping strategies discussed in the group. And finally teachings on the cultivation of compassion for caregivers as offered by Chokyi Nyima Rinpoche and David R. Shlim in *Medicine and Compassion* (2004) showed the possibilities of a way of relieving the suffering of others without incurring "burnout."

This particular group program was organized around six weekly 75–90-minute sessions, and the number of participants (caregivers) varied between eight and twelve. The caregivers included spouses, companions, parents, and adult children of people living with a neurological condition. Number and length of sessions and number of participants are by no means fixed guidelines. Therapists adapting this approach have the flexibility to structure the group experience in a way that is most appropriate for their setting and the needs of the participants. The program was offered as a psychoeducational experience and each session was structured with an organizing theme and four components. The themes reflected the challenges and opportunities involved in caregiving, and the components included a didactic portion, an experiential exercise, a discussion period, and suggestions for the week. The group facilitator would begin each session by inviting the participants to take a few moments to center their awareness in the present moment by bringing their attention to the flow of their breathing (approximately 2 minutes). The first part of a session would be a brief presentation by the group facilitator on a topic reflecting the theme of the week (approximately 20 minutes). The presentation was followed by an experiential exercise of a guided meditation (approximately 15 to 20 minutes). Next the group would be invited to share their experiences with the previous week's suggestions, pose questions, and suggest possibilities (approximately 15 to 20 minutes). The final component would include suggestions to try in the upcoming week (approximately 10 to 15 minutes). These recommendations would be based on the group members' experiences and questions, and would also include methods for expanding mindfulness (e.g., walking, eating, driving with mindfulness). Each session would then conclude with a silent meditation (approximately 2 minutes).

The next section is an outline of a group program for caregivers that includes a schedule and agenda items from one such experience. The intention is not to suggest a particular format to be followed in a specific way, but more so to offer one of many possibilities that may be tried and adapted in providing information and support to caregivers. Each session's theme reflects a topic that we have considered in the book and so I will not elaborate upon them again in this outline. These key themes for the group facilitator's presentation are noted as Presentation Points.

A PSYCHOEDUCATIONAL GROUP PROGRAM FOR CAREGIVERS

Session One: "Challenges and Opportunities"

Welcome: Centering awareness in the present moment.
Presentation Points:
1. Challenges and risks in caregiving.
2. "You can't stop the waves but you can learn to surf."
3. Introduction to the "attitude of mind" approach.

Practice Opportunity: A meditation exercise of following the breath.
Group Discussion: Reactions to the meditation exercise and an overview of the program.
Taking the Practice Home (suggestions to try): Pick a time each day when you will not be disturbed and practice the meditation of following your breath as we have today. Set aside 10 to 15 minutes each day for your practice and make the commitment to do so whether you feel like it or not. Other than this promise to yourself, you do not have to try getting somewhere or accomplishing anything special with your practice. Just follow your breath and when your attention wanders away, just notice where it has gone and gently escort your awareness back to your breath without judging or criticizing yourself.
Closing and Transition: Each session closes with a few minutes of silent meditation and the positive intention to bring a mindful attitude to caregiving and daily living.

Session Two: "Acceptance and Uncertainty"

Welcome: Centering awareness in the present moment.
Presentation Points:
1. Reactions to change and uncertainty: attachments to the past and fears of the future.
2. Acceptance as a process.
3. Guideposts—the "five elements of a way":
   • Open mind
   • Active orientation
   • Present-moment awareness
   • Process perspective
   • Balanced view

Practice Opportunity: A guided meditation for awakening the senses and expanding awareness to the sense of the body, touch, and sound.
Group Discussion: Reactions to presentation and meditation exercise.
Taking the Practice Home (suggestions to try): Continue your practice of daily meditation and you may want to try expanding your awareness in meditation to include the physical sense of your body and then the sounds that surround you as we did in today's meditation. Your practice of daily meditation also is providing you with a foundation to cultivate a mindful attitude in daily living. You may cultivate this mindful attitude in any activity that you do. Try eating a meal mindfully, bringing your careful attention to your food and drink—its appearance on your plate, the aroma, its taste and texture. Focus on the moment to moment process of eating your meal. If you find yourself thinking about future plans or beginning to rush your meal to get somewhere else, just notice those actions or thoughts— just as you would in meditation—and simply bring your attention back to your meal.
Closing and Transition: Silent meditation and the positive intention to bring a mindful attitude to caregiving and daily living.

Session Three: "Cultivating Positive Emotions"

Welcome: Centering awareness in the present moment.
Presentation Points:
1. Connections from research to living:
   • Positive emotions and thinking.
   • An open mind sees options and possibilities, and with possibilities there is hope.

2. Cultivating positive emotions and resilience:
   - Positive reappraisal.
   - Problem-focused coping.
   - Finding positive meaning in daily events.
3. Guideposts for living with challenges—complementary perspectives:
   - The "elements of a way" and "mindful living."
   - Coping strategies for cultivating positive emotions.

Practice Opportunity: A guided meditation on creating space and placing challenges within the context of a larger life held with gratitude and lived in the present moment.

Group Discussion: Reactions to the presentation and meditation exercise.

Taking the Practice Home (suggestions to try): Continue your practice of daily meditation. You also may want to try another way of expanding your practice into daily living with a walking meditation. Try to remember that this is a walk without a destination. You are not trying to get anywhere other than where you are. As you begin your walk you may want to connect your steps to the flow of your in-breath and out-breath. You don't need to force any pace of walking or breathing. Simply bring your attention to how your breath and steps synchronize themselves. For example, there may be four steps to an in-breath and five steps to an out-breath, and this pattern may change as your walk unfolds. You may consider expanding your awareness to the sense of your body walking, the touch of your step on the path or sidewalk. You may then expand your awareness to the sights, sounds, and scents that surround you; and then bring your attention back to your steps and your breathing.

Closing and Transition: Silent meditation and the positive intention to bring a mindful attitude to caregiving and daily living.

Session Four: "Working with Difficult Emotions"

Welcome: Centering awareness in the present moment.

Presentation Points:
1. Depression: loss and the attachment to what was.
2. Anxiety: the nature of worry and the attempt to control an uncertain future.
3. Anger and frustration: overload and forcing solutions.
4. Guilt and the burden of responsibility.

Practice Opportunity: A guided meditation on working with difficult emotions. We allow our feelings to emerge, neither suppressing them nor getting carried away by them; we note them and let them pass.

Group Discussion: Reactions to the presentation and meditation exercise.

Taking the Practice Home (suggestions to try): Continue your practice of daily meditation. Our lives are filled with challenges that can stir our emotions, and with your daily practice you are developing the capacity to find stillness in the waves, a space to work with turbulence of difficult emotions and runaway thoughts. Painful feelings frequently stimulate reactive tendencies of getting carried away with a personal storyline (e.g., depressed mood leading to thoughts of being inadequate, worthless, unlovable), or attempts to deny, minimize, or suppress that which is uncomfortable or unacceptable. Our reactive tendencies create their own problems, such as depression being magnified by negative thoughts or suppressed feelings manifesting in somatic symptoms. In our daily meditation we can practice interrupting the momentum of our reactive tendencies, and instead allow our feelings to emerge—neither fueling them nor denying them—and letting them pass. For example, if feelings of frustration or anger emerge then note the feelings for what they are. Your practice will help you recognize reactive tendencies of getting carried away with thoughts about the feelings, either inflaming them (e.g., "I'll get back at them") or perhaps minimizing them (e.g., "I have no right to feel this way"). When you notice this reactive momentum building, you can interrupt it by bringing your attention back to your breath. With your breathing you will be able to create a space around the disturbing feeling, which will allow you to know your experience for what it is and decide how you want to relate to it.

Closing and Transition: Silent meditation and positive intention to bring a mindful attitude to caregiving and daily living.

Session Five: "Awakening Wisdom and Compassion"

Welcome: Centering awareness in the present moment.

Presentation Points: Highlights from *Medicine and Compassion: A Tibetan Lama's Guidance for Caregivers*, by Chokyi Nyima Rinpoche with David R. Shlim, M.D.

1. Wisdom and seeing things as they really are.
2. Compassion and being present for another.
3. Awakening wisdom and compassion with positive intention and ongoing practice: an "attitude of mind."

Practice Opportunity: A guided meditation making a transition from focused meditation to "thought-free wakefulness."

Group Discussion: Reactions to presentation and meditation exercise.

Taking the Practice Home (suggestions to try): Continue your practice of daily meditation and you may want to try the transition to "thought-free wakefulness" like we practiced today. Begin your regular practice by bringing your attention to the flowing of your breath, beginning with the unfolding moments of your in-breath and out-breath. When you have settled into a calm and relaxed wakefulness, you may let the focus on your breath recede into the background and simply let yourself be open and present to what is. If a thought arises, simply note it as a thought and let it pass like a cloud moving through the spacious sky of your awareness. If a feeling arises, you may do the same, simply note it and let it pass. Rest comfortably in the calm space you have created.

Try bringing your attitude of wisdom and compassion to the care you are providing. You have been developing a growing foundation to see things as they are and live with the truth of what is. You have also been developing a resilience to cope with stress and a calm and restful space to restore yourself. Perhaps your loved one needs assistance in putting on their socks and shoes. Bring your positive intention and mindful attitude to the task. With your nonjudgmental presence and without rushing to complete the task, bring your attention and care to the moment by moment process of gently lifting a foot, pulling up a sock, slipping on a shoe, and tying a shoelace, with gratitude that you still have the ability to do such things. Before you know it the task is done, and you may just begin to notice that what may have felt like a burden to you and your loved one is becoming an opportunity.

Closing and Transition: Silent meditation and positive intention to bring a mindful attitude to caregiving and daily living.

Session Six: "Self-Care"

Welcome: Centering awareness in the present moment.
Presentation Points:
1. Open Mind: With an open mind we can see possibilities and with possibilities there is hope. Allow yourself to have your experience as it is, without negative self-judgment.
2. Active Orientation: Read, listen, gather helpful information, and above all continue your practice. The wisdom, compassion, and resilience needed for caregiving are cultivated with practice.
3. Present-Moment Awareness: Multitasking is overrated. Life is occurring now, one moment at a time for you and the person you are caring for. Slow down and take your time. You'll get to where you're going a lot faster, and you won't miss your life on the way.

4. Process Perspective: Everything changes and nothing stays the same. Take your practice into life not so much as a means to an end but as a part of the unfolding process of life itself.
5. Balanced View: Knowing your limits is not to be defeated by overload. Providing care to others at the expense of self-care leads to burnout and ultimately the inability to provide care to anyone. Take the time to restore yourself. Rest. Take care of your body, eat well and exercise; but don't forget to take care of your mind—that is what our practice is about. Your breath is the connection of mind and body. Give it your careful attention.

Practice Opportunity: A guided loving kindness meditation. Building upon our meditation practice and the foundation of following our breath, we allow ourselves to have our experience with nonjudgmental positive regard. Our breathing creates a space of loving kindness in which our experience is held with the care and attention that we try to offer to others. *Meditation for Optimum Health* (Weil and Kabat-Zinn 2001) is an excellent audio resource for a guided loving kindness meditation as well as other mindfulness meditation exercises (available from Sounds True, P.O. Box 8010, Boulder, CO 80306-8010).

Group Discussion: Reactions to the presentation and meditation exercises.

Taking the Practice Home (closing comments): As our experience together for the past six weeks now comes to an end, may your practice continue to be a part of the unfolding process of your life, providing you with resilience to confront challenges, helping you cultivate wisdom and compassion to provide care, and allowing you moments of peace and contentment.

> May God bless and keep you always,
> May your wishes all come true,
> May you always do for others
> And let others do for you.

—Bob Dylan, "Forever Young" (2004)

REFERENCES AND READINGS

Dylan, Bob. 2004. *Bob Dylan lyrics, 1962–2001*. New York: Simon & Schuster.

Folkman, Susan, and Judith Tedlie Moskowitz. 2000. Positive affect and the other side of coping. *American Psychologist* 55 (6): 647–654.

Fredrickson, Barbara. 2001. The role of positive emotions in positive psychology: The broaden-and-build theory of positive emotions. *American Psychologist* 56 (3): 218–226.

Glozman, Janna M. 2004. Quality of life of caregivers. *Neuropsychology Review* 14 (4): 183–196.

Murrell, Rachel. 1999. Quality of life and neurological illness: A review of the literature. *Neuropsychology Review* 9 (4): 209–229.

Rinpoche, Chokyi Nyima, and David R. Shlim. 2004. *Medicine and compassion: A Tibetan lama's guidance for caregivers.* Somerville, MA: Wisdom Publications.

Weil, Andrew, and Jon Kabat-Zinn. 2001. *Meditation for optimum health.* Boulder, CO: Sounds True.

13

Epilogue

What is one to do on the day when thoughts cease to flow and the proper words won't come?

—Sigmund Freud (Bloom 1994)

AN UNFOLDING PATH

In bringing to a close his grand novel *In Search of Lost Time*, Marcel Proust (1992) leaves us with the character Marcel set to work on the book we have just completed, or perhaps more accurately, have just read. Might we take away a message about completions being parts of an ongoing process—an unfolding path—where endings cycle back to beginnings and where others now will write the story that I am closing? For more than three decades residents, interns, and graduate students have allowed me the role of a teacher. They now will continue on the path, and I would like to offer some final thoughts to take along the way.

Be smart but grow wise. As best you can, try to maintain the open mind of the beginner who can see many possibilities. You then will offer your patients a bridge of hope when it is most needed rather than the narrow view of the "experts" who see reflections of their own concepts but are blind to patients' experiences. Learn from your mistakes; you invariably will make them because that is the nature of things when dealing with uncertainty in psychotherapy. But be curious and let a growing understanding of the process replace your self-judgment and criticism. You will find yourself in interactions with patients that are reminiscent of their problematic interactions with others. In such moments, what may feel like failures of technique or understanding are actually opportunities for growth and transformation, as long as you can step back with awareness and be curious about how you and your patient arrived at this point.

Stay active in your learning; training in psychotherapy doesn't end. I have known some masterful psychotherapists but they were the first to admit psychotherapy could no more be mastered than human nature. Read in your respective disciplines of psychology and psychiatry; your professional colleagues past and present have much to offer from their clinical experiences and research. Be careful not to succumb to dichotomous thinking in our current climate of empirically validated psychological treatment, with its emphasize on measurable outcomes and "scientifically" grounded therapies. I am not suggesting ignoring the usefulness of empirically validated cognitive-behavioral approaches, but our patients are more than collections of symptoms to be treated, and as Adam Phillips (2006) recently stated in an op-ed piece in the *New York Times*, "One of the good things psychotherapy can do, like the arts, is show us the limits of what science can do for our welfare. The scientific method alone is never going to be enough, especially when we are working out how to live and who we can be." Stay current with the scientific literature and be open to wisdom found elsewhere. Has Shakespeare's genius in representing the complexity of personality ever been outdone?

"Only that day dawns to which we are awake." Take Thoreau's words to heart and make them your daily mantra. Lost in our minds, in our preoccupations about one thing or another, we miss the life we will regret not living; and it is all in the moments, in this present moment, right now. Honor the moments of your experience with gratitude, and the simplest activities become a celebration of living, a way to contentment. As you cultivate this mindful respect for your own experience you will become increasingly present for your patients' experiences, and they will know it and it will make a difference.

Everything changes and all that we know will one day come to an end. That's just the way it is. The moment to moment unfolding process of our lives has a parallel in the unfolding process of psychotherapy. The course of a therapy session, and for that matter, the entire course of psychotherapy is an unfolding process that is not always amenable to a predetermined plan of what is supposed to happen. Somehow the vicissitudes of our patients' lives do not always conform neatly to our best-laid treatment plans. Of course, we may force the issue with proscribed strategies and assignments, and attribute our patients' so-called failures to noncompliance or resistance. Might it be more fruitful, however, to wonder just what this resistance is about, and what its meaning is for the patient, and for our interaction with the patient? Be careful not to let methods of assessment take the place of the real thing—something like having a patient complete a depression symptom checklist while tears are streaming down her cheeks. Therapy sessions are not isolated events in time that lend themselves to easy quantification in terms of success or failure. So-called failures like a missed session or perhaps an atypically quiet session are parts of a process because more frequently than not they are statements—albeit behaviorally expressed—about patients' experiences of what has transpired or feelings about what is to come. Be open to what your patients are trying to tell you about their experiences; their messages come in many forms.

Just like your patients are more than their illness, you are more than your career. Psychotherapy is as demanding as it can be rewarding, and if you are going to be helpful to your patients you really have to be there. And by being there I don't mean 24/7 availability, but instead being truly present at that time when you and the patient are together. I have come to learn that being present for others is less a matter of willpower and more an issue of balance. If we are able to honor our own experience, we are better prepared to honor the experience of someone else. And balance requires time for rest, restoration, and engagement in activities other than those that pay the mortgage. Irritability, fatigue, and depression are among the more obvious signs of imbalance; trust in the perceptions of loved ones or colleagues who may recognize these signs in you before you do. Psychotherapy for the psychotherapist can be good medicine, but you also may want to consider some preventative approaches. There is no one size fits all formula, but I can offer some ways that have been helpful to me:

- Try meditation, yoga, or maybe tai chi and incorporate the practice into your daily living.
- Practice mindful living and let your senses be your openings to the present moment.
- Spend some time in silence each day. It doesn't have to be long. Don't go to sleep; just be quiet.
- Spend time in nature wherever you can find it. Read Wendell Berry's poem "The Peace of Wild Things" (see chapter 10).
- Take the time to notice your family and loved ones in the simplest acts of living.
- Walk through an art museum on a rainy Sunday afternoon. Take in a college baseball game in May.
- Try reading a poem aloud. You may have your own favorites or you can try one from the book. Check out the Writer's Almanac online for a daily poem.
- Listen to music. Right now for me it is Beethoven's late piano sonatas; another time it could just as well be Bruce Springsteen. Whatever your spirit calls for is just fine.

Dare to answer Freud's question and do not be deterred by the challenges of patients living with neurological conditions; they will need your services, and you have much to offer. And along the way, may you know moments of peace and joy, and may we all grow in wisdom and compassion.

REFERENCES AND READINGS

Berry, Wendell. 1998. *The selected poems of Wendell Berry*. Washington, D.C.: Counterpoint.

Bloom, Harold. 1994. Freud: A Shakespearean Reading. In *The Western canon*. New York: Riverhead Books.

Phillips, Adam. 2006. A mind is a terrible thing to measure. *New York Times*, Feb. 26, 13(L).

Proust, Marcel. 1992. *In search of lost time*. Translated by C. K. S. Moncrieff, T. Kilmartin, edited by D. J. Enright. New York: Modern Library, Random House.

Thoreau, Henry David. 2004. *Walden*. Boston: Shambhala.

Index

About the Author

Albert S. Aniskiewicz, Ph.D., ABPP, is professor of psychiatry and neurology at Michigan State University. He is a diplomate in clinical psychology with the American Board of Professional Psychology and a diplomate in assessment psychology with the American Board of Assessment Psychology. He is a fellow with the Academy of Clinical Psychology. Dr. Aniskiewicz has been on the faculty of Michigan State University for many years where he has taught in the areas of psychotherapy, personality assessment, and neuropsychology. He coauthored with Dr. William J. Mueller, *Psychotherapeutic Interventions in Hysterical Disorders*. He maintains a clinical practice at the Michigan State University Psychiatry and Neurology Clinics.